THE HUMAN EQUATION:

SCIENCE AND SPIRITUALITY

VOLUME I

Donald D. Powell

PUBLISHED BY THE HUMAN EQUATION INC.

Copyright © 2004 by Donald D. Powell and The Human Equation Inc.
Printed in Canada
First Printed in 2004

All rights reserved. No part of this work covered by the copyrights hereon may be reproduced or used in any form or by any means–graphic, electronic or mechanical–without the written permission of the publisher, except by reviewers, who may quote brief passages.

Publisher: The Human Equation Inc.
11740 - 133 Street
Edmonton NW, Alberta
Canada T5M 1H6

Library and Archives Canada Cataloguing in Publication

Powell, Donald David, 1938-
The human equation / Donald David Powell.

Includes bibliographical references and index.
Contents: v. 1. Science and spirituality.
ISBN 0-9736103-0-1 (v. 1)

1. Interdisciplinary approach to knowledge. I. Title.

BD255.P68 2004 001 C2004-904519-9

Printing: Quality Color, an RR Donnelley Company, Edmonton, Alberta, Canada
Cover Design: Ivan Stewart, Digital Reaction Studios
Cover Illustration: The Human Equation Inc. ®
Illustrations of Metalogical Constructs: Copyright © 2004 by Donald D. Powell and The Human Equation Inc.

THE HUMAN EQUATION: SCIENCE AND SPIRITUALITY

VOLUME I

Contents

THE HUMAN EQUATION:

SCIENCE AND SPIRITUALITY

VOLUME I

Dedication

My grandmother, Alma Rogers, who partook of the cultural life of Toronto, Canada, around 1900, incarnated a profound generosity. She was one of those unique individuals who could quietly help others without compromising their self-respect. She was a quintessential 'third person' in the manner of Socrates. This work is dedicated to the memory of Mary Alma Elizabeth Rogers, 1875-1970.

The riddle of The Human Equation:

The Philosophers' stone is both fire and water.

THE HUMAN EQUATION:

SCIENCE AND SPIRITUALITY

VOLUME I

Introduction

Perhaps the principal motto of this text should be, we have no secrets. Despite the pretense of cosmic censorship, religious dogma, arcane scientism, secular humanism and moribund aesthetics, *free & open systems of choice & action are the essence & substance of The Human Equation.* And, when the anamnesia & paramnesia of forgetfulness are overcome, our memories become restored to their youthful prime. Accordingly, throughout this text I will be acting as a pathfinder for the progressive ideas and feelings of New Wave philosophy. And, whether or not the content herein passes muster, as an expert rating, is not as important as the behavioral guidelines provided. Thus, the object is not to lard the reader down with a questionable triad of ready made answers, solutions and results, but to provide "General Guidelines" supportive of the process of personal 'individuation' (Carl Gustav Jung).

While introducing the concepts & percepts of important terms and relationships, I will be using many single and double *scare quotes.* Some people may find this technique to be a little campy, but until The Human Equation has been completely fleshed out, scare quotes are an effective way of focusing the reader's 'attention' where it belongs.

This work is generally concerned with *information implosion,* although hopefully it avoids the irrational reaction implied by Alvin Toffler's 'Super-Simplifier'. Up to the present, the detailed analysis of the specialized texts of the modern era has produced an *information explosion* that is crying out for General Guidelines. Nevertheless, we must proceed carefully, for the paleontologist Stephen Jay Gould is essentially right in saying that we have no 'general principles'. Thus, to combat complexity one cannot simply substitute simplicity, or, extrapolate from complexity using static principles purported to explain dynamic processes. For as the American psychologist Susan Oyama states, in *The Ontogeny of Information* (1985), sometimes it is the simple 'solutions' that are the problem. And yet, according to the Canadian media mogul, Marshall McLuhan, every subject, if studied in depth, relates to every other subject. He took a cross-disciplinary approach that is close to my heart.

I hesitate to use the more popular term 'transdisciplinary', because its usage implies an almost encyclopedic knowledge & understanding of each and every area of learning. Few of us can take such a polymathic approach. Fortunately, the mature integration of any given discipline sets out relationships that lend themselves to understanding the naturally progressive measures of other disciplines.

In other terms, the complexity of modern life guarantees that there will never again be a truly Renaissance person, capable of the synoptic powers necessary for integrating a multitude of specialized interests. Nevertheless, if one takes a naturally holistic approach within a given discipline, General Guidelines tend to make evident the cross-disciplinary relationships of integrative modes of learning. The wave of the future, then, is in the orchestration of specialized interests so as to bring about their common utility. By sharing resource bases, expertise, and research & development costs, in a commonsensical approach, the philosophy of "Integrative Discipline" not only empowers individuals, but also engenders a greater measure of social cohesion.

In the twentieth century, physicists, mathematicians and other scientists have frequently made the transition to become philosophers, artists, teachers and politicians, etc. Similarly, business oriented individuals, and industrialists, often become purveyors of democratic rights, as well as benefactors of educational reforms. Accordingly, normally isolated categories, managed on a need-to-know basis, are no longer adequate for The Human Equation. Modern people are constantly assailed with prefixes such as "inter, trans, supra, cross, poly, multi", etc. What had its beginnings during the nineteenth century as metalogical research, in hopes of discovering the underlying scientific processes for all aspects of our existence, has now shifted its focus toward the more feasible *psychology of relationships.*

I will be presenting numerous new terms, generic to The Human Equation, some of which have been included in the Glossary. Many of these terms will be immediately self-evident, because the contextual clues of Integrative Discipline, through repetition and variation, will help integrate new concepts & percepts into the reader's personal frame of reference. As mentioned, Carl Gustav Jung, who studied psychology under Sigmund Freud, referred to this developmental approach as individuation. We each have our own individual path to development, motivated by a personalized process of "opinionation" that gives every learner a unique approach toward complex learning. Thus, to facilitate the educational principle of *overlearning for transfer of training,* this work has many recurrent and overlapping themes, which, in the fullness of time, seem to support in-depth learning. And, most importantly, for that is the saving grace of this work, all concepts & percepts will be related to colored models, called "Metalogical Constructs". What

The Human Equation does best is organize the relational 'aspect ratios' of Metaphor, as an overall strategy that is amazingly efficient at integrating different modes of learning.

Importantly, the cohesive logic of Metalogical Constructs is established through the careful interrelating of shape, color, quality, order, meaning, scale and number, etc. Accordingly, paired relationships are ubiquitous, and, to focus upon these special dualities, I will often tie them together with an "&" instead of the more normal "and". As a further example, the vertical modes of *psychological oppositions* are contrasted with the horizontal modes of *recombinant appositions.* And, Universal Dualities, such as time & space, energy & momentum, and becoming & being, etc. are the precursors of what I refer to as the "Recombinant Third System". Congruent progressions, like the diatonic music scale, set up a chromodynamic spectrum that blends together the 'objectivity' of complementary relationships. One begins with the *Vertical Mosaic* (work by John A. Porter, 1965) of *levels of awareness*, or is what is called the 'first system', &, the *Horizontal Mosaic*, of *degrees of recognition*, as what is referred to as the 'second system'. Then, the two are recombine for the meaningful *recomposition of attention*, as the 'third system'. All the dynamic patterns in this work lead toward this third alternative, built up through what I refer to as "True Trinitine Patterns" or "TTPs". The third system is always a work in progress, similar to the Buddhist 'awakening'.

Isaac Newton simply stated that one can not deterministically solve this 'three-body problem'. Nevertheless, the German astronomer Johannes Kepler tended to see these dynamic processes in a manner similar to my TTPs. The latter take on a kind of "diagonal X" approach, neither rhetorically vertical on the y-axis, nor dialectically horizontal on the x-axis, but recombinantly diagonal on the z-axis, similar to the physics of 'angular momenta'. *Rate & range* become resolved through *ratio* (a TTP), just as human *controversy & conflict* can & may lead to a *breakthrough in learning*. Resolving the three-ness of such "Crossover Patterns" requires learning the eternal temporalities of the first system, as the **Verification of Knowledge**, along with the infinite spatialities of the second system, as the **Validation of Understanding**, and then, searching for the **Viability of Correspondence**, through the third system. The first is Einstein's 'E_1', and the second is his 'E_2', which are the "Two Competencies" that Human Beings never fully realize. It might help to think of these two as button & string, which I find more helpful than Einstein's 'straw & marble'. 'Ortho' as a button & 'para' as a string are also good analogies for the first & second systems. The third, as the either and both of the other two, is Einstein's 'E_3', which he referred to as the 'natural system'. Like Buddhist koans, the trick is to resolve their independent natures. Many of us are more familiar with the terms 'this & that' and 'such-and-such'.

The natural system is self-emergent and self-evident, and hopefully, for us at least, it proves to be reliable, viable and genuine. However, this "proof" as such, must depend upon the experiential growth of evidentiary objectivity. Accordingly, excessive aggressivity & passivity, as the basis of human adventurism, can & may be overcome through participation in the Real Human Adventure. The process grows on us, if we are willing to fully engage ourselves in the such-and-such of a miraculous Quest. Importantly, through the Quest of The Human Equation the reader will have ample opportunity to experience each concept & percept, many times, from many different angles, following the example of The Great Crystal of Light, represented by Metalogical Construct No.12.

By way of example, few people have a real appreciation of Darwin's 'natural selection'. Natural selection is button & string, as implying perfect knowledge & understanding. Unfortunately, this & that, through the distorted vision of humanism, have tended to become obviated as the folly of social Darwinism, which pretends that the extremes of competition are most fitting for human survival. In reality, the Two Competencies, of the first & second systems, are not within the *rate & range* of perfectly resolvable *aspect ratios*, leaving the third system as indeterminate, and yet potentially progressive in nature. That is, in the manner of consummate politicians, if people insist upon deterministic control-&-denial patterns, *Sense and Sensibility* become tokenized as *Pride and Prejudice* (two novels by Jane Austen). Central to The Human Equation, then, is an attempt to avoid an *unfortunate turn of events*, by nickel & diming the assumptions & suppositions of the "Two Determinisms". (See the inverted heart of Metalogical Construct No.4.) Any given person can be absolutely brilliant, and yet have a tragically intractable personality. One only has to look at criminal law, as practiced by many legal systems, which often plays upon the systematic doubt of an unfortunate public, while coercing judgements through the use of legalisms. The Indecision/Confusion of a rigid legal process, usually jumps to the false efficacy of automatic progress, when the biases & prejudices of influential people are brought to bear. Just because the law works for the "right people" doesn't mean it reflects progressive legality. The influential and wealthy can afford button-&-string defenses, which are apt to use & abuse the public sensibility, while making mockery of the undeniable legality of the full correspondence of evidence. Any legal system that pretends that one can really 'tell the whole truth and nothing but the truth' needs the application of a good laxative.

One dimension that we will be exploring is how the presence or absence of 'positive law' relates to the way in which The Human Equation supports the humane development of the 'spirit of the law', based upon what is called 'natural law'. I take the position that natural law has its roots in the natural system, which implies that, for us, legality stems from the same rigorous development as the scientific method.

To begin at the beginning, all developments of The Human Equation have their foundation in the propagation patterns of light quanta, as the source of Universal Dynamics. In that light is self-polarizing, Universal Duality develops much in the manner of a Buddhist koan. What is important, is to resolve the ambiguous feelings generated by a given koan-set, through some sort of associative process. Unfortunately, because of the foibles of the Human Observer, Duality often becomes translated as antinomy, dichotomy, complicity, duplicity, collusion and conspiracy, etc. The result is a dualism that leads to the meaningless dehumanization of The Human Equation. If *ambiguity & arbitrariness* lead to *absurdity*, the recombinant third person fails to emerge from the fundamental Duality of the 'I & thou'. (Universal Duality is modeled by Metalogical Construct No.13.) Certainly, empirical systems, based upon the development of experience, facilitate work with evolutionary processes, but they often fail to escape the captivating rendering of the biased subjectivism of obviation & the prejudicial objectivism of the so-called facts. Then, in order to compensate for the libertine excesses of so-called free association, dictatorial coercion & convergence usually result in artificial legalisms. (See Construct No.4) Without the careful recomposition of what physicists refer to as 'associative production', the end product becomes a lifeless travesty of justice.

Ergo! the importance of 'arguing from design' (Canadian philosopher, Northop Frye); i.e., universal design, in order that Subjectivity & Objectivity are not subject to & object to our normally limited sense of recombinant relationships. One usually juggles feverishly with the E_1 of time & the E_2 of space, separately, and then often fails to appreciate the naturally emergent dynamics of E_3. The latter is not simply three spatial distances, as 'metric space', but shares both spatial & temporal modes by blending space-time characteristics. Physicists use the term 'Euclidean space-time object' (my Construct No.7), to render what I refer to as "Associative Justice". In other terms, the *entities* of time & *events* of space become the recombinant *states* of a legal space-time object (a TTP). Simply put, temporal 'length' in the vertical mode & spatial 'distance' in the horizontal mode, become, through the organized discipline of a democratic, coextensive association, a shape with 'volume', as a viable third alternative. In other words, energy & mass recombine to be experienced as the "Side Effects" of a natural system. Importantly then, when 'energy/mass densities' commingle to make up the volume of a quantum state, they naturally maintain the 'unitarity' of the universe. Such-and-such supports the general viability of empirical evidence, as experienced naturally through the third system. To bring us back to earth, one simply needs to visualize what has been called 'God's caterpillar'.

If the object of our attention no longer "breaths" naturally, then the Christian Commandment of 'Thou shalt not kill.' comes to mind. Again, not taking that fundamental tenet in a childishly literal manner, how we talk about the dead is of considerable importance. (Most of us take this latter admonition in an overly simplistic manner.) Individual and social progress is not possible if the lessons of the past are not fully understood. And, if after the death of a remarkably humane person, his or her work is viewed with a distorted perspective, then, effectively, they die again.

As above, God's caterpillar seems to be eternally hung out to dry. To intuitively appreciate where the human psyche picks up on this Reclining Figure, it is imperative to revisit the topic of 'Minkowski space'. Sadly enough, this concept has generally lost the fully fleshed-out meaning originally intended by its advocate Hermann Minkowski (German mathematician, 1864-1909). He was the predecessor and mentor of Einstein, and his evocation of the 'four-dimensional double light cone' is the basis of my Metalogical Construct No.7. Such is a much better representation than the single 'light cone' that Stephen Hawking presented in his work *A Brief History of Time* (1988). Significantly, my model overcomes many of the dilemmas which have confronted theoretical physics since the misinterpretation of Minkowski's work. The 'evidence' is there, and easily visualized in Construct No.7, but until The Human Equation the philosophy has been lacking. As part of the same process, we can all appreciate the four seasons, and yet until my work no one has been able to properly render the fourth dimension in a manner fit for public consumption. Minkowski gave us the clues about the experiential fourth dimension, except, in the past, we have not paid attention to how the natural system becomes *trustworthy.* My term for these natural transitions is the "Four Phases". An example of these integral relationships, other than the four seasons already mentioned, is: *gambit, habit, ambit, probit.* Many more later.

As per Construct No.7, with the four-dimensional double light cone one can not move left or right in *apposition*, or up or down in *opposition*, without including the *conjugal blending* of space-time properties. Reciprocal oppositions vertically (the colors red-black, blue-yellow, green-white and orange-purple), and the complementary appositions horizontally (red-green, blue-orange, yellow-purple and black-white) render the recombinant aspect ratios of the third system. The secret of the eight harmonic relationships lies in the diagonal lines produced by the complexities of various Crossover Patterns.

Take off the head/tail or the tail/head, and the system fails. That is, in point of fact, this caterpillar is really both genders rolled into one magnificent creature, going in two directions at the same time & place. By convention, the masculine analytic extension evolves toward the right, and the feminine synthetic extension devolves toward the left. Thus, the door swings both ways regardless of the physics of the orientation of '*spin & charge*' and/or the admixture of '*mass & energy*'. And, to avoid living too much on the edge (No.4), we just need to escape from the great soap opera of becoming 'tragically hip in La La Land', with the middle ground taken as the be-all and end-all of all things essential. Construct No.4 is a tragicomic vertical mode where one gets stuck going up & down between the peak of the highest mountain (transcendent sentiments) & the bottom of the deepest sea (subliminal sympathies). Like a consummate villain, this model is the greatest of all bad examples, as the rigid humanism of a devil incarnate. Perfect, here & now, dualisms leave no room for humane progress.

Construct No.13 models Universal Dualities that are 'supersymmetrical', which physicists refer to as 'Susys'. Something well begun becomes properly resolved, with Construct No.13 naturally keying Construct No.7, as the third alternative. That is, the Universal Duality of supersymmetrical pairings goes much further than the invocation of any particular 'ism', regardless of the area of inquiry. To talk of odd without even, essence without substance, or a photon without a graviton, etc. is to misunderstand the very nature of the "Antithetical Vortices" of Minkowski space. As the song says, 'You can't have one, without the o-t-h-e-r.' For example, to think that one can completely polarize something in a single, isolated direction is to misunderstand the very nature of the physics of diffraction & interference, such as between entities & events. We will come back to this topic, and similar analogies, many times, in order to complete the healing process. What No.13 gives us, is an epistemological basis for establishing well-made koans that can be resolved in a legally viable manner. Until The Human Equation, this process has never been properly rendered. For the reader, this means that past dilemmas will simply pass away, providing each person with a growing sense of self-esteem.

Although the Universal Duality of E_1 & E_2 is the basis of Construct No.7, this model really only represents E_3 as Einstein's natural system. In terms of the modern philosophy of physics, No.7 is recombinantly, the Euclidean space-time object. In point of fact, it is *decombinantly devolutionary* to the left, and, *recombinantly evolutionary* to the right. And, its two Side Effects are the proverbial hare and tortoise, with the first ending up last, and the last eventually coming in first. Such and such is a naturally bilateral, coextensive process that avoids the unhealthy extremes of taking this & that too seriously (No.4). Hence, just like Darwin himself, I devoutly avoid representing the exact Temporality (now) & Spatiality (here) of natural selection. The latter Two Competencies are well beyond my level of knowledge & understanding, and so I work with the propagation of light quanta along a 'world line' that continually blends space-time relationships. Hence, we do not have Leibnitz's 'best of all possible worlds', locked into the idealism of the Vertical Mosaic, as there is always room to do better.

Accordingly, I get along well with men like Minkowski and Darwin, but am at a loss as to what happens to their teachings after their demise. As previously mentioned, the question poses itself, about the meaning of the Tenth Commandment: 'Thou shalt not kill?' Certainly, how & what we remember, about the teachings of our forebears, is indicative of either the well-being of human nature, or conversely the decadent state of the Human Condition. 'Progress' is not something that modern society can easily quantify and monopolize. There always remains the possibility that Human Beings, in the future, will become less humane than their ancestors. That is really what the constant 'warning' of the Glorious Koran is all about. Not just physical death but *cultural death* is a real possibility in this world of irrelevant interests, irreverent humor and licentious disrespect for the Maintenance of Innocence. This erroneous triplet reflects the Koran's 'three pillars of the devil', as modeled by the Vertical Mosaic of Construct No.4.

Logic (possible) & reason (plausible) must be constantly recombined in order to discover the diagonal variables (probable) of a viable argument: an important TTP. To obviate The Human Equation, I will be demonstrating the possibility of blending the logic of 'antimatter waves' with the plausible reasons of 'matter waves', in order to resolve the probable relationships of all 'ten field equations' (Einstein). Thus, having 'good args' involves much more than simply quarreling or debating. So let's pick up and continue developing the decalogical thread – as a ten-dimensional space-time that reflects *any objective system* built upon legal argumentation. It's just that, as Einstein rightly claimed, the simplest possible system must have at least ten field equations, with each 'wave train' being made up of what he called 'three functions'. Three-ness, then, seems to be following us around, on many different levels, as though the metaphor of the "Universal Triangle" just might reflect a measure of real viability. I will be making these ideas so easy to understand that the reader will be amazed at how beautiful life really is! It all fits together, with everybody swimming in the same stream.

The second system is substantially objective as qualitative and feminine, for the Soul of Spatiality, &, the first system is essentially subjective as quantitative and masculine, for the Spirit of Temporality. Hence, for a start, we can resolve the dilemma about who is the Significant Other (yang), &, who is the Symbolic Other (yin). (See Construct No.9, for the colored rings labeled "Sign & Symbol".) As an example from physics, the exact position of the 'rest energy' (Einstein's 'E_0'), or magnitude of Temporality, &, the exact momentum of the 'rest mass' (Einstein's 'M_0') or range of Spatiality, are not really at issue here. That is, the exact vertical length of time & horizontal distance of space remain indeterminate, but what they are, blended together, we can live with, like a man and a woman rediscovering 'compatibility' (Einstein). For Freud this progressive association was the 'Heterosexual Stage' that I refer to as the third person: neither and both male & female. Such-and-such mirrors the way the universe unfolds itself, as the constantly emergent New Wave of the third system. Accordingly, what is really represented in Construct No.7 is the orientation of the interacting charge and spin of *electromagnetic waves*, not the exact nature of matter & antimatter. Hence, the eight harmonic colors, with two colors associated with each of the Four Phases, does not reveal the extreme relationships of an "&", but mirrors the more gradual 'Associative And' of classical transitions that we can measure *and* experience.

In No.7, by convention, the 'unit of electron charge' originates to the left and naturally moves toward the right, while the 'unit of magnetic spin' originates to the right and naturally moves toward the left. Together, they produce helical Crossover Patterns. That is, the symbiont of electricity and symbiont of magnetism produce symbiotic '*traveling waves*', whose Side Effects blend with each other as a kind of proverbial apple. In other terms, these symbionts interact decombinantly toward the left *and* recombinantly toward the right, producing naturally symbiotic processes that give life to inanimate objects, *and* allow living plants *and* animals to continue living. Realistically then, there can be no extreme shearing gradients (&). Otherwise, local organic life would cease to be viable. In other terms, Phases I *and* III make up Side Effects that behave like two halves of one apple; coextensively, rather than the self-destructive extremes of matter & antimatter interacting directly. In simpler terms, spring and fall act like "buffer zones" between the more extreme values of the summer of Phase II & winter of Phase IV.

Further, in No.7 the very Essence of Time is a theoretical hyperplane (button) within the red-to-green Means of Phase II, and the exact Substance of Space is a hypothetical split (broken string) between the two black-to-white Ends of Phase IV. In other words, in Phase II matter doubles up through the *obvious* meeting of 'wave fronts', and in Phase IV antimatter doubles down through the *hidden* separation of 'standing waves'. Of course, we are not normally *aware* of the red-to-green Paradigm shift going on all around us. The graciousness of the Paradigm shift acts like a kind of covariant electrostatic field that supports the stillness of all the 'things' around us. Sparks do not normally jump from one object to another, and without the Earth orbiting within the solar system's ecosphere, there would be no biosphere on our planet capable of supporting human life. The Paradigm shift within Phase II (red-green) is an everlasting miracle.

Conversely, we do not normally *recognize* the black-to-white Doppler shift going on within the core of nonexistence, in deep space. Those rapid shifts to the nature of matter, are, fortunately for us, mainly hidden within the true Doppler shift of outer & inner space - safely removed from normal existence. For example, we don't normally realize that the 'unbounded curvature of space' (Einstein) operates not only *within*, between the poles of a planet, but also curves around *without.*

Importantly then, what we generally experience avoids the extreme button-&-string parts hidden without (field) & within (particle) Phases II & IV. More naturally, three-dimensional transitions (ground state) allow harmonious change. Of course many of us have been erroneously led to believe that we can see in three dimensions!? That is, to imply that our environment is made up of 'three spatial dimensions and one temporal dimension' is simply misleading. Three-dimensional metric space (length, height and width), as we normally treat it, has little to do with the volumetric blending of measurable space-time characteristics. Looking in the center of No.7, at the heart of Temporality, one finds a small "hourglass" of black-to-white spatial 'curl', which lies hidden, without & within the range of normal experience. It is the *implicit function* of gravity. Similarly, split between the two Ends of Spatiality there is a small temporal aberration as a red-to-green hourglass. This is the *implicit formation* of 'omniformity', or pure matter that can take any possible shape. Together, these two hourglasses are respectively the subliminal (my 4 & 6) and transcendent (my 11 & 9) characteristics of space & time folding within & without each other. They do influence and subject our existence to potential & implicit contingencies, but as 'nonlocalities' they are not part of what we call local or normal measurements. So with a pattern such as 2 & 4 + 3, the 3 is a locally measurable, odd ground state, which, naturally, must be paired with an even implicit function (2 & 4 in this case) as a quantum mechanical nonlocality. That is, whatever 3 is, it has a 'Higgs mechanism' (2 & 4) giving it a certain weight. With this example, one has a "bread donut" (+ 3) of positive matter, dunked in coffee (2 & 4), which is both within the hole and without the donut – often referred to as a torus or toroid.

But, as with 2 - 1 & 3, one can have a "chocolate donut" (2 -) as a real space, with positive matter as milk without & within it (1 & 3). These ideas will become patently clear as the text progresses. (See Metalogical Construct No.14, which treats the ten, donut-like triads holistically.) Portraying the donut-like, toroidal metaphors of the third system depends upon the gradual progressions of such even/Odd or Even/odd triplets. Importantly, there must be an even pair, as "Outer Field & Inner Particle", attached to an Odd Torus, as a "Middle Ground State". For example: 6 & 8 + 7. Inversely, with 6 - 5 & 7, the Middle Ground State is an Even Torus (as a black donut), and the Outer Field & Inner Particle are odd (as the milk). The implied directions are agreed by convention. The TTP is *acceptance* (by convention), *access* (by encoding) and *agreement* (by procedure). Except politicians usually try to control & deny, acceptance & accession, and avoid getting consensual agreement, unless the dynamic, evolving state of 'general democracy' is healthy.

I'm very good at making these complex ideas easy to understand, and importantly, knowing & understanding these relationships *will set you free!* Once the reader has digested my book, there is really no limit to what a given person can do, from an educational point of view. It will primarily be a question of motivation.

Because big Time has little space within & without it, and big Space has little time within & without it, things move along in good order. Accordingly, the *continuous* flow of flat Temporality itself must always retain some degree of *discontinuous* spatial curl. (On the humorous side, this makes us all partly dysfunctional: No.4.) Such is Einstein's infamous 'cosmological constant' (or c.c.), portrayed by the black-to-white hourglass of nonlocal, spatial characteristics, as an implicit function. Hence, the local Explicit Formation has the nonlocal implicit function without & within it. What this means is that one cannot shield any given chunk of positive matter, from the force of gravity. Gravity, as a nonlocal, quantum mechanical implicit function, penetrates all things. Hence, it appears that the nonlocal remnants of antimatter seem to want to play in matter's ballpark as a discontinuous implicit function, while conversely matter remnants remain a discontinuous *implicit formation* without & within the realm of Spatiality. That is, space is never really empty, but has some form of matter zipping through it as a *form* of radiation. In other words, space & time are independent of each other, but never fully mutually exclusive. There is always some matter left over as discontinuous time without & within continuous Spatiality, and some curl left over as discontinuous space without & within continuous Temporality.

The psychologist Carl Gustav Jung referred to these factors as feminine 'anima' (my 4 & 6) within the 'Celestial Magus' (my + 5), &, masculine 'animus' (my 11 & 9) within the 'Celestial Muse' (my 10). However, there remains evident within these metaphorical relationships, a very serious flaw that The Human Equation must overcome. There are really six relationships here, not just Jung's four. Einstein also missed part of this full set, when he wrote $E = Mc^2$. No matter who you are, if you are not able to work out these difficulties & problems, you will never become master of your own self, and thus remain a threat to the progress of human nature. Good intentions are not enough. Terrorism has its roots in the misconceptions and distorted perceptions of each and every one of us. It is broken. I will fix it. We will develop a better Social Consciousness.

The famous physicist Murray Gill-Mann is fond of saying, "Keep your eye on the donut." As implied, Outer Field & Inner Particle are not part of what we normally experience. They are nonlocal, quantum mechanical operators. It is really the Middle Ground State that reveals whether the donut is "bread" or "chocolate". In other terms, if a torus is made of matter, and is expanding, through what we call 'emissions', its positive energy can be represented as "white time". Inversely, if a torus is made of antimatter, and is contracting, through what we call 'absorption', its negative substance can, for metaphorical reasons, be represented as "black space". And yet, it is 'gray matter', as making up the moderation of experience, that is of most concern to Human Beings.

For The Human Equation, then, the 'truth' is never unalloyed, just as 'meaning' is always an admixture of temporal & spatial characteristics. Further, the best of ideas are usually partly dysfunctional, and certain concepts, which at first might be held in derision, could eventually prove to be reformative. Hence, the nature of significant & symbolic relationships is such that there is *never a completely true or false set of decision modes.* Therefore, in mathematical terms, Gödel's theorem establishes that the up & down extremes of Construct No.4 are far too metaphysical to be of real help to human nature. And yet, most of 'us' never overcome the inadvertence of controversial & conflicted relationships, bicycling between unconscious & subconscious alter egos.

Looking at Metalogical Construct No.13, those dimensions which fold out oddly are shown as white, and those that fold in evenly are shown as black. Black & white represent extreme values, referred to as the true Doppler shift. That gives the impression that the creation mode is primarily tied to the objectivity of a Phase IV set of relationships, which produces *dialetheism* (9-11), or what the Greeks called the River of Lethe (lethal). No.13, in the form of a cross, resembles Einstein's concept of looking along two intersecting, self-polarizing light waves. If traditional figure/ground Gestalt patterns are tied to No.13, giving the impression of just two factors for each part of the cross, then *human epistemology becomes perverted.* However, if the two vertical black lines are treated as my 4 & 6, and the two horizontal white lines as my 11 & 9, then, with 5 as the vertical white line and 10 as the horizontal black line, there are three terms to each side. But, we are not out of the woods yet, because the Duality of No.13 can still be prostituted to an unhealthy dualism. Firstly, we must realize that 'this' is like the Greek River of Styx, in the vertical mode, as an aspect of existence. Hence, the epistemology of proper supersymmetrical patterns must include both the vertical 'rhetorical syllogism' (3 factors), of the Subjectivity of Existence, &, the horizontal 'dialectical syllogism' (3 factors), of the Objectivity of Nonexistence. In the past, these two basic syllogisms were not usually treated in a manner that facilitated their recombination as a third alternative.

In No.13, I introduced the colored circles to Einstein's Susy in order to avoid the perversion of basic epistemology. The supersymmetrical arms of the cross, if set up as a true creation mode, should naturally lead from No.13 to No.7, or, from Einstein's E_1 & E_2, to his E_3. Thus, instead of the extremes of the two arms, positive matter can be represented in a more moderate manner, as folding out oddly with 'fermions' (after Enrico Fermi, Ital.-Am. physicist, 1901-1954), which are shown as orange-red-green-blue. Antimatter relationships, that fold in evenly with 'bosons' (after Satyendra Bose, Indian physicist, 1894-1974) are shown as yellow-white-black-purple. (Note the order of the colors.) Fermions are usually represented as clockwise in No13, and rightward moving in No.7; bosons as counterclockwise in No.13, and leftward moving in No.7. Physicists portray these conventions of directionality through the dynamics of 'chirality'. As per the Quarteron Pattern (Construct No.1), I refer to 'up' as folding out oddly, analytically rightward, and to 'down' as folding in evenly, synthetically leftward. Without my models, these aspects are not representable in a manner that facilitates them being learned by the general public.

The koan-like, paradoxical relationships between fermions & bosons are the heterogeneic (folding out oddly as fermions) aspects of 'quantum electrodynamics', or QED, and the homogeneic (folding in evenly as bosons) aspects are 'quantum chromodynamics', or QCD. QED & QCD are the modern versions of the *two basic ancient syllogisms* that are fundamental to all epistemological theories. Note in No.13, that the method of calculating inverts the nature of the message: that the 'constituents' of double black lines *differentiate* the white 'forces' of QED, and that the 'constituents' of double white lines *integrate* the black 'forces' of QCD. 'This' as QED places 4 & 6 with + 5, and 'that' as QCD places 10 - with 11 & 9, together making up the two fundamental syllogisms of supersymmetrical interplay. Thus, the vertical *rhetorical syllogism* becomes modernized as 'special relativity' & the horizontal *dialectical syllogism* is rendered as 'general relativity'. Together, these two syllogisms intimate the idealism of the Subjectivity & Objectivity of Universal Duality, as the would-be Certainty Principle.

It's just that, in Einstein's famous equation, of $E = mc^2$, there are supposed to be two syllogisms, for a total of six factors, blended to produce the compatibility of the natural system. However, the *dialetheism* of general relativity (mc^2) dominates the equation as a nonexistent creation mode, while the *diatheism* of the special relativity side (E) remains incomplete! (Physicists say that Einstein did not fully 'geometrize' special relativity.) And, as we have stated, if the basic epistemological relationships are distorted (within No. 13) then No.7 becomes unresolvable as a natural set of doctrinal arguments. Such is likely the reason why Einstein never fully completed his ten field equations. With the decalogical spectrum of Construct No.14, I at least give a very simplified, but importantly, *complete set of ten field equations.* So dear reader, you and I together, will not only finish Einstein's basic equation but also complete all of his field equations, for the full development of 'superstring theory'. Once, only a few people on this planet could work out these patterns. Soon almost everybody will be talking about them.

Particles, like solid-white donut centers (trade name Timbits), are the Inner Particles of fermions. White fermions can also constitute an Outer Field of positive matter. Affectively, a black boson donut is being dunked in white fermion milk, which fills in the areas around the black donut with a white Outer Field & a white Inner Particle, making up a positive pair of constituent fermions.

Thus, positive field-&-particle patterns can be represented by odd numbers such as 1 & 3, 3 & 5, etc. These are nonlocal integral derivatives, that begin with the 11 & 9 of the v.e.d., as the most basic example. The black donut (10) itself is the magnetic ground state of antimatter 'force', as the 'wave function' (Erwin Schrödinger) of a Middle Ground State that can only be known by the white constituent fermions which surround it with milk – in the Outer Field & Inner Particle. (Two white 'constituents' to *know* a single black 'force' become an 'enigma' [11 & 9]. And, these patterns of *dialetheism* (9-11), as 'enigma', still mystify modern thinkers. In No.4, they are at the top.) Thus, in No.13, the horizontal black line is the black donut as the Middle Ground State of nonexistence, and the two white lines are the milk without & within 'that'. (Hence, the Christian 'immaculate conception' seems enigmatic for 11 & 9, 'when' it becomes an intellectual abstraction at the top of No.4.) And, the vertical white 'force' is a white bread donut as the Middle Ground State of existence, with the two black 'constituents' as the coffee without & within 'this'. (Two black to *understand* a single white becomes the *diatheism* of a 'conundrum' [6-4] in the bottom of No.4. In modern society this becomes the 'false belief syndrome'.)

In other terms, QED is the vertical white line of 'covariance' between two black lines, &, QCD is the two white lines of 'contravariance' about the horizontal black line in between. (Note that *only* the white lines can be identified as "existing", which presented early Western philosophers with an enigma, especially concerning the essentialism & evolutionism of the Christian Trinity. (We must 'look to the light'.) Further, the same enigma also presents problems for modern particle physics. Thus a neutral particle cannot be identified directly, only by its interaction with charged particles. Hence, a 'neutrino' is best sought in the area of 'antineutrinos', which would have a measurable 'charge equivalence'. The trick is for the supersymmetries of QED & QCD to produce a system of measurement similar to No.7, so that the Dynamics of Streaming support the natural system on a fundamental level of analogy. ***The***

Human Equation will be proclaiming the thesis that the basic Susy leads to the natural 'teleology of physics', as fundamental to trusting that democracy is the most efficient form of government.

Make no mistake, this work is not just about physical principles. Whatever the area of inquiry, The Human Equation provides procedural protocols that render General Guidelines appropriate to *any area of human inquiry.* For example, through what I call "grammatics", the follow decalogical pattern is extremely advanced: interjection, article, preposition, conjunction, verb, adverb, pronoun, adjective, noun, and the ineffable Word itself. You may prefer to get your doctorate on 'The Relationship Between Pronoun Use and Mental Health', or, simply check my models to see in what orbit "pronoun" lies: the 7th orbit. Then, compare that aspect with similar attributes for the same orbit, such as wisdom, Buddhahood, or teleology, complex numbers, etc. Hence, I don't need to preach, bang on a drum, launch into an ethnic cant, or, have an axe to grind. Whatever you do, dear Reader, with the relationships of The Human Equation, is your own business. Nevertheless, what *we* must do together, is reexamine fundamental patterns, such as 'inference' (deduction) and 'interpretation' (induction). But, I don't leave you out in the cold. Basic epistemology is as simple as pretty colored models.

It is only natural that a truly epistemological model begins with intersecting light waves as a set of First Principles. In No.13, if the metaphor for Reason is given as white, then for Logic it is black. Thus, the two vertical black lines are 'inductive logic' (4 & 6), and the vertical white line is 'deductive reason' (5). Correspondingly, the two horizontal white lines are 'inductive reason' and the horizontal black line is 'deductive logic'. Thereby Reason & Logic move within & without each other, in the manner of Universal Duality. There is a kind of thirteen-dimensional character about the vertical 'bar', and a similar thirteen-ness about the horizontal 'bas', making their Mutuality fundamental to all harmonic relationships, based upon the divine nature of marriage. (This Duality relates the Hebrew teachings of Urim & Thummim, to the mind/body harmony of Buddhahood, and to the Susys of physics, etc., etc.) In a symbolic sense, two unlucky thirteens become one lucky fifteen (5 & 10), which could be based upon the supersymmetries of twenty-six dimensional space-time. The Cabalistic patterns of Susys, as 'lights & values', certainly tickle my fancy. Recombinantly, portraying the fifteen-ness of this Poetic Kiss is the stuff of greatness, due to the reputable interplay it provides between the ground states of Eminence vertically (5), & Distinction horizontally (10). But here there is a special proviso: the torus of the Significant Other (5) cannot *become* a single 'one' of mutual inclusion & the torus of the Symbolic Other may not *be* an exact 'dyad' of mutual exclusion. In No.7, the 'one' is the real, unknown Paradigm shift (red-green) of Phase II, in the Means of Existence, & the 'dyad' is the true, unfathomable Doppler shift (black-white) of Phase IV, in the Ends of Nonexistence. These terms, the 'one and the dyad', produced by Xenocrates (a student of Plato) are still viable – even for modern civilization. Importantly, they must not become niggling politics, cycling between the sentiments of mutual inclusion (up) & the sympathies of mutual exclusion (down), as modeled by Metalogical Construct No.4. In the latter case, the Universal Duality of No.13 becomes the dualisms of No.4, or what is commonly called 'having hang-ups'.

Still looking at No.13, Carl Gustav Jung referred to the figure/ground relationships of the vertical triplet as the Celestial Magus (white line) and anima (two black lines), & the horizontal triplet as Celestial Muse (black line) and animus (two white lines). The reader will no doubt notice that I have modified these Taoistic Antithetical Vortices by introducing the dimensionality of three-ness as an extension of Universal Duality. Accordingly, I have six terms instead of Jung's four, because using four allows *Gestalt psychology to get hung up on figure/ground patterns that move within & without each other, in an unhealthy manner.* Using six terms provides for a naturally viable approach, founded upon two triads, both made up of Outer Field, Middle Ground State and Inner Particle, based upon my field-ground-particle pattern. Such three-ness is integral to the development of all aspects of modern philosophy. However, we are not out of the woods yet. Triplets, like dualities, can still be misconstrued. In No.4, there is a dominant masculine triangulation in the upper transcendent, parapsychological mode (9-11-5), & a subservient feminine triangulation in the lower subliminal, paranormal mode (6-4-10). Here, psychology boarders on becoming a science.

Interestingly enough, I probably was also strongly influenced by Jung's mandala-like, colored models, which he left incomplete upon his death in 1961. My hunch is that Jung based his circular "fermions & bosons" on the mathematical Hamiltonian functions of Sir William Rowan Hamilton (1805-1865), a British mathematician and astronomer whose vector analysis was fundamental to modern statistical dynamics. Combine the ideals of Hamilton's math, Jung's mandalas and Johann Wolfgang von Goethe's holistic color theories, and the result is my Quarteron Pattern, which became Metalogical Construct No.1. Interestingly, the 'eightfold way' that is evident in the Quarteron Pattern operates much like the systemic relationships developed by physicists in the 1960's. This aspect of the 'standard model' or SM, resides mainly in the vertical mode, like a button, *orthogonally.* 'This', like the theories of the static universe, seeks to define the 'one' as what physicists call a 'single symmetry classification'. Naturally, such a philosophy is moribund. 'This' alone, as the only 'one', would make being politically correct a determining factor, establishing the legalisms of *obviation & evidence*, and making science into the quasiscience of empiricism. Obviation & evidence is one of the suspect dualisms of No.4, while *observation & experiment* is a proper duality, as modeled by the First Principles of No.13.

Further, continuing the influence of Hindu and Buddhist mandalas, Construct No.7 is a good metaphor for the Eightfold

Path. The latter works like a "fat string", mainly in the horizontal mode, through what has been referred to as angular momentum. Physicists need this model to complete their SM, because the Quarteron Pattern is better understood when it is related to the horizontal 'smear effect' of matter. Nevertheless, the interactions produced by the physics of particle collisions are best modeled in relation to the vertical mode. We will be discussing this verticalized dimensionality of particle physics under the philosophical term of Mimesis. Just remember that the vertical 'eightfold way' is not the horizontal Eightfold Path. The former is like 'ortho-hydrogen', on a button, while the latter resembles 'para-hydrogen', on a string. Thus, the orthogonal tends to *become* exaggerated vertically & the paralogical tends to be reduced horizontally, as part of the alienation of Human Nature: ***for ever & anon.*** Importantly, Life Cycles can move in two distinctly bilateral directions, devolving leftward and evolving rightward, as appositions. The reciprocals of oppositions move upward to a larger scale & downward to a smaller scale, primarily on one orthogonal plane of action. The horizontal mode or Horizontal Mosaic is referred to as a 'cross channel', & the vertical mode or Vertical Mosaic is called the 'direct channel'. Horizontally, one has self-evident Middle Ground States, and vertically the crust & crumbs of reciprocal derivatives are Outer Field & Inner Particle, or *field-particle interactions.*

Here, we must introduce a revolution in human learning! Traditionally, figure/ground Gestalts have plagued human nature. For example, if one looks at the stripes in a shirt, it is not possible to notice details such as buttons or loose threads, etc. And, inversely, when examining that shirt for soiled spots, the overall pattern is not part of conscious perception. Clever people have erroneously barked up this figure/ground tree as being a fundamental 'duality' that human nature cannot escape. In reality, following the Universal Triangle, there are three relationships. Firstly, the style, cut, price, material and quality of the manufacturing of the shirt is the conceptual Outer Field. Then the overall, usually uniform pattern becomes the Middle Ground State. Thirdly, various details can be brought into focus by shifting one's attention to the specific aspects of an Inner Figure (Particle). This example may seem trivial, but the Field-Ground-Figure pattern (Don Powell) is crucial to the ***educational reforms necessary to bring Human Beings into the modern era of progressive scientific measures.***

Even great men have been, and still are being taken in by traditional figure/ground Gestalts. Taoist models tend to be given this same dualistic interpretation. Manichaean dualisms, based upon Persian dualism, have strongly influenced the fundamental philosophies and spirituality of human thinking. Einstein talked about the 'homomorphic and isotropic', while the modern 'isotopic' must be added in as an Outer Field. William Shakespeare, Karl Marx, Carl Gustav Jung, and many others have struggled with these same inconsistencies (Construct No.4). Jung's influence can be directly perceived when looking at the *Hamiltonian torus functions* of Construct No.9. The torus function is shaped like a donut and is normally split into a 'transport phenomenon', between the crust of the Outer Field & the crumbs of the Inner Particle. (For the wave train 6 - 5 & 7, the 5 & 7 make up the transport phenomenon, of field & particle, while 6 - is their ground state.) In No.9, the donut-shaped portions are the Middle Ground State, and the donut holes are Inner Particles. However, keep in mind that for the emergent three-ness of modern chaos theory, Jung's dualistic modes need modification. Each torus, to complete the 'discriminant function' between the outer & inner portions, must be fitted with an Outer Field reflecting the same colors as the Inner Particle. It's like blowing a smoke ring. And, just as my epistemological model has a built-in three-ness not represented by Jung's dualistic colored rings, so the Four Phases in No.9 require the triad of a field-ground-figure pattern for each torus. If the reader would be so kind as to imagine an Outer Field for each donut, with the same color combination as the respective donut hole or Inner Particle, then the models will meet the standard three-ness of modern theory. The Middle Ground States, as the donuts, are what we experience developmentally. As per No.7, they usually share two colors for each stage of development. Thus Middle Ground States are paired, odd with even, as a *heterotic association*. The Outer Field & Inner Particle are a 'reflection principle' – for want of a better term – as the nonlocal reciprocals of a *field-particle dualism* that is not normally experienced. Now, everything clicks into place, for all ten field equations. My genius, if I may use that word, has been to combine Goethe's theory of comprehensive color relationships with the rings of Jung and Hamilton. I have yet to find anyone, other than myself, who can get all the wave-train triplets into one consistent, decalogical system.

At a later point in this work, we will be looking at Jung's anima & Celestial Magus as the figure/ground of an incomplete Phase II, &, his Celestial Muse & animus as a similar pattern for Phase IV. Further, looking at Construct No.6 as a Phase IV pattern, we can envision Einstein's homomorphic (10 - , yellow-white-black-purple) and isotropic (9, blue-green-red-orange) for general relativity. Einstein has made the same incomplete supposition as Jung, likely due to the traditional figure/ground relationships of Gestalt brinkmanship. Now, we know that mc^2 or M_oc^2 requires ten-ness for M_o as a rest mass for 'supergravity', and, the transcription, transformation or transfusion of eleven-ness & nine-ness, for c^2. Hence, by adding an Outer Field (11), of the same coloration as the Inner Particle (9), the dialectical syllogism of Phase IV is completed as the traditional 11-10-9. As a complete torus, Phase IV combines the 'isotopic outer field' (11) to go with the 'isotropic inner particle' (9), around the Middle Ground State of the homomorphic (10). 11 & 9 are the field & particle of 'environment & corpuscle'. When we get around to doing a similar triplet pattern for 'this' as the special relativity of Phase II, we will have to add two more terms to 'E_o' so that Einstein's equation will finally be completed at the level of the rhetorical or 'demonstrative syllogism' (4-5-6). Except that the traditional syllogisms of 4-5-6 & 11-10-9 need to be given a modern twist, as 4 & 6 + 5, &, 10 - 11 & 9, to show their direction of intent, or chirality.

It behooves me at this point to remark that the mystical teachings of the ancients of all human societies are not to be summarily discounted. For some, historical studies like alchemy, mystical numerology, astrology and metaphysics have bad connotations, but the ancients were really every bit as intelligent as modern humanity. Except, they lacked an integrated system of communication to help each other overcome the glitches of their learning processes. Without *peer review* it is difficult to twig onto a consistent approach. Further, because of the dominance of antagonistic relationships, they often threw the baby out with the bath water, by excessively criticizing individuals and failing to incorporate their discoveries into a system of Integrative Discipline. Accordingly, I will tend to take only what I find appealing and useful, from the great individuals of the past, and try to avoid impugning their *reputations*, which have a sacred quality.

Another interesting aside is that most developers of scientific principles, at an early stage in their careers, become interested in optics, or some related topic of light theory. Personally, I came to such realizations through the study of aesthetics, including the history of art and literature, as well as color theory. However, having purchased a manual, single-lens-reflex camera certainly provided a stimulus for thinking about the nature of light propagation.

In this vein, let's return to the First Principles of Construct No. 13. For the German philosopher Immanuel Kant (1724-1804), the vertical white line would be ***a priori reason*** as deductive reason, or a reasonable inference. The two black lines would be ***a posteriori logic*** as inductive logic, or a logical interpretation (differential calculus of the 'discriminant function' as the 'logic difference equation' for the closed loop). Otherwise, the horizontal black line would be ***a priori logic*** as deductive logic or a logical inference. And, the two white lines would be ***a posteriori reason*** as inductive reason or a reasonable interpretation (integral calculus as the 'closed form integral' of an open system). Note that the three vertical aspects have an open method for calculating the Closed system, &, the three horizontal aspects have a closed method for the calculus of the Open system. Physicists often call 'Type I' open and 'Type II' closed, which implies that they are dealing inductively with the constituents of Outer Field & Inner Particle, as the derivatives of the two nonlocal hourglass-like structures hidden without & within Phases II & IV (No.7). However, the operatives or derivatives of the method of calculation, between Outer Field & Inner Particle, do not determine the Middle Ground State. (This is called the 'law of excluded middles'.) The open-Closed first system is operationally opened by the discriminant function (4 & 6) for the covariance of Closed Heterogeneity (+ 5, vertical white line). To balance the universe, the Open-closed second system is closed by contravariance (11 & 9), as separating out oddly from Open Homogeneity (10 -, horizontal black line). Thus, the first system doubles up & the second system doubles down (see No.7). Hence, to summarize, if we go inductive-Deductive to show the quantum operatives and the nature of the first system, Type I is open-Closed for matter (4 & 6 + 5), &, as Deductive-inductive, Type II is Open-closed for antimatter (10 - 11 & 9). (Note that the chirality is finally correct for each syllogism of three terms.) That is, + 5 is Closed (rightward, positively) & 10 – is Open (leftward, negatively), as the respective deductive inferences that reflect the Real Means & True Ends of the Middle Ground State for each of the two systems. In other terms, Type I is spatially discontinuous (4 & 6) for Temporal Identity (+ 5, Closed for existence), &, Type II for Spatial Continuity (10 – , Open for nonexistence), is temporally discontinuous (11 & 9). It will be worth marking this page in some manner so that the reader will have a handy reference for further discussion.

The way in which the Outer Field & Inner Particle of the 'inductive method' reverses the deductive Middle Ground State can be confusing unless one has Construct No.13. Here, we are getting into the secret of the Poetic Kiss. That is, the two thirteens of Construct No.13 can become lucky, in that they provide: 1) for the wedding of one's inner personality (intrapersonal), 2) for the marriage of two individuals with each other (interpersonal), and 3) for the overall compatibility of the universe (suprapersonal).

With the vertical rhetorical or demonstrative syllogism (4-5-6), inductive logic is without (4) & within (6) Deductive Reason (5), &, with the horizontal dialectical syllogism (11-10-9), inductive reason is without (11) & within (9) deductive logic (10 –). In more complete terms, inductive logic embraces Deductive Reason (4 & 6 + 5), &, Deductive Logic is embraced by inductive reason (10 – 11 & 9). And, after having properly completed the Universal Duality of a fundamental set of Susys, we are now ready to move from No.13 to No.7, and work out a decalogical system of 'punctuation' for many topics, such as the proper order for the Ten Commandments – among others. The object is to give the reader a passion for the study of tenfold taxonomical progressions, so popular in the nineteenth century.

Apparently St. Augustine toyed with numerological relationships in an attempt to establish Universal Systems Theory. He originated the Christian Trinity, in order to avoid some of the pitfalls of dualism. More recently, the Oxford mathematician Roger Penrose entertained the idea of using 'integers' to portray Universal Dynamics. Thereby, one could construct recombinant processes through simple arithmetic operations such as addition, subtraction, ratio, combination & permutation, etc. This is the simplistic approach I have taken in all my models, for the purpose of making fundamental relationships self-evident. Besides, like the general public, I am not very good at math. However, with the inception of modern computing science the power of 'complex numbers' has now been linked operatively to ordinal systems of normative measurement. In other terms, each one of the eight Middle Ground States of No.7 would be considered an appropriate 'rest frame' for a given 'complex plane', within a unified system. Things like wave functions, field equations and inertial progressions, can be used to help define translations, transductions, transitions and transformations, etc. between different complex planes. Within a given Life Cycle or dynamic spectral range, each quantum state maintains the 'unitarity, consistency and invariance' of the overall system. In No.7, I refer to the overall pattern of such relationships as the Dynamics of Streaming. And, each odd-even pair marks a transition between a given Phase, with the eight harmonics covering the Four Phases of complete phasal space. Hence, each quantum state shares in the complete phasal space of Constant Unity Factors.

To return to the previous analysis, physicists refer to Type I as an open system, but looking at the vertical lines in Construct No. 13, and their development in the central Means of Construct No.7, we are ready to remove confusion in this regard. As the Means, the first system is not an open system, but is open-Closed in Phase II for the semiconducting solids of "Matter Resonance". The planet Earth is not the planet Mars, etc. Each planetary system is materially closed, although unbounded spatially. In the Means, electrodynamic waves dominate as an *Explicit Formation* (+ 5), with magnetic characteristics as an *implicit function* (4 & 6). The Explicit Formation is deductively electrostatics (+ 5), because the wave fronts of 'electrostatic covariance' dominate the implicit function of what is inductively 'paramagnetic' without & within them (4 & 6). Again, the inductive takes a back seat to the Deductive, for the latter obviates the Middle Ground State and is not just the derivative of a differential operation. Similarly, the horizontal lines of Construct No. 13 are developed about the Ends of Construct No.7, in Phase IV, making the second system into a Open-closed system of "Antimatter Resonance", not the closed system advocated by Type II. Here one has an antimatter relationship as an *Explicit Function* (10 -), along with an *implicit formation* (11 & 9). The 'diamagnetic', based upon 'magnetostatic standing waves' (10 - 0), is the dominant, deductive ground state, and the 'paraelectrical' is the inductive derivative of an implicit formation that produces contravariance (11 & 9) as a closed form integral. When a 'magnetostatic accretion disk' (black button, disk or torus), produced by magnetostatic standing waves, becomes the Ends of Antimatter Resonance (10 - 0), then environment & corpuscle (11 & 9) must break spatial symmetry through 'adiabatic expansion'. (No absolutes are allowed. As mentioned at the beginning of this text, there is no pretense of cosmic censorship without & within Antimatter Resonance in Phase IV, just as there is no pretense of the static universe as the fixed 'one' of Matter Resonance in Phase II.) *What this means is that a so-called 'singularity' or 'null point' of zero dimensions is really only a 'point defect' of very-limited dimensionality; i.e., less than a one-dimensional line.* In other words, black holes are not dimensionless points, but are 'contingent' as a kind of 'worm hole', too small and too highly pressurized to allow safe passage for normal matter. In Phase IV, Antimatter acts as a Universal Solvent, and matter is reduced to PRP, as the omniformity of uniform inertia.

To show the duplicitous nature of the unbounded curvature of the Ends, I will be using a doubled-down ground state: 10 - 0 as the diamagnetic standing waves of 'condensation'. Such Spatiality 'warps' around between the legitimate poles of a world system, especially in the example of Jupiter, which is dominated by its 'magnetosphere'. Jupiter is essentially an Open system, for the 'electric flux' that passes between the poles internally, and then curves back around from the southern geographic pole to the northern one. That typifies the second system as an Open-closed system (10 - 11 & 9). The closed form integral (11 & 9) is a derivative of its dominant Spatiality (10). In contrast, Earth's planetary system is dominated by the Temporality of matter and electrostatic relationships (+ 5), with the 'geomagnetic system' (4 & 6) acting like the implicit function of the logic difference equation. This typifies the first system as an open-Closed system (4 & 6 + 5). In the latter case, matter develops the Means through the Explicit Formation of a 'covariant, electrostatic accretion disk' (white button, disk or torus), which doubles up in existence. In point of fact, the electrostatic accretion disk cannot normally be observed directly for the exact identification of *Verification*, &, the magnetostatic accretion disk cannot be established through the exact processing of the evidence of *Validation.* (Astronomers have recently come to recognize the distinction, within deep space, of white & black accretion disks.) Importantly, the buttons of the real Paradigm shift & the true Doppler shift remain indeterminate, in contrast to the harmonic congruence of the eight, colored buttons that make up the self-evident *Viability* of No.7.

The horizontal cross channels transitioning through the local ground states of the Four Phases are a very different story from the vertical direct channels linking the nonlocalities of quantum mechanical operatives. The latter are directly reciprocal, based upon exponential inversions, while the former are experienced directly through symbiotic recombinance. (In string theory, the former is a horizontal 'heterotic string' and the latter represents vertical 'superstrings'.) Construct No.14 shows all 30 terms for complete phasal space, with each wave train triplet having a quantum mechanical, correlated nonlocal pair associated with a classical ground as their corollary. Even-odd and even-Odd sets of three terms make up the complex numbers of associative development that work through integral transitions in the way expressed by Roger Penrose.

In Construct No.8, the patterns on the lower left, which are similar to No.7, have been modified at the upper right to reveal toroidal relationships. I have tried to begin with natural numbers to discover real numbers (positive) and imaginary numbers (negative), and then recombine them through complex numbers, to produce a unified, odd-even space-time. Penrose refers to such an operation as 'projective geometry'. In No.8, the Phase III self-evident aspect ratios are shown by the blue-purple torus floating up like a cold donut of 'magnetic spin' in a vat of hot "Electronic Resonance" (negative anions without & within the positive anode, or torus of the nucleophilic ground state). The Phase I toroidal formation shows a yellow-orange donut floating up in a green-blue-purple-black area of "Magnetic Resonance" (positive cations without & within the negative cathode, or torus of the electrophilic ground state).

The former nucleophilic torus, as a Phase III pattern, represents the 'moment of magnetic impedance', as a factor of 'magnetic spin orientation', which is 'positronic', and contains within the 'fast electron' or 'free electron'. In Phase I, the electrophilic torus is the 'slow electron of electrical resistance', also referred to as the electron's 'unit of charge', which contains within it the 'holes' of positive current flow. The negative free electrons within Phase III and the positive holes within Phase I are exchanged as the current flow that we experience through our use of electrical appliances.

As a planetary system, our Earth produces a 'heat ring' that helps make the Arctic generally warmer than the Antarctic. Apparently the two symbiotic tori (electrophilic in Phase I and nucleophilic in Phase III) differentially influence the separate polar openings in Earth's ozone shield, making the northern opening smaller (incoming) and less dangerous than the southern one (outgoing). Many animals in southern Chile are developing cataracts and in the future, if our planet gets even more hostile, someone will soon develop a sunvisor for animals. For humans, getting less direct sunlight is in order.

We will come back to these concepts again, relating them to other examples such as the operation of old-fashioned electronic tubes, microcurrents within DNA, transistor circuits, etc., etc. In contrast to the gray matter of the traveling waves of Phases I and III, the white & black tori of Phases II & IV are often less directly evident. More recently, the Hubble telescope has made available images of the various kinds of white & black accretion disks, involved in star and planet formation. The button-string or ortho-para patterns of deep space are quite remarkable, with white accretion disks (Phase II) centered by black holes, &, black accretion disks (Phase IV) centered by white holes as quasi-stellar objects that are radiation sources.

Construct No. 13, as purely II & IV or button & string, is flawed and yet still one of the best epistemological models ever built. Nevertheless, it is not possible to distinguish the orientation of 4-5-6 for the vertical triplet, and thus the QED pattern of 4 & 6 + 5 is not *conventionally obvious* as the Arrow of Time. And yet, Phase II is part of an organic system, and the Paradigm shift must open its window to future development. Similarly, the Phase IV orientation of 11-10-9 cannot be established for the horizontal triplet and thus the QCD pattern of 10 - 11 & 9 is not *actually evident* for the Space Vector. In a complete system, the Arrow of Time & Space Vector must have the same classical orientation, which is basic to the historically important EPR experiment debated by Albert Einstein, Boris Podolsky and Nathan Rosen. With my models and my system of ten field equations, this debate is finally resolved, and easily understood. Within a given system, Phases II & IV, and Phases I and III, are all tied together in a holistic manner, just like the four seasons. Thus, the II-&-IV fundamentals of No.13 must lead to the natural I-and-III extensions of No.7. (Think of voltage & amperage as recombining to produce wattage: a TTP.) And, as per No.13, it is no longer possible to *prevaricate & equivocate*, to convince & convert through controversy & conflict, when moving naturally from the Universal Duality of Susys to a given argumentative development as an organic process. Hence, proper science always remains democratically viable.

To go over No.13 again, the three vertical lines are the demonstrative syllogism of Aristotelian origin, as the 'one' of Xenocrates. The 'one' places Rhetoric where it belongs, in the Vertical Mosaic of the Means of existence, as Subjectivity. This becomes a window in time (4 & 6), in the area of physical Transportation (+ 5). In other words, ***'this' as the Window of Time is the Becoming of Transportation, or Body.*** Further, 'this' is the Story of all plausible stories, as a vertical profile or 'behavior field' that reveals the mythological 'narrative line' of historical existence. Common sense has these three lines as 'when' (4, black Outer Field), 'how' (5, white Middle Ground State), and 'why' (6, black Inner Particle). They produce subjective inadvertent inversions on the *prima facie*, or button of the Means, with the black particle inverting to the black field and vice versa, while the white ground retains its 'isometric centricity' as a white donut. The latter tends to double up as 'conformal matter' (when the donut cooks). This is shown in the center of Construct No.7 as "+1/2 & +1/2". Except that if we don't solve the problem of orientation, and 4-5-6 becomes interchangeable with 6-5-4, then a static 'syndrome' could be associated with the fixation of existence, as per No.4. That is, the orientation of the Window of Time must relate to the orientation of the Door of Space; which are the A-&-B particles of the EPR debate.

To pick up the Phase IV side of No.13, for traditional Dialectics Aristotle's *dialectical syllogism* places 'cause' where it belongs, in the Horizontal Mosaic of the Ends of nonexistence, as Objectivity. That, as Xenocrates 'dyad', is Actuality, or what is called 'experiment' or 'work'. However, those First Principles, stemming from the 'infinity of values' within deep space, as She, must not become the prostitution of feminine beauty, the preciosity of objects, the anarchy of revolution, the commoditization of values, success as its own measure, the purchase of moral consent, prejudicial evidence, or immutable facts. We are talking about pragmatic democracy leading to fascism. And thus, it is very important that the 'dyad' avoids taking part in cycles of violence, because it is the most active mode. And, equally important, for scientific investigation, nothing is perfectly predictable. Further, common sense has these three horizontal lines as 'where' (11, white Outer Field), 'what' (10, black Middle Ground State), and 'who' (9, white Inner Particle). They are subject to the syndrome of the white particle becoming the white field & vice versa, while the black ground retains its 'allometric centricity' as a black torus. ***'That' as the Door of Space is the Being of Communication, or Mind.***

Unfortunately, as with the Arrow of Time in Phase II, the Space Vector of Phase IV presents problems with orientation, because No.13 does not show how the 11-10-9 or 9-10-11 pattern fits into the Ends of Phase IV. We must work with 10 - 11 & 9, and then expand that fundamental triplet to a larger triplet pattern as a recognizable 'sequence'. The Ends double down as 'disjunctive antimatter', which is shown to either side of Construct No.7 as "-1/2 & -1/2". Those Ends of Phase IV are magnetostatic standing waves as the contravariant *materia secunda* of antimatter, while the Means in Phase II is an electrostatic wave front as the covariant *materia prima* of matter.

Unfortunately, when Duality becomes dualism, The Human Equation naturally bases existence upon the **assumption** of essence and form, and plays down, through **supposition**, the nonexistence of substance and function, to produce the *prima facie* of Construct No.4. That is, through the mind/body syndrome, *materia prima & materia secunda* fail to blend into a natural system as a material object that relates to the other aspects of objective development. 'We' (No.7) get lost, and become 'us' (No.4). In the same manner, the Quarteron Pattern represents the standard model (SM) as a single symmetry classification, by advocating the dominance of 'sufficient reason' over 'necessary logic', when the SM might be better understood through the coextensive sets of No.7. In other terms, because of string-like reductionism, substantial relationships, which although they remain an implicit function, are still important for providing the logical glue that ties together The Human Equation in a developmental manner. That is, it is very difficult to see "function", even though we can not do without it.

Properly handled, Masculinity, time, Means, Likeness, existence, matter, form, essence and the like, make the Vertical Mosaic compatible with the Horizontal Mosaic of Femininity, space, Ends, Difference, nonexistence, antimatter, function and substance, etc. Such an arrangement resembles the physics of Gabriele

Veneziano's 'dual resonance model' (1968). Thus, The Human Equation *should be* based upon the commingling of the first & second systems. Except that patterns like differences-in-Likeness (Vertical Mosaic), or 'separate-sameness' as open-Closed, and, patterns of likenesses-in-Difference (Horizontal Mosaic) or 'same-separateness' as Open-closed, usually have their antithetical natures combined in an inopportune manner. This becomes the Tree of Good & Evil, with one not able to distinguish which, the ascendant or the descendent, is good or evil, true or false, proof or disproof, etc. One is left bedeviled, in a quandary. That is, as per Construct No.4, how one construes the demonstrative syllogism (Rhetoric, 4-5-6) & the dialectical syllogism (Dialectic, 11-10-9), through 'androgynous inversion', becomes *habit forming*, as an absolute triplet of oddness (9-11-5) over an absolute triplet of evenness (6-4-10). (The "9-11" pattern of 'naming before meaning', has been, unfortunately, engraved into the human psyche rather forcefully since the terrorism of 2001, in New York. I like the message, but the misguided messenger did not need to kill others in order to drive it home.) 9-11-5 is the proverbial 'three princes', over 6-4-10 as the 'diva triformis'. For physics, one can invoke the erroneousness of the 'spin-3 particle' over the 'spin-3 force'. Einstein's twin-paradox is the eventual, deadly result. That is, the *specious reason* of the obviation of answers (9-11) & the *spurious logic* of the evidence of solutions (6-4) revolve about the control (5-10) & denial (10-5) of a meaningless result, detached from the larger reality.

The central twist is like a loophole within a button, or a no-spin-zone that acts as the political optic of an 'orthocentrism' or a peephole of reductionism. For example, it is meaningless to narrow down one's options by pretending to be fair, tolerant and equal (a TTP), which becomes a deceptive entanglement that is both contemptuous & malicious. One might be niggardly punctilious and mean spirited, all the while pretending to advocate fairness, equality and tolerance, while really working coercively on a fixed agenda. Such is the sleight of hand of sophisticated necromancy, as the Death of Innocence. Shame above & guilt below, lead to scandal in between as a false trinity. In other terms, enigma (9-11) over conundrum (6-4) precludes the vertical mode of *metalepsis,* and then, the dilemma of control (5-10) begs the dilemma of denial (10-5), which retrocludes the horizontal mode of *prolepsis.* The result is the contemptuousness of Indecision-Confusion (5-10) & maliciousness of Confusion-Indecision (10-5), as the artificial marriage of static controversy & censorial conflict: both disarming & alarming. Which; this or that; becomes Einstein's twin-paradox, based upon the two dilemmas (5 & 10) becoming the two syndromes of ambiguity (5-10) & arbitrariness (10-5), to make up the absurdity of one paradox. Life loses all meaning. Thus, the vertical inversions of Shakespeare's ease & lust, within metalepsis, shrink down to the hyphenated reductionism (5-10) of a false prolepsis, made up of *religious theocracy* (5-10) & *scientific technocracy* (10-5). People become aloof, jaded and complacent: another false trinity. (It was the Muslim faith that alerted me to the patterns of the 'three pillars of the devil'.) So, instead of Jane Austen's *Sense and Sensibility* (1811) as the Duality of the Divine Comedy (No.13), we get her *Pride and Prejudice* (1813) as the dualism of the Demonic Parody (No.4). Rhetoric as observation & Dialectic as experiment, no longer truly independent, undergo the sophistry of the doppelganger of two demiurgic alter egos, as the androgynous inversion of biased obviation & prejudicial evidence, centered about an unresolvable bipolar complex of ironic detachment. Such an impossible middle position becomes an inharmonious barrier to reasonable progress, through what I refer to as "Xenogeneic Contingencies".

Construct No.4 will be the center of interest for this unfortunate turn of events, wherein the autocratic (9-11) is over the meritocratic (6-4), vertically, with the theocratic (5-10) & technocratic (10-5) interacting reductively, in between. A four bladed fan results in the twin-paradox of a cruciform pattern, by which humanity tends toward a feeling of hopelessness. To describe the patristic roots of this pattern, I like to use the expression 'bent of mind & body in a time'. This 'one' alone is "Temporal Infusion", which takes on mythic proportions that excuse doing something upon ideological grounds. 'One' seeks to control history & deny destiny – except for the privileged few who have the 'correct' political connections. That is, acceptance is controlled through political inclusion & accession is denied through political exclusion, while agreement becomes a question of dictating 'affirmative action'. Discordantly, the topological interplay of intellectual & emotional landscapes is reduced to a social *duopoly* between monolithic control & monopolistic influence, to produce 'one note persons' whose variation of feelings & loyalties is restricted under the duress of a repressive *oligopoly*. Temporal Infusion invokes the irrecusable interaction of ingenious lies & disingenuous secrets, making reality into the oscillating hobbyhorse of an artificial 'virtual reality'. Just because something works, doesn't make it right.

The interplay of human spirituality and science is crucial, but historically it has been distorted by the disharmonious interaction of the Book of Scripture & Book of Nature. Apropos, I learned of Leon Lederman through his work with Dick Teresi, on *The God Particle* (1993). Dr. Lederman is an accomplished physicist who once headed up the Fermilab accelerator at Batavia, Illinois and is now promoting the construction of the Superconducting Super Collider at Waxahachie, Texas. In the above text, he sometimes draws analogies between science and other areas of human endeavor, such as art and religion. And, like myself, he doesn't like to meander too freely between subjective & objective modes, such as one witnesses in the work *The Tao Of Physics* (1975) by the physicist Fritjof Capra. Similarly, I will be maintaining a distinction between the natural system and the "surnatural system", which, progressive or not, brings out the importance of the sociopolitics of scientific developments. Surrealistic, spiritual, transcendental, metaphysical and aesthetic modes of thinking and feeling may be less directly objective, and yet despite the preternatural roots, The Human Equation produces a progressively recombinant association. Except that nonscientific ways lend themselves more easily to the dishonest TTP of exploitation, manipulation and coercion. Preternatural propensities, for building up a surnatural system, are seldom disciplined and harmonious. And, although scientific investigation can also become corrupt, it tends to follow the "c's" more readily: consistent, comprehensive, congruent, corresponded, correlated, coherent, confluent, etc. Appropriately, I hope to make evident that a moral approach differs very little from the general organic thrust of the scientific method.

Arguing from 'universal design space' makes the third system a natural extension of the first & second systems, allowing it to be analyzed in a manner similar to quantum statistical mechanics, which is basic to probabilistic measurements. However, Western modes of development have tended to emphasize the formal, orderly, essential, structured, periodic and temporal, etc. One can see this positivism reflected in the conversion of St. Augustine (354-430 AD), from Manichaean dualism to a Christian approach based upon the spiritual Trinity. Combining the *allopatric* Being of Father (11-9) for the second system, and the *sympatric* Becoming of Son (+ 5) for the first system, the Belonging of the Holy Spirit imbues the third system with a dynamic form of essentialism. (The logical positivism of essentialism has often been questioned by scholars, but, on the other side of the coin, we must 'look to the light'.) In a more complete manner, for the Dharmakaya of Buddhism and the Braham of Hinduism, the spiritual & the physical become intertwined, much like the modern conception of the double helix. Accordingly, the Book of Nature, as the Objectivity of Being, & the Book of Scripture, as the Subjectivity of Becoming, must be blended in order to give meaning to terms such as success, progress, evolution and predestination. When, as adults, we reach maturity, in the fullness of time, it is the 'ethology' of the Italian philosopher Giambattista Vico (1688-1744) that sets the standard for social progress. In other terms, based upon the Ethos of Greek teachings, an ethological approach allows for the recomposition of the democratic state. In the modern era, such has become the sociopolitics of scientific progress. Accordingly, moving from dictatorial affirmation, to democratic agreement and professional peer review, effective change requires the empowerment of individuality, whether male or female.

Coming out of the Greek anatomical conception of time as discontinuous bits of *opaque substances*, &, space as the extended emptiness of *transparent essences*, a mechanistic/idyllic viewpoint of life took hold. (Note the unconscious & subconscious inversions of the italicized tautological word pairs. In No.4, *opaque substance*, as up-down, moves from the manic to the depressive, &, *transparent essence*, as down-up, moves from the obsessive to the compulsive. A better mousetrap will never be invented, because it guarantees that the mathematics of the Julia set [1906, inverted heart shape] will lead to Einstein's twin-paradox, like Freud's 'reaction formation'.) Traditionally, there existed the perception of having to repress natural and animal aspects using a supernatural machine, which lead to a denatured style of education. The epic surrealism of a masculine sense of authority reigned over mechanical certainty. Unfortunately, the jailer built the cage for the bird's security, only to become enslaved to the folly of having to mind his own miscreance. Hence, both the animal and the machine became psychopathologically interdependent as the 'animal-machine' (Susan Oyama). Ironically, the 'machine' became parapsychologically contemptuous, through biased obviation, &, the 'animal' became paranaturally malicious, through prejudicial evidence. This is my "romantic-mechanism". (In reality, we do not know about love, &, we do not understand the nature of a machine.) In Metalogical Construct No.4, psychological opposites "spin-flip" up-to-down through liberalism & flip-flop down-to-up through conservatism, and so on. Tricky inversions resemble the tokenism of a turncoat inadvertently changing sides between the 'metaphysical conceit' of Hubris above & 'metaphysical humility' of Nemesis below. Thus, there are two tautological outlooks as demiurgic alter egos, which can cycle unconsciously from above & subconsciously from below, so that the unconscious &

subconscious pivot about the unconscionable. This two-headed pattern, as an *amphisbaena*, resembles the traditional rendering of two snakes wound around a rod. Such a diathesis acts like bias & prejudice combining to become self-deception, or, enigma & conundrum converging to produce dilemma, or exploitation & manipulation resulting in coercion, or complicity & duplicity combining as virtuality, etc. In the prevalent, bicameral duopoly of most political systems, liberalism & conservatism keep the center disarmingly indeterminate, as bipartisan about nonpartisan, so as to control & deny the resolution of social issues. For the diathetical pattern to produce the false trinity, 'one' expects answers & solutions to produce the final result of a fixed agenda. Unfortunately, the combinatorial result becomes the doppelganger of Mimesis, for the palliation of hate & fear through the monolithic-monopoly of automatic progress as the confabulation of narrow-minded policies. Fatalistic modes take over because the up-down/down-up, twin figure-ground patterns of Gestalt brinkmanship lead from the vertical diatheism of the *convenient & expedient* to the dialetheism of the *efficacious*, as dictating results. With the miscreance of diatheism, the Word of God becomes the lost word, and history takes a turn for the worse as the Mythos of Mimesis, or, the Iconographic Simulacrum. Idolatry wins the day and with life as strife, through the meaningless 'acting out' of unconscious & subconscious tendencies, antagonists stake out their demiurgic territory, by capturing the doppelganger in the middle as the romantic-mechanism of the "Hyphenated Person". Scary isn't it?

In modern terms, 'fractal patterns' add in the quantification of mathematical finesse without a sense of either substance or direction. The sowing machine needle goes up & down through the hole in the cloth without a thread of logic to follow the path. This might become a gay & lesbian crisis, a psycho-biological stalemate, a bipartisan standoff, a nonpartisan truce, etc. leading to the fatal combination of aestheticism & adventurism, or revisionism & revolution. Strange 'population inversions' occur, alternating accidentally up & down, with *classical individualism* sitting on the fence, and no real *individuality* for discovering the 'otherness' of the third person. Discordantly, the Classical Alienation of the romantic-mechanism can make civilizing modes, such as assimilation & acculturation or irrelevance & irreverence (Greek Pathos & Bathos), into the diathetical false leads of the two primary ultimatums of Gestalt brinkmanship, as a lost cause. Reciprocity produces gridlock as a syndrome between two tautologies, with intellectual complicity & emotional duplicity pivoting about a center of indifference & violence. Such is the nature of the *prima facie* of Temporal Infusion. People tend to hide within the flattened response patterns of gradualism and relativism as a virtual reality, and then deny that small, but significant-&-substantial changes could possibly add up to real progress. That is, a kind of verticalized "reactionary reflexology" replaces the small analytical incremental steps of more responsible modes.

Responsibility for this impasse is shared between both masculinism up & feminism down, with the result being esotericism as a nefarious complot. The Human Race generally lacks the recombinant "Transmodal Inference" (5 & 10) for breaking out of such a double-plotted syndrome. An appropriate example is evidenced by the Scottish novelist, Robert Louis Stevenson's (1850-1894) *The Strange Case of Dr. Jekyll and Mr. Hyde* (1886). The author was ready to accept the 'active aggressivity' of masculine hate, but not the 'passive aggressivity' of feminine fear. The syndrome takes place between loving hate as homicide & hating love as suicide. Then, a dissociative solution presents itself: dignifying suicide to excuse killing others, while avoiding accountability.

Hating the idea of losing power seems just as real as the fear of facing up to the scourge of the powerful, which gives the impression that 'cycles' are unnatural and unhealthy. Hence, I will be using the more adequate references of "Mr. Jekyll & Mrs. Hyde", so that blame is shared, for the inefficient dissolution of the folding out of oddness

& folding in of evenness (No.4). "He" thinks that he is 100% sure of his manic-depressive, up-down tautology, &, "she" emotes that she is 100% sure of her obsessive-compulsive, down-up tautology. (Psychologists who enjoy their influence over a captive audience bark up the tree of a 50-50 relationship.) To paraphrase the game of *Monopoly*: 'Do not collect $200. Go directly to jail.' Each point of view is tautologically inverted, with the twin-paradox forming from the two heads of the 'direct syndrome' in between. Such, causes the 'lapsus inversion' of the up/down spin-flip of liberalism & the down/up flip-flop of conservatism, thereby combining enigma & conundrum as a bipartisan/nonpartisan dilemma - with no bilateral, postpartisan resolution. (John Fitzgerald Kennedy Jr. advocated "postpartisan politics".) The orthogonal button seems to expand to Eternity in the here, &, the string is reduced to Infinity in the now. Sadly, this false trinity, of Hubris, Nemesis and Mimesis, becomes the Three Fates of Greek infamy, which, not so surprisingly, still plague modern societies. 'Us' are too clever by half.

An interesting aside here, is that the German philosopher Hegel's TTP of 'thesis, antithesis, synthesis' (ca 1821), much to his chagrin, tended toward reductionism, to what is called 'the squared universe'. Hegel really sought continuous self-resolution by advocating the monotheistic third person that recombines the spiritual & natural, the individual & universal, the real & ideal, the Body & Mind, etc. Unfortunately, his triplet pattern tended to become a flattened-response pattern, based upon divisive control, discontinuous denial and artificial fixation. Similar to the 'three pillars of the devil' in Muslim teachings, these relationships reflect exploitation, manipulation and coercion. In terms of physics, we tend to think that the universe is expanding; viewed from our diathetical nexus; and that the dialetheistic plexus came from a big bang centered in our neck of the woods. Discordantly, diatheism as conceived obviation, &, dialetheism as perceived evidence, fail to provide a natural methodology for observation & experiment.

In the latter case, the Human Observer seeks knowledge & understanding of the Natural Language (Ludwig Wittgenstein), in order to continually rediscover the Laws of Nature, through the scientific method. Hence, the playful commingling of observation & experiment produces an every-improving rendering of what we all share, through the dialogical development of empirical experience. The dynamic TTP is observation, experiment and experience. Evidentiary objectivity must avoid the Hegelianism of dictating an unnatural synthesis between empiricism & scientism, by advocating a thorough-going approach, through ethological legality, as a viable work in progress.

The Human Equation must resolve the conflict presented by Construct No.4, before it is possible to move beyond self-righteousness (up) & self-justification (down), and, self-deception (between). One of the most fundamental roadblocks is presented by the cyclopian vision of the illusion of seeing three-dimensional space. The latter is really a recombinant association of different 'energy densities', accompanied by their complementary 'mass densities', and thusly, is not just an ethereal image. The visual illusion becomes extended from the physical aspect of the optical chiasma, in the brain, to the abstraction of a mental chiasmus, by assuming & subsuming such things as *uniform & empty metric space.* The Divided Mind results when the said visual dominance is channeled vicariously through various public media, with the thematic weighting of content becoming reduced to an ethereal state through 'rapid comprehension'. Thus, the Human Condition tends to become a real rush, with a horde of hares attempting to cut the tortoise off at the bridge, without recognizing that he is already on the other side. Discordantly, people look for quick, easy solutions to all their problems. There comes the impression that being rich and influential allows one to do anything with impunity. Discordantly, rationalizing explaining & idealizing complaining results in excusing any sort of behavior, no matter what the situation. There is the impression that, 'I am innocent,' and, 'It's not my fault.' But, should one's own thoughts & actions be allowed to determine another's existence, and is a particular language or ethnic outlook really the measure of 'all possible worlds' (Leibnitz)? Importantly, each person's 'interior monologue' (James Joyce), just might nickel & dime others to death, unless the self regenerates through the interplay of the universal & the particular. That is, *intrapersonal dialogue*, within the self, is a potential source for personal growth. And, following the 'healing circle' of intrapersonal dialogue, individuality soon acquires social consciousness, through *interpersonal dialogue.* Hence, the healing circle expands to include others, within a larger, eusocial Circle of Well-Being.

A simple set of three spatial dimensions, without any consideration of recombinant three-dimensional space-time properties, is a meaningless and nonsensical artifact of pure quantification. One can see 'this' in the triplet of thought, emotion, and projection. *Anthropomorphic projection* produces the idealism of all 'saints' and no 'angels'. Except that the projection of speculative conclusions is not conducive to the natural recombinance of thematic development. That is, unconscious behaviorism (up) & subconscious introspectionism (down) tend to fixate 'attention' without encouraging the emergence of in-depth learning. A truly three-dimensional progression translates psychology into *behavior modification*, through a voyage of self-discovery, as symbolized in the Arabic story about the *Three Princes of Serendib* (source of the word "serendipity" coined by the English man of letters Horace Walpole, 1717-1797). If society & the individual develop bad habits, and the 'fascist-communist conspiracy' (Russian President Boris Yeltsin, 1995) fails to promote the communion of individuality, then adolescent structuralism tends to jump to unfounded consequentialism. For example, Western society is always working on 'The Reform of the Young Offenders Act', which is symptomatic of the closed loop of interior monologue producing delayed judiciality. A prolonged adolescence, for a middle-aged *puer aeternus*, is the basis of all terrorism, with intemperancies exploding from overly structured situations, to claim that others are evil, and then make war on them, as unwarranted constructivism. Even St. Augustine, in his youth, did not want to give in to the requirement of personal behavior modification. As a priest, he would not be able to have his way with women. Similarly, most parents and societies perpetuate the prevalence of their innate faults, by unconsciously & subconsciously, through opportunism & permissiveness, imposing their own biases & prejudices on their children, and others. Further, it is very disappointing that specialized learning and professional ethics often do not produce the 'progress' necessary for a more humane society. If 'higher learning' were as effective as it should be, The Human Equation would be able to link discipline with the empathetic treatment of others, while maintaining a commonsensical approach to advanced learning.

Terrorism as such begins with pharisaic tribalism, linguistic hysteria, and incomplete social conditioning. 'This' is based upon the homicidal lies of explosive behavior ('fission' above as a mechanism), & the suicidal secrets of implosive behavior ('fusion' below as romanticism). Subsequently, the main problem for modern society is an increasingly more delicate infrastructure, with the 'slow-breaking asymmetry' of real change held back, due to superstructure & substructure colluding to produce anarchistic structuralism. The latter becomes the quadrivium of autocratic above, meritocratic below, theocratic left, and technocratic right. Thus, the autocratic & meritocratic make *metalepsis* into an ambiguous diatheism as the River of Styx, in the Vertical Mosaic, &, the theocratic & technocratic make *prolepsis* into an arbitrary dialetheism as the River of Lethe, in the Horizontal Mosaic. The ambiguous & arbitrary currents do not a real river make, because diatheism & dialetheism only produce the absurdity of meaningless superstitions. In the past, Roman armies would invite 'success' by passing through the four-way arch of the *Janus-gate.* But 'one' invites disaster if the vertical Form of the 'strait gate' remains static, from side-to-side as controversial, &, the horizontal Function of the 'round gate' is made discontinuous by converging upon cycles of violence. Hence, advocating the static universe & cosmic censorship leads to convincing & converting, or, controversy & conflict. Evidently, arguing from the wrong design theory, like the four-way arch, produces disastrous personal and social consequences. However, because the spiritual and scientific are naturally associated, there is always a measure of hope.

Like St. Augustine, it is to everyone's advantage to overcome the dualism of the 'terrible two's', commonly identified as a stage through which all human children pass. And yet, by never really coming to grips with two-ness, most people remain both overly controversial, &, prone to conflict. For example, the German poet and dramatist, Johann Wolfgang von Goethe (1749-1832) tried to work out a 'double sanity check' for the human race. That is, it wasn't so much the 'white matter' of existence or the 'black matter' of nonexistence that interested him, as the 'gray matter' of what went between. Not the isolated assumption of the opaque, or the deep supposition of the transparent, but the recomposition of a translucent admixture. Like my Metalogical Constructs, Goethe *saw each color as requiring all the others in order to have its unique identity.* In the same manner, democracy itself reflects the local in the global, and vice versa, which mirrors the checks & balances of Goethe's double sanity check. He sought to avoid Jane Austen's *Pride and Prejudice* as a twin-paradox, and resolve Universal Duality based upon recombining her *Sense and Sensibility.* As per No.13, the four-way arches of fermions & bosons make up the angular momenta of Crossover Patterns that eventually reflect a progressive Life Cycle. However, unless monitored by a community of well-meaning persons, the famous Roman gate, the Janus Geminus, could not be a model of healthy recombinance. It acted like a flower sifter, with the Phase II side as a static, and the other side alternately mobile, similar to the 'dyad' of Phase IV dialetheism. If Goethe's double sanity check, like my Double Passover, resolves Einstein's twin-paradox, through Diacritical Consciousness, then enhancing personal self-esteem will naturally lead to the respect of others, through what I call

Associative Justice. Such is remarkable similar to the teleological physics of associative production.

The omniformity of dialetheism as Perfectly Random Patterns (PRP), like Carl Gustav Jung's 'archetypal patterns', is able to assume any given form as a 'body plan' (American paleontologist Stephen Jay Gould). That is, a Phase IV creation mode is purported to be the cause of First Principles, as an ultimate source of 'universal design space', for such things as the almost unlimited number of body plans that existed, on Earth, in the pre-biotic, primordial soup. That is really a one-sided assumption, because nonexistence as such has its birth within the existence of matter, in the Means of Phase II, just as the birth of matter takes place within nonexistence, in the Ends of Phase IV. (In No.7, compare the small hourglasses with their larger counterparts of the same colors.) Accordingly, the Life Cycle is based upon a Means-End Continuum, with matter & antimatter folding within & without each other, with the different 'histories' of No.7 reflecting their origin in the Certainty Principle of Universal Duality, as per No.13.

Thus, using a 'sum over histories' (Am. phys. Richard Feynman, 1918-1988), as placing individual design within the argument from universal design, one is less inclined to be specious & spurious, and more likely to keep things in good proportion. And, the way in which our body plan reflects the *Corpus Universalis* becomes a matter of blending both Objectivity & Subjectivity within the natural system. That is, using Construct No.2 as a good "bad example", the traditional idea that the objectivity of the Book of Nature totally separates the objective Mind of Being, in nonexistence, from the subjective Body of Becoming in existence, just doesn't ring true.

Keeping in mind the danger of anthropomorphic projection, modifying the human behavior field allows us to nurture but not dictate our own development. Discordantly however, one could treat life in the manner of the Janus-gate, producing a wicked limp by attempting to fix the Subjectivity of Verification & push the Objectivity of Validation, through legalisms such as empiricism & scientism. In modern terms, one could exercise coercive 'selection pressures' (Phillip E. Johnson) through the *evolutionism* of dictating choices & actions. Add these selection pressures, based upon a high-minded surnatural outlook, to natural tendencies such as Darwin's 'selective evolution', and the recipe for change becomes overly complicated. It's just that, for The Human Equation, Subjectivity may be even more important than Objectivity, at least concerning the never-ending search for the Natural Language, as a better and better way of processing information.

Surprisingly, the aesthetics of the Reclining Figure (No.7) is not really that different from the Corpus Universalis. (No.7 can be viewed sideways, as a female figure with the head to the left, and as a male figure with the head to the right. The two are fatalistically 'joined at the hip' in the Means of existence, which could result in uncontrolled & unrestrained 'population inversions', such as the diatheism of No.4.) The major point to be made here is that for the Universal Duality, of Subjectivity (4-5-6) & Objectivity (11-10-9), as the Two Competencies, The Human Equation cannot totally separate out the Verification of Subjectivity from the Validation of Objectivity. (In No.4, subjectivism [9-11-5] is up & objectivism [6-4-10] is down, through androgynous inversion.) Just as the *application* of our reasonable interpretation (9-11) usually taints Objectivity (10 - 11 & 9), so the *methodology* of our logical interpretation (6-4) tends to distort Subjectivity (4 & 6 + 5). That is, subjective observation becomes difficult due to the bias of obviation, & objective experiment presents problems because of the evaluative nature of prejudicial evidence. In other terms, defining the *application of laws* & describing the *methodology of principles*, for establishing the *perfectly empirical*, is no walk in the park. In other words, the Verification of Commutative Justice & the Validation of Distributive Justice must be tempered by the Viability of Associative

Justice. Hence, two-ness is nothing to be shrugged off as easily resolvable, making the legality of natural processes into a kind of unfinished symphony, as a work in progress. Instead of the Two Competencies of Validation & Verification, in isolation, legality is a process by which to gradually establish the Correspondence of Viability. That is, there is never; despite the fact that adversarial legalisms give the impression that one can have a clear verdict of guilty or not guilty; a perfect rendering of justice, because of the nature of Associative Justice. Similarly, the *omniscience* of a Phase IV pattern & the *omnipotence* of a Phase II pattern recombine to produce the *omnipresence* of Phases I and III. Accordingly, the perfect TTP of omniscience, omnipotence and omnipresence would be Heaven on Earth, because everyone would live along the *River of Gods* (Roman sarcophagus, dating from the 3rd century A. D.). That is, poisonous Styx & noxious Lethe should rightly recombine as the River of the Garden of Eden, or the River Canathus, in order to restore the innocence of, the free will of humanity as a whole.

In Metalogical Construct No.9, the 'Mobius strip' (Germ. math. 1790-1868) shows the direct channel, as the red-to-green Paradigm shift, overlying the black-to-white Doppler shift. When Temporality as a formal 'strait gate' opens, Spatiality as a functional 'round gate' closes, and vice versa. The red-to-green Explicit Formation, essential to the conjunction of our existence, makes the black-to-white implicit function into a subjunctive mode that places Femininity under masculine rule, as a '*sosie*'. And yet, for the Mobius strip, to either side stretches the more gradual cross channel of real Side Effects, between Phases I and III. The vertical mode intimates Darwin's natural selection as the perfect supersymmetry of the Two Competencies of Phases II & IV. But, better yet, the Side Effects reflect natural organic processes. For The Human Equation, the orange-yellow pattern of Phase I and the blue-purple pattern of Phase III, are coextensively symbiotic, as an orderly, bilateral development. The two vertical direct channels make up the untouchable Duality of the Commutative Or as Commutative

Justice & the Distributive But Not as Distributive Justice. As per No.9, they are the combinations of the Sign of the 'either/or' above as 'all are', & the permutations of the Symbol of the 'neither/nor' below, as 'all are not'. Better yet, to the left is the "Negative Associative And" as 'some are', and to the right the "Positive Associative And" as 'some are not', with Side Effects making up the Associative Justice of the *gender issue.* That is, Side Effects involve the symbiotic Crossover Patterns of "co-ordination", which appear as a double helix. From a spiritual point of view then, He & She recombine through the recomposition of correspondence, to share in human development as companion partners.

As part of Construct No.9, we will be working with Solomon's Seal to reveal the recombinant patterns of what is referred to as 'Androgynous Reinversion'. If each of the two triangulations shown in No.4 is flipped once horizontally & vertically, and then interlaced one with the other, a rather remarkable Pivotal Experience is produced. Now, there is *no demand for a static universe & cosmic censorship as a perfect system,* a perfect legal case, the demonstration of an exact science, the formation of an all-powerful corporation, or a divine right to convince & convert others. The supersymmetries of Pivotal Experience advocate the natural system as basic to all empirical processes, and, eventually include such things as conventions, codes, norms, laws, rights, morals, rules, regulations and measurements, etc. The implied perfection of obviation & evidence must be filtered through experience based upon observation & experiment, or it will simply reflect the structuralism of empiricism & constructivism of scientism, as a form of tyrannical and totalitarian behavior. To deliver a dualistic ultimatum, through the androgynous cycling of Gestalt brinkmanship, is to expect the perfect mind & perfect body as an actual Mobius strip. In No.13, as a 'symmetry group', the Apocalypse Now in the upper half expects Verification (red-green) & Validation (black-white) to *define perfect laws* (intellectual bias), while the lower half is limited to the Armageddon of side effects that are 'always late', by expecting the *exact description of the facts* (emotional prejudice), rather experiencing the evidentiary objectivity of progressive Side Effects.

However, the silver lining of quasiscience, advocated by the rhetoric of the silver- tongued devil, tends to become a fool's gold. We must be careful of the obfuscation of mesmerizing charismatics, clever lawyers, bad teachers, convincing salesmen, brilliant actors, confident politicians and unscrupulous scientists. Those with a mellifluous style and artful delivery, who give the impression they have reached gnosis, are not to be trusted. The Gordian knot of Greek fame is not that easily untied. A truly Pivotal Experience is more closely related to the spontaneous revelation of Diacritical Consciousness, rather than the cruciform arches of the Janus-gate. Unscrupulous individuals can play upon the susceptibility of others. Generally, a personal lack of vigilance is demonstrated by false hopes, based upon excessive caution and careless actions. We are never completely *sure, secure and safe*, and will never achieve a perfectly accountable approach that is fully *open, transparent and clear.* Therefore, the survival of the fittest depends upon the ethological we of the 'royal metaphor'. That is, talking positively about such things as faith, prayer and good luck mainly indicates a willingness to work things out through the 'phylogeny of the group' (7th harmonic, purple). Sociologically, such is the human community. As the expression goes, one may talk the talk (metalepsis), but one must also be ready to walk the walk (prolepsis).

St. Thomas Aquinas (1224-1274) is purported to have said that 'the ends are inverted in the execution of the means.' (Note that the central hourglass of No.7 appears to invert the white-to-black Ends.) The Verification of Means (4 & 6 + 5 or red-green) & the Validation of Ends (10 - 11 & 9 or black-white) present antithetical design features. In the Ends, the dyad experiences the overlapping of two sets of convergent relationships as reductive 'interference patterns', resulting in the unpredictable Doppler shift. In the Means 'diffraction gradients' are prevalent, and are associated with the ortho-parallel crystalline structures of the indeterminate Paradigm shift. Interestingly, with the pattern 4 & 6 + 5, 4 & 6 act like 'lower-order interrupt', &, with 10 - 11 & 9, 11 & 9 resemble 'higher-order interrupt'. Newton apparently envisioned some kind of odd/even pairing of wave trains, but not likely as involved as the foregoing. And, Einstein never fully recognized that a pattern like 4 & 6, resembling 'quantum mechanical effects', could be associated with the classical measurement of slow-breaking asymmetry (+ 5). Fortunately, our existence is blessed with a moderated Means, graciously referred to as the 'weak anthropic principle'. Einstein used the term 'inner illumination', and, the Cambridge physicist Stephen Hawking calls this aspect a 'free lunch'. Hence, our zone of existence is essentially the subjective "Affective Domain" of the Book of Scripture, and 'us' worries about who dispenses 'authority', through politics. For Human Beings then, politics often becomes a combative arena for antagonists, because it tends to rend asunder the 'seamless robe' of healthy, progressive measures.

Moving from the whole to the part, the force of nonexistence (10 -) as an Explicit Function, becomes a smaller set of constituents as an implicit function (4 & 6) without & within our changing existence (+ 5). Thus, in the special case of the Vertical Mosaic, in the center of the Means, the direct channel of Antimatter Resonance is without in space as an Outer Field, like the force of gravity, & hidden within matter as an Inner Particle, like a center of gravity. Hence, the origin of the Ends (10-0 as the 'strong force') becomes the *mediatrix* of an implicit function (4 & 6 as the 'weak force'), or the black-to-white hourglass in the center of No.7. On a psychological level, 4 & 6 acts as the instinctive moral compass of tactile orientation within: the proprioceptive sense of directionality. Externally, in the mind, the universal guidance of Synaesthetic Global Intelligence returns within the individual to provide a source of kinesthetic extension, in a particular direction. (This sense of orientation is commonly lacking in civilized peoples.) In other terms, the Soul of Symbol (10-0) is the origin of objective innocence, in relation to the current Maintenance of Innocence (4 & 6) as the true meaning of chastity. That is, one may look upon the mediatrix (4 & 6) as a sort of black touchstone for the Maintenance of Innocence within each individual, such as the spiritual center of orientation for Muslims in Mecca. This black stone of physics is supposed to be a perfect 'periodic crystal', while for the Muslim faith it is the Moral Compass. In one sense, chastity motivates the Crux of Choice, that, through faith in Allah, prevents the sophistication of adultery from becoming a materialistic contragradient, in the manner of dialectical materialism. In terms of physics, 4 & 6 are the operant constituents of the 'weak force' as SU(2). Hence, my pattern of 4 & 6 + 5, in physical terms, becomes SU(2) + U(1) as quantum electrodynamics or QED.

However, as St. Thomas Aquinas mentioned, the imposition of human willfulness can impose a reverse, artificial Doppler shift as a 6-4 back-formation, or what is called 'postdiction', as reasoning after the fact. Historically, this type of relationship occurs when a usually complacent middle class seeks anarchistic solutions, as with social revolution, pragmatic democracy and rampant capitalism. As a material example, with the Earth's geomagnetic system the implicit function becomes a typical compass that reverses the polarity of the external magnetosphere. Symbolically, 4 & 6 have a *methodological function*, like the magic hands of the Reclining Figure. Unfortunately, people often become astute at secreting away the magical functions of methodology because of a perceived need to control processes of development. Discordantly, there might be a proliferation of secret societies that enshrine magic rites and rituals as part of their normalization process. Such unconscionable gatekeepers often disregard legitimate alternatives, that go beyond habitual, reflexive behavior. Further, romantic love has this same backward, paranormal nature, which literary types refer to as 'necrophilia', when individual chemistry and getting too personal cloud over the spiritual 'copulation of intimacy'. On a deeper level of analogy, is the c.c. as a 'contragradient representation' (m*) of quantum mechanical effects, which is referred to as the 'Higgs mechanism' (Peter Higgs, Brit. phys., ca. 1960s). Other aspects are the 'nuclear magnetic dipole', the 'exciton' that mediates electromagnetic interactions, and the algorithmic mathematics of what is general called 'artificial intelligence' or AI. Myself, for 4 & 6 I prefer the term "paramagnetic worm hole", which acts as a mediatrix for what is called 'neutral current processes', down the center of No.7. Poetically, implying the presence of a Jezebel (6-4), one might intone the phrase 'Mary, Mary quite contrary'. Society is riddled with such gatekeepers, who restrict the access of others to needed services and contacts. Otherwise, on different levels of analogy, the 4 & 6 pattern resembles Heisenberg's 'uncertainty principle' (Werner Heisenberg, Germ. phys., ca. 1927), the mathematics of the discriminant function and other computational derivatives of an exponentially reciprocal character that have a divisive nature. From a psychological point of view, people tend to feel the fractionating effect of the information explosion. Further, a particular method implies the action-reaction pattern of simplistic, artificial situations wherein the 'can' of success seems to justify what is done, and/ or gives the impression of being able to predict direct consequences through post hoc reasoning. Often the 6-4 pattern leads to the false belief syndrome, and it may also lock into a pattern that justifies the simple 'psychological closure' of a very short attention span.

Positively, these computational, nonlocal derivatives (4 & 6) can act in support of the developmental ground states of the 'complex plane' (+ 5). That is, as the c.c., a kind of Mary Magdalene sustains and supports the emergence of essential change. And, if the natural emissions of a given system begin on the left and move to the right, by convention, then the 'collapse of the wave packet' (4 & 6) as SU(2) will be asymmetrical for U(I) as the electromagnetic interaction (+ 5). Thus, the weak force centered in Phase II acts as an Outer Field & Inner Particle for the Middle Ground State of slow-breaking asymmetry. It becomes *effective & correct* (4 & 6), when associated with what is *professional* (+ 5). Hence, SU(2) + U(I), as the combined 'electroweak theory' of Sheldon Glashow, Abdus Salam and Stephen Weinberg (1964), makes up the 4 & 6 + 5 pattern of QED for quantum electrodynamics. And, the different metaphors can all be interrelated through the dynamic, asymmetrical streaming of the semiconducting properties of solids, centered in Phase II, as the Means of Matter Resonance.

Following such a pattern, psychologists sometimes overemphasize 4 & 6 as the psychological profile of a quasi-stationary behavior field, but generally the term 'just noticeable difference' can be applied to these theories of behavior modification. Unfortunately, what is called 'free association' often fails to provide acceptable guidance. In the same vein, journalists who must constantly report on the nonsensical nature of social interactions, have coined the phrase 'never green', for some people who just can't (4) or won't (6)...take a hint (+ 5).

As mentioned, the Paradigm shift is a fundamental triplet of *serialization or realization*, just as the true Doppler shift is a fundamental triplet of *sequentialization or speciation.* Thus, 4 & 6 + 5 can be extended to a larger series of three sets as *mean* (4 - 3 & 5), *median* (6 - 5 & 7), and *mode* (4 & 6 + 5). Just as 10 - 11 & 9 can be extended to a larger sequence of three sets as 10 - 11 & 9, 0 - 9 & 1 and 0 & 2 + 1. Generally speaking, the Vertical Mosaic involves the demonstrative metaphysics of the Serialization of History, which is only indirectly linked to the independent Horizontal Mosaic as the Sequence of Speciation. The two systems being 'independent but compatible' (Einstein) is important, because otherwise the vertical repression of structuralism, for the static universe, could lead to the horizontal transference of constructivism, as cosmic censorship. In a safer, more general way, the physical systems of 'Fermi-Dirac statistics' cover the Vertical Mosaic & 'Bose-Einstein statistics' cover the Horizontal Mosaic. One could also refer to the combinations of the Commutative Or, &, the permutations of the Distributive But

Not. These two are the Means & Ends as the two systems. The first is 'significant' without involving immanentism, &, the second is 'necessary' without invoking interventionism. Together, the two systems offer what is called the Transmodal Inference, in order to come up with the Associative And as the third alternative. The TTP is Commutative Or (Phase II as + +), Distributive But Not (Phase IV as - -) and Associative And (Phases I and III as - + and + -), with the latter developing through experiential transitions. Later, I will be adding to Boolean logic when we discuss these two antiparticle aspect ratios of the Associative And.

In No.7, the *enthalpic source* of the larger Paradigm shift (+ 5, red-green) in Phase II is the distant and independent red-to-green hourglass (11 & 9 and 9 & 1) split between the two Ends of unbounded space (10-0) in Phase IV. This nuclear kernel of primordial positive matter in the Ends, acts like an *enthalpic rosebud* (11 & 9) in relation to the mature rose (+ 5) in the Means of existence. Effectively, the 'deuterotype' (10-0), in two places at once, begins as a dyadic 'oblate condensate' (fattened sphere, 10 - 11 & 9), making up the supposed mirror-image 'parity' of Spatiality. Except that parity undergoes 'spontaneous symmetry breaking', which produces a 'prolate dilate' (narrowed sphere, 0 - 9 & 1) as an asymmetrical material 'archetype'. For my triad of three sequential wave trains (p. 54), stemming from nonexistence, physicists refer to 'time-asymmetric quantum gravity'. (See Penrose, *The Emperor's New Mind*, p. 458). For biological sequencing, these patterns are called 'heterozygous dihybridization', and the American biologist Seymour Benzer likes to refer to the 'recon' (my 10 - 11 & 9), the 'muton' (my 0 - 9 & 1) and the 'cistron' (my 0 & 2 + 1). Returning to the level of general relativity, the most fundamental 11 & 9 pattern is the 'dilaton photon' of c^2 in Einstein's formula of $E_o = M_oc^2$ (5 = 10 - 11 & 9). C^2 represents the basic values of "quantum mechanical affects" (11 & 9) as the *archetypal enthalpy* of omniformity, or the PRP of the infinity of values: the finest knitting needles possible for the production of positive matter. After funneling upward through Wolfgang Pauli's 'exclusion principle' as 'higher-order interrupt', at a nonlocal and nondetectable level, an infrared signature emerges from the 'blackbody radiation' of the v.e.d. (10 - 11 & 9 and 0-9 & 1), based upon a kind of 'magic radix' for prescribing fundamental 'superconducting currents' (Brian Josephson, ca. 1970). Hence, 'preformationism' (Susan Oyama), although still primarily an undetectable part of speciation, is prescriptively inferred to be a 'messenger photon' (0 & 2 + 1) as a *species of protomatter*. And, as mentioned above, the horizontal Sequence of Speciation must have at least 'three arbitrary variables' (Einstein), or 10 - 11 & 9, 0 - 9 & 1 and 0 & 2 - 1, as per my simplified numerological system. The dyadic graviton of supergravity (10-0), is intertwined with the parity of the quadrupole of the 'dilaton photons' (11 & 9 and 9 & 1), resulting in the emission of the messenger photon (+ 1), to make up a total of five fundamental photons.

Often there is much confusion between horizontal speciation, based upon the allopatric 11 & 9 of 'preformationism' (Oyama), &, vertical 'cladistics', based upon the rest energy of the sympatric 5 of 'interactionism' (Oyama). Here, The Human Equation gets into all kinds of deep doo-doo. (Note above that the actual fundamental five in the second system transitions to the real + 5 in the first system, as 'light' that we can actually see: five wavelengths.) In contrast, most people forget all about the orderly way in which the supersymmetrical Transmodal Inference naturally builds up the third system, called 'logos made flesh' in Christian metaphors. They go wacko over what is called the 'nine-to-five inference', which supposedly turns the rosebud of reincarnation (9) into a perfect rose as a real saint (5), that we would all hate for showing us all up, all the time. In other terms, remember how geneticists promised that the human genome would give direct access to curing diseases? Further, note that the very people using perceptualism to work back to the actual dating of the creation of the universe (15 billion years), are the same ones suffering from the conceptualism of obviating the expanding universe based upon the Hubble theory: 9-to-5 again. Then there are the advocates of vertical cladistics, who claim to be able to trace current species back to a common ancestor in the primordial soup of the distant past: 5-to-9 this time, but still an untenable claim. Horizontal speciation becomes tied to the idiotic lining up of a *historical series* of vertical body plans, from which the claim is made that there is a *logical sequence* linking humans back to certain prehominids. With this aspect of the nine-to-five inference as the 'greening of the gold', linear tree-like branches are assumed to descend back to a single common ancestor in the distant past. Such *vertical cladistics* tend to deny the independent role of speciation in the horizontal mode. This is like saying that God, Allah or Shiva etc. looks exactly like us, when we really mean that the Corpus Universalis is our causal source. Wisely, Darwin did not want to play with the Transmodal Inference of supersymmetrical *natural selection.* That is, the permutations of the unknown 'contingencies' (Stephen Jay Gould) of Phase IV & the combinations of the misunderstood 'tentativity' of Phase II, do not allow one to make a direct inference from the second system to the first. Today, the Phase IV contingencies of horizontal DNA, as duplication, are seen as being distinct from the Phase II tentativity of verticalized RNA, as replication. Further, if one examines my numerological relationships, the *inductive interpretation* of 9 is based upon the 'isotropic' as a generic Inner Particle, and the *deductive inference* of 5 relates to the 'isomeric' as a Middle Ground State. Hence, one cannot 'infer' from one system to the other, because both of the essential terms (odd) are not inferences. (This aspect vindicates the physicist John Bell's theorem that 'nonlocal' quantum variables must be included.) Thus, the ninth harmonic can be an Inner Particle (11 & 9) or Outer Field (9 & 1), but, and this is an important but, there is no deductive inference for 9 as a Middle Ground State. Hence, we cannot 'know' the ninth harmonic as the Acoustic. For philosophy, moving from the first system to the second, this means that within our Means of Existence 'we cannot know the exact consequences of our actions'. And, moving from the second system to the first, for genetic engineering isolated gene traits cannot be directly projected to the exact physical characteristics of an adult creature. And yet, traditional religion has often speculated that it is possible to make a *direct axiological link* between the Soul of the creation mode (interventionism) and the Spirit in the world around us (immanentism), as proof of the existence of God. Either way; that directly to this or this directly to that; just ain't true.

As mentioned previously, if we don't get a hold on our espistemological dualities, whatever subject area one is dealing with will become falsified by dualisms. Regardless of whether a person is a brilliant scientist, a devout religious leader, a respected judge, or a dynamic politician, the 'terrible two's' can still make individuals the willful agents of Gestalt brinkmanship, as backward, retarded, always late, and/or retrogressive.

Appropriately, Susan Oyama's bugbear is that 'preformationism' (11 & 9) might become an inference for predetermining the 'interactionism' of a fixed body plan (4 & 6). Accordingly, the biotechnology of gene therapy could be of great benefit, but genetic engineering just might have monstrous results, as symbolized by the novel *The Hunchback of Notre Dame* (1831, Victor Hugo). This is where human cloning comes in, with frightful results. Slight changes in the genetic code could result in the transmogrification of a mature entity, and upset the natural balance of more general selection pressures. It is not really possible to know exactly 'what's behind the green door', by vaingloriously stealing a moment of glory (9-to-5). Transgenic interference could eventual have disastrous results, because one cannot anticipate all the interactions, when introducing inadvertent changes to the Life Cycle. Some things are best left alone.

Eventually, with the wave trains of all ten field equations in place, and many different examples given, a holistic approach should become self-evident. Unfortunately, the metaphorical effects & facts of 4 & 6 usually result in a fatalistic back-formation, through the symbolism of end products, with genuine ideals turning into disingenuous pragmatics as a back-formation. The philosophical term is 'deontology', wherein the limit cycles of interactionism, as a closed, coplanar loupe, tend not to be progressive. Thereby, Temporal Infusion becomes an anathematic act of miscreance and fatalistic regressiveness develops, reflected by the characterization of the *regressus ad uterum* as undermining reevaluation. (Literary ladies might say that they have a 'reluctant womb'.) Literature refers to the inadvertent *peripeteia* (sudden reversals of fortune) of such decision modes as reflecting a 'tragic flaw', which mirrors the Greek *hamartia.* In the same manner, modern psychology, preferring to define & describe the psychological profile of individualism, often fails to promote the progressive behavioral shaping of individuality. Further, effect of information (4) & invention of facts (6) become an example of artificial intelligence, implying the Chinese curse of 'May you live in interesting times.' Often the simplistic closure of narrow-minded *limit cycles* produces a kind of sententiousness, wherein the 'signifier' (4), through the 'significant' (5), becomes the 'signified' (6). Or the 'referrer', through the 'referent', leads to the 'referred'. One may be dealing with political correctness, or making the profit motive more important than human lives. Similarly, a specialized outlook tends to find what it is looking for. Often, quantitative solutions and knowledge-based learning fail to produce satisfactory, long-term results. The Temporal Infusion of these modern mousetraps is much more difficult to debunk, because it is generally intangible, and, invisible to the naked eye. Subsequently, the agape of stormy atmospherics, as the triplet of Hubris, Nemesis & Mimesis, become a crucial Test, with most people never getting beyond, to the ambiance of an irenic state. They get caught up in the limit cycles of Circles of Vengeance, going nowhere faster and faster, between the parapsychological (9-11), &, paranormal (6-4), and then, in no-man's-land in between, they fall for the artificial entanglement of the *deus ex machina* (5-10/10-5). As the expression goes, you reap what you sow, and to sow the wind is to reap the whirlwind. God is no dummy, so why wouldn't She/He make up the best game in town, and then provide everyone with a 'free lunch' or a 'get out for free pass'...if they are pure in heart? Discordantly, if moral turpitude sets in through dismissiveness, idealism and preciosity, or accommodation, indulgence and appeasement, etc. a penchant for meaningless activity develops. And, most unfortunately, because of the distractions of aestheticism & adventurism a general breakdown in communication occurs. Then, to relieve a feeling of entrapment, people often turn to systematic doubt, codependent romantic love, artificial stimulants, psychiatric palliation, soap-opera dramatics, mystical cults, the work ethic, and other confabulations that stem from the internecine politics of the 'nuclear family'. Stuck in the Vertical Mosaic, compromising fails to produce real compromise, being vindictive is not vindicated, fitting in is not fitting, what is committed shows a lack of commitment, being an adult is not mature, individualism is not yet individuality, synchronism fails to reach 'synchronicity' (Jung), etc. It is only through a *breakthrough in learning* that the individual comes to realize that, doing one's 'best' can be an excuse for not doing better. And, trying too hard often becomes simply trying, especially for others, without producing significant results. The only real fact of our existence is that everyone is bedeviled in one manner or another.

To get back to our models, looking at Construct No.8, the pattern in the lower left is similar to No.7. As pairs of ground states, Phase I is yellow-orange (Negative Associative And), Phase II is red-green (Paradigm shift), Phase III is blue-purple (Positive Associative And), and Phase IV is black-white (Doppler shift). Outer Fields are the six points of the respective hexagrams. Then, at the upper right, I added Inner Particles by folding the Outer Fields into the interior of the Middle Ground States. Surprisingly, Phase I became a yellow-orange torus formation, floating in Magnetic Resonance. And, Phase III a blue-purple torus function, floating in Electronic Resonance. Hence, the electron torus to the left produces heat, and is symbiotically paired with the positron torus on the right, that produces the impedance of magnetic cooling. And thus, between the two Side Effects, the *net thermal energy* is relatively constant. Hence, together, as the two primary Side Effects, these two *symbionts* are symbiotically volumetric, with a cooling effect moving toward the left, synthetically, and a heating affect moving toward the right, analytically. Further, Phase II is centered by an electrostatic wave front, that is home to 'temperature', &, Phase IV pivots about magnetostatic standing waves, as home to 'pressure'. In contrast then, Phases II & IV are strongly antithetical to, and primarily independent of, each other. However, as symbiotic self-evident Side Effects, Phases I and III are experienced as the two halves of the one proverbial apple. Accordingly, Phase I, as the future in the past, is a symbiont called the 'unit of charge', for the slow electron of hot resistance. And, Phase III, as 'the past in the future', a symbiont called the 'magnetic moment' or 'Bohr magneton' represents a unit of magnetic spin, or cool impedance. Contrary to Phases II & IV, I and III are not relatively static, and therefore are called '*soliton traveling waves*'. It is the commingling of their helical Crossover Patterns that becomes the associative development of heterotic co-ordination. These relationships are experienced as the Side Effects of natural growth and decay, and as bilaterally coextensive are not just accidental spin-offs or 'bad side effects'.

Returning to dualities, traditionally the Affective Domain (4-5-6) is the Book of Scripture, in existence, as the Body, &, the "Effective Domain" (11-10-9) is the Book of Nature, in nonexistence, as the Mind. Independently, they are Subjectivity as observation, centered in Phase II, &, Objectivity as experiment, centered in Phase IV. Otherwise, they are Verification & Validation as the Two Competencies that make up the "Haptic Extension of the Hands of God"...which is not ours to have & hold. As per Construct No. 13, knowing & understanding the foregoing brings together the 'good sorts' of two spiritual thirteens, wherein religion beholds God as the principle arbiter of marriage. Traditional philosophy refers to these antithetical relationships of Mind & Body, which, unfortunately, tends to become locked into the Temporal Infusion of the mind/body syndrome shown in No.4. 'This' becomes strictly a Vertical Mosaic, without a horizontal equivalent, when the brilliant Superego Self represses the Shadow Self through disingenuous reductionism (makes me think of Virginia Woolf's novel *To The Lighthouse*, 1927). Anything not forbidden is compulsory, leading to repression & transference acting in collusion to produce conspiracy. That is, the expansive tautology of the up/down-down/up syndrome of Temporality leads to the reductive tautology of the left/right-right/left syndrome of Spatiality. Thus, in the manner of the Quarteron Pattern (No.1), a moral dilemma develops between the syndrome of *materia prima* (orthogonal button) & the syndrome of *material secunda* (parametric hole), to produce an intractable *prima facie*. Discordantly, a control-&-denial pattern locks the Phases into one GUT ('grand unified theory') as the closed-loop system of a single symmetry classification. Then, as per No.4, Side Effects become assumed & subsumed within a Vertical Mosaic. Hence, through the bipolar nature of Gestalt brinkmanship, the ultimatum of the static universe is in league with the ultimatum of cosmic censorship. In other terms, misinformation & disinformation collude to mistake the vertical *metalepsis*, as a 'have in the now', which leads to mistaking horizontal *prolepsis*, as a 'hold in the here'. Then, without Goethe's double sanity check, the two dilemmas lead to Einstein's twin-paradox. That is, the orthogonal 'one' in the vertical mode becomes the replacement the autocratic, as *misinformation*, over the displacement of the meritocratic, as *disinformation*, with the parametric 'dyad' in the horizontal mode rendering the theocratic to the left, as *misrepresentation*, and the technocratic to the right, as *misdirection*. Grid lock arrives, with misinformation over disinformation, &, misrepresentation beside misdirection.

The fact that the pestilence of the cruciform pattern, as a Gordian knot, makes up a twin-paradox is no myth. It is serious business, because personalism goes hand in hand with ungodliness.

Four-ness as a quadrilateral fixation, &, ten-ness as perceptual centering, become entangled as the fourteen-ness of the Greek Hades. That is, when the fourth dimension is no longer rendered through commonsensical relationships, a healthy sense of self-sameness is lost. Only the full *awareness* of metalepsis vertically, as the before & after of space, &, the complete *recognition* of prolepsis horizontally, as the before & after of time, recombine for the progressive *attention* of four-dimensional experience. And, only after learning to appreciate how the triplet of awareness, recognition and attention recombines, is it possible to be conscious of our humanity.

Through the twin-paradox, Diacritical Consciousness can either come to side with the Divine Comedy, or slip into the Demonic Parody. Such a Double Passover requires that the two thirteens, as the Significant Other & Symbolic Other, come together in harmony. And, unless the correspondence of Universal Duality allows compatibility to reproduce the 'we' of the third person plural, there is an excessive burden placed on society to police the individual. Thus, the Universal Duality of the She/He must avoid dualism and become a heterosexual gender issue that makes survival a truly liberating experience. Correspondingly, my rendering of the Christian decalogue begins with the 'prescription' of the I & thou, as species, followed by the 'ascription' of respect for father & mother, as genus. These two, dual sets are the fundamental heterosexual relationships of associative co-ordination, and are not to be undone by any male hierarchy.

Unfortunately, the Word of God tends to become a Tower of Babel as the lost word, due to the inflationary expression of many specialized languages, special interests and special persons. When acting out becomes explosive, actual communication is shifted to the background as a waste of time, and may be directed toward adversarial 'antinomies' (Kant) rather than progressive issues. In reality, the one Acoustic (9) as a creation mode becomes many different acoustics (+ 5) in real time. In other words, the Sovereignty of God as represented and directed by Human Beings tends to take a 'linguistic turn' (Wittgenstein), and becomes translated as territoriality, ethnocentrism, legalisms, quantification, 'dialectical materialism' (Karl Marx), the market economy, etc. What begins with the Intelligence of the 'round gate', as the **Mixed Metaphor** (11-10-9), becomes part of the 'strait gate', as the field operations of the **Split Metaphor** (4-5-6), and usually features only select parts rather than a complete sense of design function. In other terms, it is difficult to decide how to apply Global Intelligence, and what proportionality to use when mixing Local & Global Adaptations. Just as Darwin's natural selection has tended to become death warmed over as 'neo-Darwinism' and social Darwinism, so Local & Global Adaptations have often been translated as 'adaptationism' (No.4). The question poses itself: can we really define something as being representative & purposive? With the approach of the 'sum over histories' (physicist Richard Feynman) each part is seen in relation to the whole, and placed appropriately & proportionally where it belongs, as in No.7. That is, the various vertical matrices (representative) are recombined in an attempt to link up all the *possible* (imaginary) *& plausible* (real), in order to produce the *probable* (complex): a TTP. Such systems dynamics came out of the 1940's physics of 'renormalization theory'. That is, the *plausible & possible* recombine to produce the *probable*, as a third system that can be experienced or normalized. In other terms, the teleological democracy of physics becomes a scientific process, through meaningful measurements that are based upon recombining energy & momentum. Thus, Local & Global Adaptations are summed up through the eight histories of Recombinant Adaptations. Similarly, modern social or general democracy is based upon recombining local concerns with the trend toward economic globalization, even though neoliberalism tends to short-circuit the process (as per No.4). Importantly, in the fullness of time, The Human Equation is learning to accept more *consistent, coherent and comprehensive* frames of reference (a TTP). We cannot expect to achieve perfect **Commutative & Distributive Justice**, but we can learn to live with the gradual adaptation of **Associative Justice**: an important TTP. From the point of view of physics, 'Feynman diagrams' are based upon the skin (field) & bones (particles) of complex mathematics, but leave us with the systematic flesh (groundstates) of orderly measurements.

Unfortunately, following a less-than-adequate reinterpretation of the ancients, like Aristotle and St. Thomas Aquinas, patristic modes of linear representation have sought to fixate theoretical laws & general principles. The Greek approach to Euclidean geometry was exemplary of this incipient idealism, which influenced other areas of learning. Such a monolithic approach produces Temporal Infusion, by narrowing the scope of operations to a closed system that only seems more *sure, secure and safe.* Instead of a pattern like Feynman's democratic renormalization, the checks & balances of the *free & open system* become a silver lining that defines the biased obviation of theoretical laws & describes the prejudicial evidence of general principles. The focus becomes whatever is efficacious in the moment, rather than truly efficient on a long-term basis. Following the Renaissance, based upon the misguided Scholastic teachings of man's misguided mastery of nature, secular humanism rubber-stamped reality. The triad of *realism, altruism and humanism* is a great mousetrap. Subsequently, the holistic teachings of scholars such as Descartes, Newton and Leibnitz failed to make their mark, while their mechanistic approach toward empiricism & scientism prevailed. Thus discordant ideologies became a quintessential fishing expedition, with a cliched approach acting out of a more general malaise, the classical 'psychic rift' (Jung). The vulgarization of science then embedded itself within the mind/body syndrome of the bourgeoisie, as the verticalized quasiscience of empiricism. Such pragmatism goes hand in hand with imperialism, with the Hyphenated Person expecting automatic progress, somewhere between indifference & violence, as a public time bomb waiting for politicians to declare the next war. Currently, New Age theories, charismatic cult religions, youthful adventurism, sexual permissiveness, scandal-sheet journalism, and *enneagrammatical patterns* (Glossary), etc. offer the oversimplified triplet of answers (sure), solutions (secure) and results (safe). Discordantly, the law becomes exploited for getting simple closure, and inflicting retrograde redressment. And yet, much of the 'retro' of the 1990's resembles the doctrines of the French Revolution, based upon the questionable triplet of fraternity (biased) equality (uneven) and liberty (inhumane). Empty slogans are ineffectual when there is too much freedom and too many choices, without General Guidelines. The implication is that immediate satisfaction can be provided through the inconsequential choices & actions of adventurism. Karl Marx's dialectical materialism was precedent to modern adventurism, based upon the same sets of antinomial brinkmanship. As another example, the interventionism of Americans in Chile, in 1973, did not really help the cause of democracy. In the same vein, the naïve experiment to force democratic reform on China, at Tiananmen Square in 1989, is another example of ill-conceived adventurism. Similarly, Russian society has become the broken glass of too many, similar quick fixes. The central problem is that expecting an immediate result doesn't require earning the trust of others, by being accountable to the people at large. Democracy is not an artificial heart transplant that depends upon the imposition of sentimental answers, the subterfuge of sympathetic solutions, and the absolution of immediate results. Working directly from the 'antecedents' of Phase II, in existence, to the 'consequents' of Phase IV, as ideal solutions, merely involves unrealistic *Great Expectations* (Charles Dickens, 1861). More importantly, the deconstructive 'precedents' of Phase I must recombine with the reconstructive 'subsequents' of Phase III, to produce Integrative Discipline. Accordingly, *precedent, antecedent, subsequent and consequent*, similar to *best, fine, better and good*, become the Four Phases of seasonable changes that can be lived with, because they untie the bipolar cruciform pattern of the Gordian knot. We will be developing many comparable sets of four.

We are beginning to throw off the pall that shrouded Old Science, by removing the scales from our eyes. To look, hear and sense is becoming see, listen and feel, leading to the *vision, judgement and consideration* of better aims, objectives and goals. For example, we no longer accept the Scholastic view of the Middle Ages that matter can neither be created nor destroyed. Matter is only one of the four currently accepted aspects of fundamental dimensionality, shown by the "Four Resonances" of Construct No.12. In our exposition of The Human Equation, we will be working to overcome the false trinity of complicity & duplicity and deception, in favor of the recombinant patterns of the New Wave. Naturally, 'defense mechanisms' will be working to fixate the entities of New Age doctrines. Some people will pay a lot of money to false prophets in order to avoid the commitment of real progress. We have to remain vigilant. There are no quick fixes, just better and better questions, in accordance with the process of inquiry, traditionally based upon the progressive measures of Platonic *aporiai* and Socratic *irony.*

A good example is the perfectly viable concept of 'liberation theology'. Social, economic and political activism in Central and South America has led to the debasement of the real principles behind this theory. Instead of facilitating New Religion through the recomposition of the gospellic community, liberation theology reflects immanentism & interventionism. Such disruptive social activism gives a new twist to revisionism & revolution. Religion, when adulterated individuals awaken to a more mature spirituality, is not meant to be threatening to either society or the individual. (There are misguided people who think that active proselytism – door-to-door or otherwise – is what great leaders like Jesus and Buddha would have wanted. Convincing & converting is not the stuff of the great religions.) Instead of the theocracy of misrepresentation, we must encourage the natural, positive empowerment of others. Religious interference in politics and economics, as prevalent in Central and South America, foments the false trinity of revisionism, revolution and disintegration, which is not an appropriate goal for a community of well-meaning persons. Similarly, in France, a popular movement of café philosophy is all the rage, with people looking for answers, solutions and results. In reality, as with Plato's aporiai, we only get better and better questions – in the manner of Geoffrey Chew's modern 'bootstrap theory' as a process of inquiry. The etymological linking of the word 'aporiai' and 'bootstrapping' shows a similar approach to theoretical development across the ages. Liberation theology must not become a fishing expedition for a paragon of perfection, based upon the convincing & converting of Xenogeneic Contingencies (Glossary). A given model for learning, setting out currently acceptable theories & principles, has it own special built-in limitations, unlike like my Metalogical Constructs which have their real value in the discovery process itself, not in the erroneous triplet of *axioms, dictums and conjectures.*

The precedents of the past, set by the 'ascription' of the 'parental generation', are deconstructive for Susan Oyama's 'ontogeny' (No.7, white-to-red). The subsequents of the future, set by the 'rescription' of the 'Generation X', is reconstructive for Oyama's 'phylogeny' (No.7, green-to-black). (Actually, I limit ontogeny to Phase I as yellow-orange [genus-family], and phylogeny to Phase III as blue-purple [subphylum-phylum]. These Side Effects are Feng-Shui in Chinese philosophy, and the 'ideal gas' and 'ideal liquid' in physical terms.) Psychologists, so far, have mainly emphasized the former as Deconstruction, without its recombinant, symbiotic partner as Reconstruction. The two halves together make up the same proverbial apple as a Recombinant Third System. Eve gave the apple to Adam and he bit out a small portion for the particulars of Local Adaptations, causing The Fall from the Garden of Eden, because Global Adaptations were left out. Thus, the New Adam of Phase I extends from the parental generation, and, he must avoid the pitfalls of the Means of Existence in Phase II, while constantly working to rejoin the New Eve of the Generation X in Phase III.

Unfortunately, the perfection of classical cause-effect tends to be limited to the Temporal Infusion of narrow limit cycles in the Vertical Mosaic of the Means. (This is the pattern of immanentism & interventionism shown in No.4) Here, cycles and side effects remain meaningless because the coplanar 'field effect' (4 & 6) turns into self-recursive entrapment. If the idealism of the proof & disproof of the field effect is impossible to overcome (see Gödel's theorem), how is one to make a leap of faith to a non-categorical classification (+ 5). Karl R. Popper referred to this vertical rift as the 'parallelism' of the 'closed society', which is a close-loup system. For Christians, this phenomenon involves taking the Spirit of Jesus Christ, too literally. Mathematically, one must invoke the law of excluded middles. In terms of physics, Popper referred to the 'collapse of the wave packet' (4 or 6, but not + 5). Surprisingly, Immanuel Kant tended to get hung up on the 'analytic proposition' of significant reason as a proof for logical positivism, making his 'categorical imperative' more prevalent than his 'hypothetical imperative'. Hegel had a similar problem, although he fought to avoid turning his thesis & antithesis into a vertical diatheism (button), followed by a horizontal dialetheism (hole). The same rift was revealed by Karl Marx's upper & lower classes of dialectical materialism. In modern times, the dominant diatheism is between monolithic synergies , followed by monopolistic convergence. Culturally, it is 'telepresence & teleportation' that we use to make up a virtual reality that we call 'reality television'. The objective is to give in to the vicariousness of being a spectator, and then if possible, interfere with the choices & actions of others, or, what is the same old immanentism & interventionism.

So how do we get away from the New Age Fall of Man, and encourage the New Wave Return to Eden? A major clue is found in the nature of the way in which the proverbial apple is put back together again. Recombinant Side Effects begin with physical causes in Phase I as the Deconstruction of the *synthetic product of anything*, and transition to spiritual causes in Phase III as the Reconstruction of the *analytic reagent of anybody.* In modern terms, Phase I is 'hardware' and Phase III is 'software'. I like to refer to the "bad donut" in Phase I and "good donut" in Phase III, because the democracy of teleological purpose depends upon delayed response patterns. (If the ingredients of the recipe are not carefully chosen and thoughtfully blended, the product will not be edible.) The overall pattern is cause/effect (- +) and effect/cause (+ -), folded between the Ends of cause/cause (- -), and split within the Means of effect-effect (+ +). The media mogul Marshall McLuhan referred to this pattern as 'egg-chicken-egg' (- ++ -), with the chicken ending up as 'toast', done on both sides, in the sun, because it was caught 'going down the road': a vertical highway with no byways. As cause/effect in Phase I, or the hare as the future in the past, and effect/cause in Phase III, or the tortoise as the past in the future, the before & after aspects of space & time are recombined by modern physics as the *Euclidean space-time object.* The Life Cycle recombines the Being of the omniscience of experiment in Phase IV, &, Becoming of the omnipotence of observation in Phase II, through the Belonging of the omnipresence of experience, between Phases I and III. The TTP is entity, event and dynamic steady state, or, time, space and real space-time object.

Some sort of evolutionary mode seems to be the prevalent regulatory standard of conduct. For sure, neither 'evolution' nor 'devolution' are provable. Patterns of emission and absorption, growth and decay, evolution and devolution, etc. do not prefer any particular orientation, which is a good argument for ultimately balancing of the triplet of the 'CPT theory' of physics (later). However, interestingly enough, the 'biogenetic law', as stated in Merriam-Wester's Collegiate Dictionary, is as follows: "the ontogeny of the individual is a recapitulation of the phylogeny of the group" (much like Oyama's). Instead of nature/nurture this pattern follows nurture/nature. The emphasis is upon Reconstruction (6-7, blue-purple) as phyletic 'descent with modification' (Darwin). Having a feeling for the teleonomic (Glossary) nature of progress, as we exit stage right, the phylogeny of the group (6-7) sets up a meaningful entrance stage left, for the ontogeny of the 'agent' as a physical cause (2-3). This transition is from the individual of Phase I (Eros), to the social of Phase III (Ethos), but the "beginning" is really in Phase III. Hence, the proper approach is firstly analytic and evolutionary, as the effect-cause of 'nurture' in Phase III, and then later synthetic and devolutionary, as the cause-effect of 'nature' in Phase I. (Note in No.7 that white-black [1-8], yellow- purple [2-7], orange-blue [3-6] and red-green [4-5], make up an acrostic of four complementary sets, that share an integral nine-ness as kind of special candle, or 'shammes'.) However, the emphasis is primarily upon analytic growth in Phase III as '*dissociative-recombination*' (7-6, Reconstruction), rather than synthetic decay in Phase I as '*recombinant-dissociation*' (2-3, Deconstruction). In terms of complete phasal space, the pattern is Phases II, III, IV and I, which follows the order of what is called the scientific method. The Human Equation must address the same approach, in order to get off 'on the right foot again'. One begins with a theoretical observation, works hypothetically through experimental relationships, and then experience is enriched with a new approach.

Unfortunately, humans tend to push *analytic evolutionism* too far, often undoing many of the beneficial aspects of our current existence. In other terms, 'analytic infinities' are attributed a rightward, evolutionary tendency, and associatively, 'synthetic infinities' become the leftovers of a leftward, devolutionary mode. Thus, it is the interplay of both symbiotic Side Effects that provides for associative production. (No.4 is change without change.) However, conventionally, the first system is given a rightward chirality, as a characteristic of asymmetrical heat flow, by playing up the adduction of evolution and playing down the subduction of devolution. In other words, we emphsize the Affective Domain, of the essential subjectivity of existence, and downplay the Effective Domain, of the substantial objectivity of nonexistence. Unfortunately, this "limp" tends to make people unconsciously denatured through the transference of intellectual *radicalism*, & subconsciously rebarbative through the factoids of prejudicial *phenomenalism*. The street angel becomes a house devil, with intellectual irrelevance & emotional *irreverence* combining to produce a measure of *irresponsibility*, that leads to the fourth nail in the coffin: being meaninglessly *irresolute*.

Unfortunately for The Human Equation, intellectual bias tends to exaggerate the process of obviation (e.g., the expanding universe), while prejudicial emotions downplay evidence that is not supported by the fundamentalism of belief structures (e.g., the big bang). That is, the preclusion of convincing conventions, as radicalism, & retroclusion of immutable codes, as phenomenalism, take on a paradoxical nature. These patterns of *transference & repression* are reflected by Freud's reaction formation. Progressive measures, such as the corroborative objectification of evidence, appear less legally viable, at first bite. The political pattern is *inquisition, overthrow and usurpation*, or, *transgression, repression and oppression.* Importantly, it is only by following the spirit of the law, through the apolitical patterns of Associative Justice, that observation & experiment can & may recombine to produce meaningfully progressive outcomes.

Expecting the exact Means of the Verification of Time, & precise Ends of the Validation of Space, always make Viability seem less reliable, at first blush. This & that, as button & string, are the Hands of God as the Forbidden Fruit, while the 'proof is in the pudding', as a gradual, empirical process of objectification. Something (Phase II, half full) & nothing (Phase IV, half empty), as defining how & describing what, are not as self-evident as the *such and such, of anything* (Phase I) *and anybody* (Phase III). That is, concepts (II) & percepts (IV) must be recycled to move from precepts (I) to "recepts" (III). In other terms, awareness (II), imbued with new information, from intelligence (IV), moves attention (I) toward consciousness (III). Accordingly, the individual, as a universe unto him or herself, learns to appreciate Universal Consciousness. There is no loss of self involved, through assimilation & acculturation. What is involved is a better understanding of the nature of self-sameness. This holistic sense of Universal Consciousness, in its most simplistic rendering, must include all Four Phases. Just the same, from a systemic point of view, with each Phase having an odd-even pair, one might feel that complete phasal space could be adequately represented by only eight field equations. And yet, the most simple system works better with ten equations, with each made up of three variables. Again, 'third level integrals', like traditional syllogisms, seem to permeate all levels of development; hence my field-ground-particle pattern.

In a similar manner, the Human Observer must work mainly with the third alternative, using Deconstruction for the *precepts of anything*, and, Reconstruction for the *recepts of anybody*. Unfortunately, striving for a Dickensian set of *Great Expectations* has tended to make Construct No.4 into a Shakespearian comedy of errors. The attempt to establish a single symmetrical classification (No.1) becomes a combination of the Apocalypse Now (radicalism) & Armageddon (phenomenalism), with the oddness of a spin-3 particle up (9-11-5) & the evenness of a spin-3 force down (6-4-10), producing *heresy* over *blasphemy* about *anathema*, as a sextuplet of excommunication. This is what we have inherited from the dualism of ancient antinomies, and which still persists through modern politics, as when pretending to be fair, tolerant and equal. The six parameters of No.4 fixate a fateful determinism, and thereby fail to represent the more adequate rendering of '*six-parameter indeterminacy*' as shown by the Susys of No.13.

The English philosopher Sir Francis Bacon (1561-1626) almost realized the fourfold nature of real experience, but for the most part he just substituted the 'inductive method' of empiricism for the authority of deduction. Importantly, Bacon sensed the danger of the cyclical pattern of No.4, when he referred to the 'preconceived attitudes and prejudices', of obviation & evidence. Further, he helped advance the theory of the scientific method by advocating that one work from the general to the specific. Such an *evidentiary process* would still require the continuing support of experience to maintain its Viability. (The TTP pattern is Verifiability, Validity and Viability, just like Becoming, Being and Belonging.) Interestingly, Bacon referred to experience as an 'ampliative inference', which appears to have been meant to string together the eight deductive inferences as the parallel corollaries of No.7. In other terms, as per No.13, each harmonic state of the third system must embrace both *correlations of inductive interpretation* (double lines) and *corollaries of deductive inference* (single lines), because reason as white can be both inductive and deductive, as may logic as black. But, neither reason nor logic can & may totally include or exclude one the other; necessitating the conjugation of the odd-even paired relationships. Unfortunately, Bacon referred to developmental experience as an 'inductive inference', when, from No. 13, we know that *there is no such animal.* However, the term 'inductive inference' could be rendered by a wave train such as 4 & 6 + 5, which is both a correlation of induction (4 & 6) and a corollary of inference (+ 5). For the open-Closed system, this would be an inductive-Inference, with analytical tendencies, to the right. But then there would also have to be an Inference-induction for a pattern like 10 - 11 & 9, as the Open-closed system, with synthetic tendencies, to the left. Nevertheless, what Bacon did of great importance was to isolate authority as mainly dependent upon deductive inference, while the scientific method is mainly, but not entirely, dependent upon inductive interpretation. The trick is to sort out Deductive Logic (10 -, the inference of a priori logic) as associated with inductive reason (11 & 9, the interpretation of a posteriori reason), &, inductive logic (4 & 6, the interpretation of a posteriori logic) as associated with Deductive Reason (+ 5, the inference of a priori reason). (A posteriori is merely 'that which follows'; the a priori inference, depending upon the chirality.) In modern terms, for 'complexity theory', as in No.7, both induction & deduction, as complementary, make up the three functors of each wave train, which always maintain the unitarity of the universe. The mathematician Roger Penrose advocates this kind of pattern, of unitary integers, because they mirror Constant Unity Factors that make up the 'gauge invariance' of each field equation.

Construct No.4, as the triplet rationalism, mysticism and idealism, is centered about the Myth of a monolithic sausage, produced by playing both ends against the middle (despite the law of excluded middles). That erroneous result, on ideological grounds, misrepresents the ground state of Essence (+ 5) as the idealism (4 & 6) of an artificial intelligence (AI). That leaves 'us' (4 & 6) with a two-headed amphisbaena that resembles the centaur of Greek mythology, which, in modern terms, becomes the collapse of the wave packet. 'Us' attempts to *derive the inductive interpretation of operatives*, as half head (field position) & half horse (particle momentum). But these two demiurgic entities are not able to re-create *the deductive inferences of complex associations*, by blending the classical orbits of the formally real (+ 1, + 3, + 5, + 7) and the functionally imaginary (2 -, 4 -, 6 -, 8 -). Of course we know that the field/particle patterns of nonlocal derivatives are the carrier medium, both too large, as skin, & too small, as bones, to be experienced locally, as flesh. The classical statistics of measurable Middle Ground States (the donuts) must be dunked in the medium of nonlocal quantum statistics. The paired grounds of associated donuts make a river, while the Styx of the fields & the Lethe of the particles, do not a river make.

Individuals like Rene Descartes, Gottfied Leibnitz, Baruch Spinoza and others, filled with the unctuousness of conceptual piety, advocated only reason as being able to directly recognize reality, without reason & logic needing to recombine for associative production. (Inverting rationalism, was the root cause of the logical fallacy of Descartes' 'universal doubt', which became the schizothymic doubting of viable evidence that still misleads empirical and legal systems even today.) As per No.4, defining the *intellectual affectation of conceptualism* (essence, form, oddness, heterogeneity) places masculinism as a white triangle with the base up and the vertex pointing down (9-11-5), which is the erroneous Assumption of Being...high minded. This is the headless, self-righteous mind of the transcendent superego (Freud), or the axiomatic 'proscription' of the Christian Fourth Commandment, as 'thou shalt not covet' (4). And, if the Freudian superego of coalescence (9-11), or replacement, becomes the Superego Self (9-11-5), it sublimates the Shadow Self for describing the effectiveness of percepts as the idyllic black triangle of feminism, with the base down and its vertex pointing up (6-4-10). The lower triplet, as a diva triformis, describes the *delusion of denotative phenomenalism* (substance, function, evenness, homogeneity). This is the 'body of the horse' as the Supposition of Non-Being, or Freud's id of condensation (6-4), as displacement, which if combined with his superego of coalescence (9-11) often becomes latently unisexual egocentrism (5-10). (Freud's 'ego love', as a natural extension, overcomes the hyphenated existence of the unisexual, through his 'parasexual', which only hints at a direct link between 5 & 10.) The two triangulations, coming together in the center of the Vertical Mosaic, represent hermaphroditic orthocentrism, like a unisexual statue as the Crux of Self-deception. (Like the Twin Towers, there is no infrastructure between superstructure & substructure.) In No.4, androgynous inversion becomes an up/down-down/up crisis in self-management, with the constituent ends of Mr. Jekyll & Mrs. Hyde, like the collapse of the wave packet, not capable of moderating, in between, the measure of a real sausage. Such an implausible, impossible and improbable center reflects the assumption of chromaticism as Mythos (5), which leaps to the supposition of modulationism as Thanatos (10). (Stevenson's Mr. Hyde was a female *sosie*, because, like in Shakespearian times, women are usually not allowed to play themselves.) Romeo & Juliet really didn't need to pivot about the accidental advice of the priest & nurse, because such monolithic Indecision-Confusion (5-10), &, monopolistic Confusion-Indecision

(10-5) was "*neither heeded nor denied...but never united.*" Thus, the monolithic & monopolistic go-betweens become the untenable diabolism of Freud's egocentrism, which is, meaninglessly irresolute. Monistic sophistication (4) & adulteration (6) banishes the 'star-crossed lovers' (5-10/10-5) from the *monotheistic stream* of Feud's ego love (which interestingly enough, resembles Bacon's ampliative inference). Thus, with a touch of finality, the hermaphroditic statue of Romeo & Juliet's fails to embody the Living Metaphor as a viable third person plural, because it does not reunite the I & thou in a natural manner. God as "personal" and united, must be based upon the coextensive co-ordination of the gender issue as naturally heterogeneic: oddly folding out & evenly folding in. The monism of monogenesis, reflected in the idiocy of terms like 'essential substance' and 'inductive inference', leads from the vertical structuralism of empiricism to the horizontal constructivism of scientism, and therefore is too irresolute to produce a recombinant third alternative. Discordantly, as per No.4, masculinism (up) suffers from chromaticism & feminism (down) suffers from modulationism, with the two combining as the unfruitful accidentals, of a nonliving kind. The monotheistic third person, as neither and both male and female, must be based upon the bilateral heterosexuality of the harmony of Mind & Body together, for the natural apotheosis of re-creative measures. Romeo's *ambiguous control* ("never heeded") & Juliet's *arbitrary denial* ("nor denied") produced the *ambivalent idolatry* of monolithic & monopolistic perfection, as a unisexual golden statue that is an apodictic idealism ("but never united"). No.4 represents this same penultimate nonsense through the modern conception of the 'three-dimensional plane', based upon token half-measures that attempt to dictate immediate answers (implausible), solutions (impossible) and results (improbable). This 'planification' of secular humanism becomes the 'Thin Man' as the monistic 'one' of the hierarchical and hieratic structures of Big Brother... watching over you. The men keep the women uninformed; the women keep the men overstimulated, and humanity goes down the tubes.

When associative production occurs, there is an natural alternation of odd and even waves, as well as an interplay of complementary states, both within and between wave trains. Accordingly, as mentioned previously, the harmonic wave states of No.7 are based upon the complementary colors of white-black (1-8), yellow-purple (2-7), orange-blue (3-6) and red-green (4-5). These complementary inferences would visually "opp" (an artistic term) if juxtaposed, which only happens obviously with the red-to-green Paradigm shift of Temporality (+ 5), because the black-to-white Doppler shift of Spatiality (10 -) is far removed, within & without. The acrostic of nine-ness is reflected in all these alternating Middle Ground States, even though the ninth obit itself can never exist as an identifiable Middle Ground State. The untenable Ninth Dream would have to combine the vertical extremals of the coalescence of matter, as chromaticism, &, the horizontal extremals of the opalescence of antimatter, as modulationism. Such implies the Transmodal Inference of the Certainty Principle, as realizing natural selection itself. But, we can & may never resolve the 'five loaves and two fish' (Christian Bible: Matthew 14:17), or 'one and dyad', by loving them to death, accidentally, as a perfect golden statue. We must back off a little, and learn to breath it.

One may think of learning as painful (**Pathos**, up as sentiment) or as fun (**Bathos**, down as sympathy), or, as the rapid comprehension of a superficial profile (**Mythos**, between as denatured). But, the desensitization of **Mythos**, as the essential inhospitality of the silver lining, instantly implicates the passion of **Thanatos** as the ideological violence of the silver bullet. (The breathable progressions of **Eros** and **Ethos**, like a breath of life flowing between Phases I and III, are left out.) Too perfect, with no room to breath, the silver lining implies chromaticism, &, the silver bullet implicates modulationism. Discordantly then, the reductionism of Leibnitz's 'impenetrables & imperceptibles' (5-10 & 10-5) becomes the Test & the Trick of a deadly Fixation, under the pretense of being what Leibnitz called the 'best of all possible worlds'

(Voltaire's *Candide*, 1759, mocked these views). The reality is, that this *bene fundatum* remains the untouchable have & hold of the Haptic Extension (Glossary). And as the indeterminate Hands of God, for the Two Competencies of Verification & Validation, such perfection remains outside our natural endeavors. We must expect, and learn to live with, a more gradual revelation of the hypothetical Ultimate Truth. Too much perfection, at once, only produces the inhospitality & violence of contrapuntal accidentals, as love gone bad. 'The evil one's must be like us (simile), or we will make war on them (copula).'

Note that, in the preceding paragraph, there is an interesting system of typology, based upon the Greek pattern of Thanatos, Eros, Pathos, Bathos, Mythos, and Ethos. Properly understood, this sextuplet is closer to 'six parameter indeterminacy', rather than the deterministic six of No.4. We will be discussing how Aristotle's concept of dynamic six-ness, as 'hexis', is closer to my monotheistic No.8, wherein hexagrammatical sextuplets make up dynamic, rather than static relationships. In fact, if the rhetorical (4-5-6) & dialectical (11-10-9) syllogisms are understood to be fundamentally recombinant, similar to modern supersymmetrical Susys, then only the outcome of a dynamic hexis could possibly be entertained. Such a paradigmatic pattern is evident in Solomon's Seal. And, with these *five loaves & two fish*, we could undoubtedly feed all the people on the planet Earth - metaphorically speaking.

In the fullness of time, in-depth learning involves volumetric shaping as the 'parallel processing' of Integrative Discipline. However, *as carbon units, what we do best is make mistakes*: 5-10 & 10-5, as all very fine & good, or forever and anon. But, what we do better is make gradual corrections and improvements, whether through Plato's dynamic 'state', Aristotle's 'efficient cause', St. Augustine's 'hypostatization of essence', Bacon's 'ampliative inference', Kant's 'noumenon', Hegel's 'synthesis', Darwin's 'survival of the fittest', Einstein's 'E_3', or my Recombinant Adaptations for recombining Local & Global Adaptations. Two antithetical absolutes too close together, like the ultimatums of Gestalt brinkmanship, born of dualism, only provide for an *ambiguous & arbitrary dissociation*; wherein faith not being tied to behavior, makes the Christian Doctrine of Justification into an absurdity. (The same goes for the Islamic faith, whose clerics have rightly intoned that 'terrorists will not even get an odor of heaven.') As per No.4, the preclusive (9-11) & retroclusive (6-4) aspects of artificial justification are not only self-contradictory, but the instant transpositions of perfect reciprocals do not lend themselves to organic growth, either physically or spiritually. As a consequence, the contrapuntal accidentals of vertical chromaticism, &, horizontal modulationism, only produce the diabolical opping of the Hyphenated Person as a automaton. The whimsical *ambivalence* of feeling, between complicity & duplicity in the vertical mode, tends to enshrine the *arbitrariness* of automatic progress, leading to the *absurdity* of seeking to control & deny unnatural *conversion factors.* The facile & idyllic, excuses & apologies of paradoxical behavior, lead to the direct syndrome (5-10 & 10-5) of self-serving double standards. Without sensible self-criticism, the implication is that others must pay for our mistakes, through our contempt & condemnation.

As a technical aside, within each wave train, field & particle are the computable reciprocals of the direct channel of quantum mechanical correlations. And, each *iterative imputable result*, based upon setting constants, into order to exponentially prove answers (field as raising powers) & disprove solutions (particle as extracting roots), becomes associated with a natural wave pattern. Of course, that ***does not mean*** that quantum operatives can *prove or disprove* classical ground states as waves (Gödel's theorem). Thus, something like 2 & 4 is a nonlocal field & particle of quantum computation, that is only associated with + 3 as a classically local analytic wave, that can be experienced but never strictly determined. In contrast, 2 - is a synthetic wave that is associated, as a complementary equivalent, with a positive 1-&-3 correlation, that has the same field-

&-particle order as 2 & 4. Hence, to complete the complementary equivalence within every wave train, regardless of whether the ground is synthetically even or analytically odd, a given classical corollary must be linked internally to its appropriate quantum correlation, *with field before particle.* Accordingly, classically local ground states are associated with quantum nonlocal field/particle dualities, so that each threefold wave train maintains the unitarity of the universe. That is, a white donut has a black medium without & within it, and vice versa. (Remember that, by convention, chirality is either synthetically leftward, for an even wave train, or analytically rightward, for an odd wave train). However, there is no mathematical 'identity principle', because quantum calculations, as operational derivatives, must comply with the law of excluded middles, and therefore Outer Field & Inner Particle cannot be used to determine a Middle Ground State. Interestingly then, as mentioned, for each wave train, internally at least, field seems to be consistently before particle. For example, with the three separate wave trains, of 2 – **1 & 3**, **2 & 4** + 3 and 4 – **3 & 5**, the three fields are **1**, **2** and **3**, followed by their correlative particles, as **3**, **4** and **5**. This conventional order, of field position before particle momentum, is *a quantum, nonlocal example of 'Bell's inequality'*. The latter works less well for the EPR claim that 'local hidden variables' can & may channel mysteriously between the 'supersymmetrical inequality' of the 'particle A' of Temporality (+ 5) & the 'particle B' of Spatiality (10 -).

However, ontologically, between wave trains, the overall pattern is another story. A French physicist, Alain Aspect, about 1980, in cooperation with many others, was able to establish that, looking at the complete set, including all ten histories of the wave trains, the pattern is generally from particle to field. In Construct No.14, the three ones, three twos, etc., up to the three sevens, all repeat a similar pattern of *particle-ground-field, from small toward large.* Generally, the reader can verify that the full set of ten wave trains; including both evenly synthetic absorption triads and oddly analytic emission triads; follows the pattern particle-ground-field, all the way up to Bertrand Russell's 'three sevens'. Typically then, as in the example above, three-ness reflects the said pattern, from particle to ground, to field, in which all terms, whether odd or even, are reduced to the left and expand to the right. (These are the absorption-emission gradients of associative development.) As per John Bell, the operatives of the quantum potential follow the 'inequality' of field-to-particle if they are within a given wave train. More importantly, based upon what is called 'Bell's theorem', all donut-like waves, for locally classical ground states, must be associated with *nonlocal, complementary quantum equivalents, as their carrier medium*, that is both larger without & smaller within.

About 1915, Einstein was in favor of dimensionless points, such as his c.c. (4 & 6), & the v.e.d. (11 & 9), but he argued against direct axiological 'action at a distance' (5-10 & 10-5). That is, he did not advocate 'local hidden variables' channeling directly between the Means & Ends of the same light cone. (The point-particles in the center of each harmonic state do not line up directly, as might be inferred by looking down the middle of No.7.) Unfortunately, with the mediatrix (4 & 6 as his c.c.) mistaken for calculating the fixed rest energy of E_o (5), Einstein could not admit to the incipient potentials of quantum mechanical effects (4 & 6). For special relativity then, this rationalization of the existence of the field effect led to the logical imputation that the interpretation of computable derivatives could actually compute the rest energy of a local ground state. (Androgynous inversion, as per No.4, is again rearing its ugly head. The eventual development of a fission bomb is implied by such rampant logical positivism.) Hence, even though Einstein regretted having come up with the computation of such an ideal 'stopper', leaving out the nonlocal quantum derivatives of the c.c. made rest energy look like a static universe. That gave the impression of a field effect (4 & 6) which could never be overcome, thereby making E_o into a Wall of Theory that was supposed to be perfectly preserved. (We now know that neither energy nor momentum is perfectly conserved.) In other terms, it was as though calculating the SU(2) of the 'aleph-null' (4 & 6) gave 'one' special dibs on the U(1) of 'aleph-one' (+ 5), by turning it into an explosive hyperplane of interactionism. This troubled approach came out of the nineteenth century's deterministic penchant for the static universe & cosmic censorship. Right up to his death in 1955, Einstein still referred to ground states as "fields". And today, many physicists still talk about the 'wave-particle duality', when they really mean 'field-particle duality'. This is where my pattern of field-ground-figure, or field-wave-particle, begins the healing process, which, spiritually, is a kind of Third Testament.

The debate on this topic became the famous EPR 'thought experiment' or Einstein-Podolsky-Rosen debate (1935). Generally, the EPR debate was confused by expecting the natural system, for the space-time object, not to require classical and quantum statistics to be intertwined. Traditionally, this confusion about 'spatial objectivity' led to expecting Phase IV relationships to be perfectly predictable, with the 'external means' giving exact experiment results, when the 'local hidden variables' of the Ends only give approximate results. (We cannot know the exact Laws of Nature.) About 1950, David Bohm eventually, rather successfully, argued in favor of the quantum interpretation of 'nonlocalities', as effecting (even derivatives) & affecting (odd derivatives) the meaningful measurements of classical experience, but not directly. In the 1960s, John Bell took a similar position – which came to be called Bell's theorem - that there were 'nonlocal variables' connecting the red-green Paradigm shift (Means of particle A) with the black-white Doppler shift (Ends of particle B), even though experiments tended to show no deterministic relationship. 'Points defects', or worm holes as nonlocalities, mean than the ground states of Means & Ends remain independent, as Einstein required, but that there could & might be *nonlocal connections on higher & lower levels of dimensionality.* For example, even constituents, such as 4 & 6, would be lower-order interrupt as a negative derivation of 'rotational spin symmetry', &, odd constituents, like 11 & 9, would be higher-order interrupt as a positive derivation of 'isotopic spin symmetry'. Accordingly, the c.c. (black-white hourglass) & v.e.d. (red-green hourglass) act like nonlocal, quantum keying mechanisms. And, generically, the odd force of 5, as a formalism (vertical white line in No.13), would remain an *indeterminate* 'heteromorphism' or 'isomorphism', &, the even force of 10, as an idealism (horizontal black line), would be an *indeterminate* 'homomorphism' or 'allomorphism'. Importantly, these two primary forces remain independent, although possibly interconnected through nonlocal constituents, such as a '*gravitational coupling constant*' (even pair), or a '*constant of kinetic velocity*' (odd pair). Of course, each wave train has a pair of correlative constituents associated with the corollary of a force, but 4 & 6 + 5 & 10 - 11 & 9, as Susys, are more pertinent to the link between the Means of particle A, for the first system, & the Ends of particle B, for the second system. And, to resolve the troubled debate of EPR, concerning objectivity and cause; including nonlocal quantum variables with local classical 'variations', does not violate Einstein's requirement, to operate at or below the speed of light, and yet it allows for *a more comprehensive treatment of complete phasal space.* Quantum theory is 'complete' then, if it includes an appropriate blending of both quantum and classical dimensions, as has been born out by experimentation.

Everybody wins, if the 'compatibility' (Albert Einstein) between the two systems means that they dovetail recombinantly to make up the third alternative (like my ten wave trains). Importantly, 'complementarity' (Niels Bohr) must be maintained, not only for the 'invariance' (Hendrik Lorentz) of each wave train, but for the total internal consistence of complete phasal space (like my ten wave trains). Also, the same associative development must allow the 'equivalence' (Einstein) between energy and mass to permeate all relationships (like my ten wave trains). Hence, Reality must be both finite & infinite, as equally expansive & reductive, within a dynamic steady state theory, based upon Constant Unity Factors, harmonizing the space-time object, as the four-dimensional double light cone of a natural third system (like my ten wave trains).

For No.7, Einstein recommended ten-dimensional space-time, with four variations of matter ground states, and, six variations of antimatter ground states (Scientific American, Special Issue Vol. 3, Number 1, 1991, p. 45). Accordingly, harmonic relationships should show the odd-even alternation of eight harmonic wave trains; not counting the dyadic Ends of nonexistence (10-11 & 9 and 0-9 & 1), which represent what Einstein called the 'unbounded curvature of space'. (Think of the magnetic north pole of Jupiter, in the southern hemisphere, and, the magnetic south pole, in the northern hemisphere, as per No.7. The black-white hourglass, acting like a compass, reverses this polarity.) No.7 shows the harmonic range of complete phasal space through the associative development of alternative ground states, as evenly synthetic toward the left, for absorption, and oddly analytic toward the right, for emission. These eight states are the measurable transitions of Middle Ground States as the waves of classical variation. (Reminds me of the theme of Zachariah's first 'eight books'.) Further, not only is the variation of the waves associative in an Odd-Even manner, but so are the quantum and classical aspects within each wave train. And, the axiological particles streaming down the center that are associated with the neutral current process of configurational space, can be generally represented by odd-even heterotic strings. (Remember the dots do not line up, as there is no direct, axiological channel.) Importantly, I will be demonstrating how string theory fits in with my simplified rendering of the ten field equations.

Strictly speaking, the constituents of 4 & 6, as fundamental to Werner Heisenberg's uncertainty principle, are typical of 'inertial mass & mass density', or the force of gravity and center of microgravity. The latter two have been shown to be nearly equal in strength. And, any field-particle pairing of even operatives (e.g., 6 & 8 + 7), when matched with the appropriately odd ground state, gives the 'weight' of that 'element', due to the fact that the Higgs mechanism instantly registers the appropriate *inertial progression.* Therefore, the weak force makes up a vertically accelerated inertial frame as a direct channel or superstring that is nonlocally connected to the strong force (10 -). In other words, one cannot shield matter from gravitational effects, because of the implicit function of the discontinuous, nonlocal quantum variables of spatial curl, that operate without & within continuous time. Thus, the global nature of the strong force of supergravity (10 -) is represented in a local manner as the gravitational coupling constant. Similarly, each ground state of "spaces", as antimatter variation, must have synchrotron radiation constituents as nonlocal quantum variables of temporal discontinuity, that operate without & within continuous space. Thus, 11 & 9, as fundamental to Wolfgang Pauli's exclusion principle, represent a constant of kinetic velocity that is associated with each even ground state. Further, as an extension of the constant of kinetic velocity, apparently each nonlocal, positive field/particle pairing contributes to what is called the '*fine structure constant*' (1/137). And, for even and odd operatives, like 4 & 6 and 11 & 9, etc. these nonlocal quantum derivations are likewise *complementary, equivalent and antithetical* to each other, much in the way that 'Planck space & Planck time', or 'Planck mass & Planck length', are considered to interrelate to make up 'Planck's constant'. That is, the odd, nonlocal 'principle of least action' of quantum mechanical affects (1 & 3, 5 & 7, etc.), and the even, nonlocal 'principle of least action' of quantum mechanical effects (0 & 2, 6 & 8, etc.) both subvene & supervene their respective, locally measurable ground states. That is the field-particles patterns are considered quantum mechanical 'superpositions', which are the operatives of what is called '*tensorial vectors*', while real vectors are a measure of matter variation, &, spatial vectors are a measure of antimatter variation. And, as mentioned, if we consider the range of 1-3-5-7 (evolution of the four waves of matter variation) and 0-2-4-6-8-10 (devolution of the six waves of antimatter variation), then each of the Odd-Even pairs of Middle Ground States would require an Outer Field & Inner Figure of opposite treatment. Thus, as shown by my simple numerological system of ten wave trains, as per Construct No.14, there must be at least 30 factors in all, when quantum and classical statistics are recombined.

Interestingly, the science of measurement has its equivalence in the spirituality of meaning, and, just as the deductive omnipotence of subjectivity seeks to reveal the *unicity* of the Holy Universal Church, the inductive omniscience of objectivity seeks to discover the *unitarity* of the Laws of Nature. Importantly then, universal design space itself is neither and both objective & subjective, because it is the interplay of science & spirituality, working together, that is responsible for the betterment of humanity. Hence, for the modern era, it is recombinant measures that bring out the dynamic progressions of the Third Testament as a sabbatical New Wave, or emergent reagent.

Figuratively, associated with Phase II is the 'alpha profile' of the ***elixir*** of Masculinity (Kant's categorical imperative, Hegel's thesis), &, dissociated through Phase IV is the 'gamma profile' of the ***manna*** of Femininity (Kant's hypothetical imperative, Hegel' antithesis). As the two systems, these are Einstein's E_1 & E_2. Then, for the traveling waves of Side Effects, the 'delta and beta profiles' are the ***ambrosia*** of Phase I and ***nectar*** of Phase III, making up the recombinant third person plural (Kant's noumenon, Hegel's synthesis). Hence, through the 'hendiadys dialogue' (Marshall McLuhan), of one through two, we get the third alternative as Einstein's E_3. Or, the hyperbolic & elliptical become parabolic.

Then, because the fourth dimension progresses as a natural system, the Four Phases take on many difference patterns of development: ambrosia-elixir-nectar-manna, or delta-alpha-beta-gamma, or charge-energy-spin-momentum, or spring-summer-fall-winter, or best-fine-better-good, etc. In the same manner, based upon Aristotle's 'four causes' and Einstein's four-dimensional space-time, Construct No.9 uses four colored tori to represent the Four Phases. Phase I is delta, Phase II is alpha, Phase III is beta and Phase IV is gamma. Similar metaphorical arrangements are found in all of the following: the Buddhist Four Truths, Hesiod's Four Ages, the Hebrew tetragrammaton, the Christian diatessaron, the Muslim maqam of Alif. Lam. Mim. Sad., the four humors of medieval medicine, the Four Laws of Conservation, and my Four Resonances as modeled by No.12. In short, a well rendered Duality produces the Recombinant Third System, which, in turn, highlights the fourfold nature of experience that underlies all systems analysis.

What is important here, is a better understanding of the nature of metaphor. It has been said that with the right metaphor it is possible to discover almost anything. Metalogical Constructs are an attempt to make metaphorical representations into General Guidelines that are patently self-evident. The synoptic view provided allows one to popularize concepts of enormous complexity, which has great educational value, because it provides a context for new learning.

Making Progress

All great thinkers, such as Max Planck and Albert Einstein, agree that the human ability to harness reason & logic in a dialogical manner provides insight into the Laws of Nature. The progressions of these associative developments become a mnemonic aid. Apropos, the decalogue of ten-dimensional space-time has proven to be a remarkably consistent extension of human consciousness. However, not surprisingly popularizing such ideas has not been easy. Take for example the Christian Ten Commandments. These rules have, for the most part, been turned into childish drivel. However, when taken as a complete set, the whole throws a remarkable light upon the meaning of each Commandment. For example, the fourth rule governing 'coveting', as my 'proscription', is a warning about accepting false assumptions. And, the sixth rule concerning 'adultery', as my 'description', denotes the *de facto values of things*, which becomes the delusional false belief syndrome. For the Ten Commandments, I will be following the pattern 10-1-2-3-4-5-6-7-8-9, using my own terms. Nevertheless, as a memory aid, mathematical, orbital, psychological and spiritual systems, etc. may vary a little, one from the other. For example, there can be no ninth atomic orbit and yet there is a Ninth Commandment, concerning 'transcription' as a warning to avoid the vanity of transference. And, as another example, in the set theory of mathematics, I agree with those who say that a *zero* must be included. Accordingly, the decalogical pattern becomes 10/0-1-2-3-4-5-6-7-8-9/10. More later.

Such progressive developments encompass TTPs such as metaphysical, social and cosmological, or physical, communal and cultural, or series, sequence and system, or time, space and space-time object, etc. The monotheistic *River of Gods*, as one stream of consciousness, is based upon triune patterns such as faith, hope and charity, or power, glory and kingdom, etc. Faith links a higher power with self, trust relates to the shared concerns of the human community, and love as supraluminal is fundamental to the Universal Marriage of First Principles. Unifying all the streams as one, the triune pattern can be intrapersonal-interpersonal-suprapersonal, or allegorical-moral-anagogical, or, Aristotle's 'peripeteia-anagnorisis-apolaustic'. Xenocrates, a student of Plato, who came up with the 'one & dyad', advocated the third alternative as 'sensibles-reasonables-intelligibles'. These liberating patterns replace the Three Fates of blind (no vision), deaf (no judgement) and dumb (no consideration). Such a miraculous transition can easily occur around the age of eleven years, according to Jean Piaget's 'systems of operations' (Swiss psychologist, 1896-1980). It is not surprising then, that a young person once said to me, "It takes three days to learn to love." Through intrapersonal dialogue, within the self, as a form of prayer, a eudaemonic disposition begins to motivate the leap of faith of Integrative Discipline, without going out on a limb, or off a deep end. That is, the atmospherics of a troubled personality can acquire the nimbus of a refreshing outlook, when the 'I' of isolated individualism gets a breakthrough in learning. There is evident a kind of *serendipitous or heuristic leap*, that predisposes an individual for the felicitous transition from paranoia to 'metanoia' (Northrop Frye). In other terms, instead of projecting speculative conclusions, and reflecting an inability to take a hint or make an appropriate guess, the power of positive thinking can bring beneficial insights. In contrast, the repression of self usually jumps to unrealistic transference, by grabbing at straws, in hopes of finding a miraculous cure-all. Consider, a society that legalizes public gambling, or, a disfranchised middle class led by the nose, to war. Discordantly, the assimilation of self, through repressive social measures, often results in a form of acculturation that is accompanied by extreme adventurism. In other words, if one goes off the deep end, perceptualism might advocate extreme measures that are culturally disruptive. Or, extreme specialization might desensitize an individual to relational patterns. For example, if a person becomes a brilliant idiot savant, paying attention to humane developments usually takes on a lower priority. Accordingly, the Integrative Discipline of the first system must join up with the Empathic Transference of the second system, in order to ensure that satisfactory relationships within the human community produce the General Guidelines of the third system. That is, by 'bringing our daughters back from the dead', the *feedback patterns* of Empathic Transference, as intelligence, become the handmaid of Integrative Discipline, as information, so that 'we' come to appreciate General Guidelines, as ethological. For Freud, the ethological pattern leads to the Heterosexual Stage as a Phase III relationship. Similarly, the *eudaemonic* 'I' of Felicity (acceptance) blends with the *eugenic* 'you' of Facility (accession), with the two recombining through the *eusocial* 'otherness' of Faculty (agreement). Science & spirituality must blend to produce the sociopolitics of legal, ethological progressions. It is the latter that are innately democratic, and which we will be discussing as having their roots within the teleological democracy of physics.

Forms of isolation need to be overcome, but not in a way that compromises individuality. As media mogul Marshall McLuhan once stated, 'All subjects studied in depth relate to all other subjects.' The same applies to knowing thyself, as a way of understanding others, or the way in which the personal healing circle joins up with the social healing circle. Instead of the codependent cycling of the coplanar & coterminal, between commensalism & mutualism (No.4), the dynamic correspondence of supportive relationships does not require a loss of independence. With the dualistic patterns of No.4, mutual inclusion & mutual exclusion set up the double fallacy of specious reason (above) & spurious logic (below), with the two ultimatums of perfect brinkmanship preventing the correspondence of Integrative Discipline & Empathic Transference. Plato's state and Aristotle's hexis both overcome this closed-form dualism, by advocating a democratic sense of *dynamic equilibrium.* Today, this same dynamic still represents a real problem for medical doctors, when caring for their patients. Further, there is a similar misunderstanding with respect to the second law of thermodynamics, referred to as 'entropic degradation'. And, concerning global pollution and atmospheric warming, many people simply become myopic naysayers. Further, often spiritual leaders find it difficult to understand that the monotheistic third person, as a Living Metaphor, requires the co-ordination of the gender issue. That is, following a Platonic pattern: beginning with the *eugenic* (Phase IV), the *eudaemonic* parental generation (Phase I) leads to the *euphenic* extension of discipline (Phase II), which engenders the *eusocial consciousness* (Phase III) of democratic practices. Accordingly, Integrative Discipline & Empathic Transference, working together, are able to get on the path of *true freedom*: the "Autonomous Complex" of General Guidelines.

Each individual is composed of innumerable universes, on many different levels of dimensionality, such as cosmic, mental, chemical, biological and atomic, etc. In fact, every living entity contains the stardust of elements developed aeons ago within the nucleosynthesis of an uncountable number of supernovas! Thus, it is not possible for an individual to fully appreciate the multitude of dimensions within one's own self, let alone comprehend how all the other universes interact. Not only is our galaxy unbelievably large, but recent photographs from the Hubble space telescope show countless other galaxies at unfathomable distances. Evidently, as Einstein claimed, there is no limit to either largeness or smallness. Just the same, there is one consistently encouraging aspect to all of the foregoing; the natural system of self-sameness is self-evident everywhere, as a kind of Universal Covenant.

Popularizing systems theory is helped by the well-known adage that a picture is worth a thousand words. All of the Metalogical Constructs in this text, in keeping with the principle of bootstrapping, need only be employed if they apply to a given situation, remain an adequate description of prevailing conditions, and provide a measure of predictability. Importantly, models are experiential, and, like a scientific flowchart, contain more intelligence than one would normally suspect. For example, Construct No.12 resembles a Persian rug, which I refer to as "Powell's carpet". I developed it independently, and was surprised to discover that the physicist Roger Penrose created similar pentagonal surfaces of five-sided 'quasiparticles', to build an ideal scalar field (points in any direction) as a sort of 'unified field theory'. Marshall McLuhan contemplated the challenge of searching for such a gateway or portal, but never claimed to have realized any sort of approximation for what has been traditionally called the 'fifth element'. Later in life, Aristotle added a sort of fifth element to his four causes, as the 'moving cause' (*Aristotle's Two Systems*, Daniel W. Graham, 1987).

Each of my Metalogical Constructs has obvious flaws and limitations, which merely add to their charm. As the English philosopher Karl R. Popper (1902-1994) maintained '*falsification*' is a fundamental scientific tenet, which is an integral part of the Phase IV relationships of experiment. However, problems occur when falsification is shifted from its "devicive" role of Facilitation within Phase IV, to a cliched methodology associated with the phenomenalism of Phase II. For example, using the principle of universal doubt as a legal methodology merely distorts the judicial process, by using Descartes' universal doubt to disingenuously *discredit any argument* that is not to one's own advantage. That is, the agnostics of 'disproving the negative hypothesis' may simply be a matter of introducing prejudicial evidence (6-4), and not really consistent with the *prescient falsification* of the neither/nor as the Distributive But Not of Phase IV. For example, the *conservative nit-picking of pragmatic denegration* is usually not up to discovering its own false belief syndrome, or that success is not its own measure, or that a question might unjustly beg its answer, or that just because something works does not make it right. The point to be made here is that Karl R. Popper decried the pragmatic belief structures of fascistic duplicity, by which the conundrum of the inductive method (6-4) promotes the confusion of displacement, in order to manipulate the subconscious down-side of 'selective retention', in support of a logical fallacy. The latter, as Freud's 'Anal Stage', is a false belief repression syndrome (lower part of No.4), wherein irreverent Bathos denies progressive understandings. This fundamentalism of immutable cultic values could lead to social suicide, through adamantine self-justification. The rebarbative emotions, of sympathetic devaluation, reflect back through a retrogressive aural-oral pattern, from the materialism of Phase II, toward preliterate neo-tribalism in Phase I. In No.4, just as the 'subjective correlative' of 'selective attention' (up) produces an anxiety transference syndrome, so the 'objective correlative' of 'selective retention' (down) produces a false belief repression syndrome.

The question becomes, do the facts speak for themselves, and, do they speak the whole truth and nothing but the truth, as though a perfect, unchanging nature were already manifest? Further, one might ask, does the law merely support the rich, famous and influential, rather than a truly legitimate sense of Associative Justice? The hidden supposition is that the permissive *breakdown of catharsis* naturally rebounds to a *breakthrough in learning.* Or, that the repression of guilt feelings makes philosophical extravagance less self-righteous. Similarly, accidents tend to happen to young people, but does having physical & psychic scars engender the quest for personal liberation? As a way out, if we get the physics right we will find the roots of Popper's 'moral rule'. For the most part, he looked upon the atonement of the moral compass as being similar to the collapse of the wave packet (4 & 6), from which to resolve a more progressive outlook, based upon the inner illumination of slow-breaking asymmetry (+ 5). The fascistic sententiousness of the demonstrative syllogism (4-5-6) must be rewritten to become 4 & 6 + 5. That is, the algorithms of the inductive method (4 & 6) must take second-shrift, as when AI works in support of a set of realistic variations that develop in context (+ 5).

Mirroring the up/down-down/up pattern of No.4, Plato and Democritus both decried the Being-&-Non-Being pattern of demiurgic entities, as token half-measures – like bipartisan politics. Thus, their *Tauton & Heteron* became a closed-loop system that modeled how not to proceed. The upper fractal would be the perfect Being of the Tauton, as a one-to-one association, &, the lower fractal the immutable Non-Being of the Heteron, as a one-to-one dissociation. This dualism becomes commensalism over mutualism, exploiting & manipulation, aiding & abetting, complicity & duplicity, defining & describing, etc. (In modern terms, computer generated fractal patterns produce the colorful arabesques that the mathematician Benoit Mandelbrodt referred to as the 'devil's polymer'. In one sense, one would have a perfect Mind & Body in the here & now, as though epistemological perfection would & could become a unisexual hermaphrodite, instead of the less perfect, mixed blessing of a heterosexual style of relationship. Demanding perfection only leads to the dishonesty and self-deception of the Two Determinisms as a direct syndrome (5-10 & 10-5). That is, the obvious agenda (up) & hidden agenda (below) become slaved to the fixed agenda between, which enables the justification of immoral conduct. Relationally, one has intellectual evasiveness & emotional deviousness as lies & secrets, or behaviorism & introspectionism, but never as truly shared experience. The result, about a core of egocentrism, is a malingering narcissism as contempt for &

condemnation of, others. Us mere mortals must take a more gradual and inclusive approach. We must go beyond worrying about perfect gnosis, while gradually working on the Buddhist 'awakening', in accordance with the development of democratic individuation. It seems that the politician that blabs the most about 'freedom', is the first to 'release the hounds' on an unsuspecting neighbor.

Historically, Alfred North Whitehead's (Eng./Am. phil. & math., 1861-1947) philosophical writings closely parallel mine. He was worried about the abuses of Old Science, which tended to favor the separation of religion & science. With Old Science, the vertical mode of authoritative empiricism becomes reduced to the horizontal device of mechanistic scientism. That is, based upon the dualism of quasiscience, as combining the Tauton of biased definitions & Heteron of prejudicial descriptions, empirical structuralism begs scientific constructivism. In contrast, Whitehead's emphasis upon a non-projective process of discovery, which like Goethe's double sanity check, involves the modern concept of the 'double blind study'. Like Jung's 'secret', Whitehead felt that the Crux of Choice & Action contained the incipient potentials of his 'prehensions', which could be marshalled for a legitimate process of inquiry. Thus, his philosophy brought out that the most important development of the nineteenth century was the 'discovery process' itself. Whitehead disliked abstraction (up) & concretism (down) as not being able to imbue immediate developments with natural methodology. Like Popper and myself, he felt that good science depended upon the right philosophical propensity. Accordingly, his *philosophy of change* was based upon Henri Bergson's sense of 'projective geometry', which links him to the modern emperor of physics Roger Penrose. My Metalogical Constructs are a continuation of this same geometric approach, wherein I use the psychology of relationships to produce General Guidelines.

The erroneousness of quasiscience is based upon the twin fallacy of the obviation of specious reason (9-11) & the evidence of spurious logic (6-4). In other terms, demanding perfect Verification merely blocks the process of Validation, with the phenomenological becoming phenomenalism. Hence, the Armageddon of Mrs. Hyde, based upon the lower triangulation of Construct No.4 (6-4-10), as 'disproving the negative hypothesis', does not represent the true falsification of an objective sequence, such as 10 - 11 & 9, 0 - 9 & 1, and 0 & 2 + 1. That Sequence, itself, as a hypothetical event, stems from what the physicist Leon Lederman referred to as 'the three major outcomes of experiment'. The first and fundamental triplet becomes part of the larger triad of an actual, but less deterministic Validation of Process. It's just that, in No.13, the three horizontal lines, as the dialectical syllogism of 11-10-9, alone, are an unattainable, sententious idealism. We will be discussing the supposition of First Principles as an 'Ideal Phase Transition', which, as Ought, Ought Naught and Might, do not allow the Laws of Nature to become know & understood as immutable facts. In No.4, the 'facts' of the feminine triangulation (6-4-10), as the diva triformis of all even numbers, are not part of a tenable disproof - despite some legal afficionados – and therefore secretly reinforces the prejudicial denotation of false beliefs. Effectively, the methodological question (6) begs predisposed belief structures (4), which then leads to the fundamentalism of general principles (10), based upon the selective retention of subconscious self-devaluation. As delusional, this self-justification becomes the down side of 'moral equivalence', which then rebounds back up to the 'ethical equivalence' of self-righteousness. Even Immanuel Kant, who knew that the down side of the '*synthetic proposition*' did not accurately concretize 'necessary logic', still did not realize that the up side of the '*analytic proposition*' does not fully constitute 'sufficient reason'. Thus, his philosophy, like Hegel's, had a wicked limp, even though he tried to avoid the double standards of a twin-paradox. Many religious people must live every day with this same sort of uneven spirituality which breeds controversy, up/down & down/up, within a narrow range of limit cycles, without finding the monotheistic *River of Gods.* In the same manner, any legal system that expects to disprove the prosecution's evidence of guilt, must avoid espousing the false belief syndrome, while keeping to a legitimate procedure that allows the consolidation of evidential objectivity, if it exists in an experiential manner.

Note that when it is *convenient*, the analytical 'one' of existence is allowed to dominate, & where it is *expedient*, the synthetic 'dyad' of nonexistence takes over. Their vertical collusion could & might become perfectly *efficacious*, as though progress can & may actually be psychopathologically automatic, without any need for human dialogue. Only Diacritical Consciousness can overcome the inevitable conspiratorial action of a Freudian reaction formation, which fills the void with what the poet T. S. Eliot referred to as the 'dissociative self', as portrayed in his poem *The Hollow Man.* For Susan Oyama 'the ghost in the ghost-in-the-machine machine' implies the need for a diacritical approach. Purely analytic Complexity (9-11-5), & purely synthetic Simplicity (6-4-10), as in No.4, imply the Greek-like unalloyed sets of perfect Entities & Events, which would be empiricism & scientism as determinism. Importantly, there are no unalloyed relationships, because legitimate relationships are always a blend of Universal Duality. Accordingly, Eminence & Distinction must learn to swim in the same stream, for the sake of human progress.

As a complete stream, phasal space requires the spring of the Negative Associative And in Phase I, the summer of the Commutative Or in Phase II, the fall of the Positive Associative And in Phase III, and finally, the winter of the Distributive But Not in Phase IV. (There! Hercules has just cleaned out the Augean stables of Boolean logic, by not allowing the donkeys of formalism [up] & the horses of functionalism [down] to reduce viable Side Effects to impotent mules. The American novelist, Ernest Hemingway would have appreciated this holistic argument.) Traveling from the falsification of experiment (IV) to the attribution of application (I), and then through the actualization of methodology (II) toward the anticipation of process (III), covers the full range of complete phasal space. The normative or regulatory pattern is 'tactics' (Phase I), 'paratactics' (Phase II), 'strategies' (Phase III) and 'intelligence' (Phase IV). It's just that, for the scientific method the preferred order is II, III, IV and I. More later.

Interestingly, Jung once entertained the idea of having a number system with the 'base 4' rather than our current 'base 10'. We will see that such an idea sometimes has merit, but would likely be more dangerous than beneficial, because the *decussative four* might be too closely linked to the *decuplative ten*, thereby attempting to determine both **Identity** (4) **& Continuity** (10). In Greek mythology Hades, as fourteenth within the pantheon of gods, was consigned to the underworld. In Construct No.1, the 4 + 10 combination of monolith & monopole, as eternal plane & infinite axis, produce the grid-lock pattern of the Four Horsemen of the Apocalypse Now (red-white-green-black) and Armageddon (yellow-orange-purple-blue). These two are loving hate & hating love.

Identity & Continuity muddy the waters of the third system, because as Newton maintained, 'we cannot solve the three-body problem.' In the same stream of thought, a French mathematician, Pierre De Fermat (1601-1665) left 'us' with the implausible formality & impossible ideal of proving 'Fermat's last theorem'. In simplistic terms, the harmonic transitions between different ground states cannot be established as the proof of a *direct axiological relationship that would hold true for all occasions.* In No.7, the axiological would not allow one to run smoothly down the axis, like 'joining up the dots', by lining up Inner Particles, without paying any attention to Middle Ground States and Outer Fields. As part of the underworld of configurational space, each bead-like Inner Particle has a different character. Thus, in 4 - 3 & 5, 5 is a particle, while in 6 & 8 + 7, 8 is an altogether different particle. Therefore, there is no way to establish an axiological proof, for one "particular" line of reasoning. Transitions (odd, stress, character) & transmutations (even, strain, trait) between different ground states, within the same organic system, are intertwined through the Crossover Patterns of the natural system. Such and such is an organic process, and we must respect the organicity of the whole system, in order to get a true measure of the separate elements. This doesn't mean that we won't discover a *neutral current process* that works fairly well for a particular system. For example, there is apparently an internal 'electron flux tube' running axiologically between the poles of Jupiter. Further, microcurrents have been discovered operating within the helical patterns of RNA and DNA. These patterns only mean that 'proof' is too strong a term to be used for *experiential progressions*, which are not an exact science. The *doctrinal ordinances* of harmonic ground states flow continuously from one inferential ground state to another, to objectify legitimate relationships, but they do not imply (4) or implicate (6) what could & might be considered as sufficient (5) & necessary proof (10) for the Identity of a field & Continuity of a particle. (This throws a kibosh into an exact determination of Bell's inequality.) We will be looking at coplanar relationships in the vertical mode, which are never quite *sufficiently closed* (static universe), & elliptically coterminal relationships in the horizontal mode, which are never quite *necessarily convergent* (cosmic censorship). In other words, energy & momentum, as A & B, are not exactly & directly convertible, meaning that Einstein's 'equivalence' does not translate perfectly from one to the other, and back again. This means that the EPR debate could not conclude the argument over the objective identities (harmonic elements) of the third system, or the nature of their causal links. It also means that the collapse of any given wave packet, like 1 & 3 or 4 & 6, neither proves nor disproves the nature of its associated ground state: in this case 2 - or + 5. Further, if particle A & B were perfectly equivalent, as between the This of energy & That of mass, that would disprove Bell's theorem, which justly requires nonlocal quantum variables to be blended with elements of classical variation, in order to establish complete phasal space.

The four major dimensions of physics seem wanting: *the weak force, the strong force, electromagnetic waves, and gravitation.* At first, my arguments may appear overly complex, but using my numerological system, along with the models, the reader will eventually get a feeling for the objective progressions of string theory. Importantly, my system, although a bit simplified, includes all four of the accepted 'forces'. Firstly, the distribution of electromagnetic energy is shared symbiotically between Phases I and III, and governs the 'lepton family' of Phase I (Construct No.3) and the 'antilepton family' of Phase III (Construct No.5). Thus, Magnetic Resonance is centered in Phase I and Electronic Resonance in Phase II. But, that still leaves the dielectric (4 - 3 & 5) and paramagnetic (4 & 6) tied to Phase II, &, the diamagnetic (10 - 0) and paraelectrical (11 & 9 and 9 & 1) linked to Phase IV. Then, centering the 'three families of particles' (+ 3, + 5 and + 7), Matter Resonance in Phase II governs the 'baryon hadron family' (See Phase II in No.9.). Phase II is built up by the *electroweak theory* governing both the SU(2) of the weak force (4 & 6) and U(I) of the electrodynamic surface effect (+ 5), to produce the wave train of QED (4 & 6 + 5). For Antimatter Resonance in Phase IV, the nucleons combine protons and neutrons as the enthalpic core of all matter elements (small red-green hourglass in No.7). Thus Phase IV, as the Antimatter Resonance of nonexistence, has at least three arbitrarily chosen variables (10 - 11 & 9, 0 - 9 & 1, 0 & 2 + 1), just as Phase II has always had a measure of 'ambiguous precision' for the mode (4 - 3 & 5), median (6 - 5 & 7) and mean (4 & 6 + 5). (Remember, because they are Susys, the basic paralogism of the sequence of 10 - 11 & 9 expands to three separate antimatter wave trains, just as the basic parallelism of the series of 4 & 6 + 5 expands to form three matter wave trains.) The gravitational strong force (10 - 0) is likely made up of 'massless vector bosons', such as gravitons, gluons and neutrinos (horizontal black line in No.13). Along with it, the 'strong color force' (two horizontal white lines) is likely a source of the dilaton photons of SU(3), for the production of quarks and antineutrinos, and other neutral current processes that have some superconducting measure of 'charge equivalence'. (Note, in Construct No.1, the gluon triplets move toward the center & the quark triplets move outward.)

Whew! That leaves Einstein's 'inertial progressions' to fit into each field equation, so that some kind of gravitational factoring is appropriately slotted into each of the eight quantum states shown in No.7. The even mass densities are 2 -, 4 -, 6 - and 8 -, while the inertial masses, associated with 'energy densities', are 0 & 2, 2 & 4, 4 & 6 and 6 & 8. That is, every shift in energy density is accompanied by a shift in inertial mass, and, every shift in mass density is accompanied by a shift in the fine structure constant of synchrotron radiation. To repeat, all together, Einstein's ten "fields" are: four for matter waves, supported by pairs of antimatter constituents, and, six for antimatter waves, again, each with its appropriate quantum operatives of complementary matter constituents. For example, 2 - 1 & 3 is a variation of antimatter wave supported by a matter field & particle, and, 6 & 8 + 7 is a variation of matter wave supported by an antimatter field & particle. Note the odd chirality of the right-handedness and even chirality of the left-handedness, for the bilateral devolution of absorption, and evolution of emission. Rightward transitions are analytic infinities, and leftward transmutations are synthetic infinities, with the two making up the co-ordination of associative production. Further, each quantum state maintains the dynamic unitarity of the universe, for a *steady state theory* that still allows for the objective regulation of ten-dimension space-time.

Naturally, some of the four Forces of Nature will be proven inadequately described, but importantly, my models clarify how the different forces interrelate. And, most importantly, *gravity was never lost, is ever present, cannot be shielded, and 'always remains attractive'* (Einstein). Further, the fourth dimension is part of everyday experience, because the Four Phases can be identified, in different proportions, at every moment, to make up the complete phasal space of the natural system.

Looking at Construct No. 13, one might argue, with the American author Ernest Hemingway, in favor of 'donkeys' as fermions (orange-red-green-blue circle), or in favor of 'horses' as bosons (yellow-white-black-purple circle). Actually, as per No.4, with the donkeys (uppermost) & the horses (lowermost), through reductionism, the 'one' donkey, breeding with the 'dyad' of the horse, only produces the unhealthy side effects of infertile mules. (When doctors talk about 'side effects' the connotation is nearly always negative.) Hence, the applesauce of artificially limited side effects is always blowing its 'entrances and exits', because the two legitimate halves, or Side Effects of the proverbial apple, are missing. By caring too much about the wrong things, the romantic love of self-reflecting donkeys & self-absorbent horses is without the meaningful coextension of the vulnerability of shared, heterosexual experience. It is coexistence (up) & cohabitation (below), without the meaningful coextension of co-ordination, in between. Hence, the Divine Comedy of the Life Cycle is often translated into a vertically meaningless Demonic Parody, without any sense of horizontal streaming. (On might even think that women should be excluded from direct participation in The Human Equation.) Always living discordantly on the edge, some people are constantly arriving late, and then never seem to leave when appropriate, which collapses viable Side Effects onto the coplanar Vertical Mosaic. (Most people want immediate, simplistic psychological closure.) Like Sancho Panza's mule in Miguel de Cervantes *Don Quixote* (1605-1615), mules are constantly disappearing before Phase III, toward the exit, and mysteriously reappearing after Phase I, center side of the entrance. (We will be discussing 'crossing over', from nonexistence to Phase I, as 'Event Inception', and, from Phase III to nonexistence, as 'Event Horizon'.) But, being infertile, they are not directly involved with the autonomous Side Effects of the heterosexual gender issue, as a viable development. Being impotent, mules levitate to living on the edge (above) or gravitate to falling into the cracks (below), but generally lack the patience to recognize more gradual, progressive measures. The Tauton of inflation, pumped up by the transference of self-righteousness (9-11), advocates shamefully opportunistic applications, & the Heteron of reduction, depressed by the regression of self-justification (6-4), secrets away permissive methodologies (No.4). Thus ambiguous choices & arbitrary actions become integrally absurd, such as the triune pattern of accommodation, indulgence and appeasement, instead of the TTP of vision, judgment and consideration, or eminence, distinction and discernment. Such a society advocates buying off people with all sorts of uncontrolled & unrestrained liberties, as adventurism, while self-liberation through participating in the Real Human Adventure, is neglected. In fact, people should get along "swimmingly".

As Shakespeare maintained, it is not so much what you do above, on and below the stage that counts, as long as you don't blow your entrances and exits. When donkeys (up) & horses (down), as *fractious & capricious*, begin to debate & quarrel like evasive crooks & devious cranks, the mules they produce become controversial & conflicted (cons), and rarely inclined toward real dialogue. The triplet pattern is foolish, silly and whimsical. (This pattern reminds me of a play by Edward Albee: *Who's Afraid of Virginia Woolf* [1962]. Like democracy, marriage may not be perfect but hopefully things will eventually work out for the better.) To have the unrealistic expectations of getting answers, solutions and results, only produces the apple sauce of explaining & complaining, and then, excusing and refusing. Sometimes our own intrapersonal dialogue, as the metaphorical donkey & horse, within each person, gets ground up within the limit cycles of a personality complex, like a kind of gay & lesbian crisis, or a Greek centaur as the mind/body syndrome. Discordantly, the extroverted street angel, as a changeling, later becomes an introverted house devil, as an underling, while making people into muted 'middlings' in between. It's the assimilation of socialism & acculturation of individualism, and, nobody to talk to about it. That is, if the dualism of switching conveniently between the outer & inner plot is maintained, then the *interior monologue* of Temporal Infusion, as the gnostic one of a closed loop of priestly intransigence, reacts ineffectually to the interiorization of intrapersonal dialogue. The pattern is irrelevant heresy, irreverent blasphemy and irresponsible anathema. Or, the excommunication of 'ring the bell, close the book and blow out the candle.' Such is the personalized basis of hypocritical double standards, which soon become imprinted through narrow-minded linguistics and socially restrictive class structures. Being opinionated, by stating one's reasons, is less than reasonable, and quite different from Xenocrates' developmental process of 'opinion', whereby reasonable arguments have their place in time. However, there is *always* an opening for the double plot to undergo the parabolic transformation of the hendiadys dialogue, with a miraculous metamorphosis taking place. That is, the universal superego & individual id, as the 'us', if able to avoid egocentrism, naturally recombine through the I'm-ok-you're-ok pattern of ego love, as the 'we' of shared response patterns. (In physics, the collapse of the wave packet does not determine the middle ground.) Such proactive measures, merging the universal & the individual, are the basis of Kant's categorical imperative (4 & 6) and Jean-Paul Sartre's 'existential action': we are becoming (+ 5) what we are doing (4 & 6), with 'existence as prior to essence' (4 & 6 + 5). Similarly, James Joyce's 'interior monologue' as a soliloquy was used to create a kind of double plot, distinguishing interior motivation from exterior occurrence. However, fatalistic tendencies are still evident, stealing a moment of glory by simply alternating between the charming Daemon of Being & the glamorous Lilith of Non-Being. Witness the claim that while the abstract analytic proposition is verifiable, though enigmatic, the concrete synthetic proposition is not considered valid, because conundral. (Note that the process word "validatable" is not normally recognized so, like the word devicive, we will have to bring it into existence.) This double plot structure, between the transcendent & unique, comes to 'us' from the epic allegories of Classical Greek theatre, where the analytic & synthetic have no viable side effects, unless a miraculous peripeteia occurs when a deus ex machina is parachuted onto the stage as an artificial denouement. The Tauton as an epic godhead above, pretending to prove the positive thesis of the changeling, is the brilliant light of the Superego Self, imposing practical reason upon the antithesis of the underling, by pretending to disprove the negative hypothesis. Thus, between the twinned fallacies of revisionism & revolution, there is no real developmental flow, because with the egocentric dilemma of the 'evil one', the precarious only leads to the pernicious.

The conundrum of the dyad is in the down position, in Phase II, as the underling, and is thus neither devicive nor validatable, and therefore not properly falsifiable as it would be if placed in a Phase IV context. (In physics, 'that' is attempting to prove the causal link of the 'external means of the local hidden variable of particle B'.) One might intone, 'I know nothing about being six feet under.' That is, the sympathetic, siren call of Lilith is the suicidal Non-Being, of the Armageddon of the 'mother of all wars' as Bathos (6). We must 'watch our six' (Freud's Anal Stage). Phenomenalism lacks the Soul of a true Madonna, by which the Great Seal, as the Womb of Theotokos 10), shelters the Immaculate Conception (11 & 9).

As part of the same metaphorical dislocation, in Junior High School, in Canada at least, geometry and logical discourse are not emphasized, leaving children with a bad attitude toward mathematical abstractions. And, even mathematical philosophers, trying to correct this imbalance, erroneously use the term 'logical reasoning' - which has no meaning – when they really mean logical discourse. Further, the mathematics of the commutative is well established, but the mathematics of the distributive is relegated to looking at 'negative numbers', black holes, the big bang, and, various false creation modes that, traditionally, give First Principles an absolute character.

Through the Two Hands of the Universal Duality of the Haptic Extension, both the commutative & distributive interact, with *real numbers* (positive) & *imaginary numbers* (negative) recombining to make up *complex numbers* (recombinant) as the third alternative. That is, both Hands work together through the

Transmodal Inference, to make up the monotheistic third system as a stream of consciousness, which, as mentioned before, is portrayed by the Roman marble relief, the *River of Gods.* Such, is the naturally flowing discourse of logical argumentation. In other words, matter waves & antimatter waves must be interwoven, so that the Four Phases of ten-dimensional space-time become a shared experience that remains essentially & substantially indeterminate.

The protocol of the following decalogical grammatics seems to hang together rather well for the Associative Justice of ten-dimensional space-time:

May/Was (+ 1)   Will (+ 3)   Can (+ 5)   Shall (+ 7)
Ought Naught (10/0)   Ought (9/10)
Might/Were (2 -)   Would (4 -)   Could (6 -)   Should (8 -)

There are four essentially conjunctive modes for matter (+ 1, + 3, +5, + 7), and four substantially subjunctive modes for antimatter (2 -, 4 -, 6 -, 8 -), with Ought and Ought Naught (9/10-10/0) set aside in the Ends, for the dyad. Interestingly, in English the subjunctive mode receives little attention. Importantly, the eight harmonic ground states are alternatively odd and even, to make up associative production. Further, through the unbounded curvature of space, the deuterotype (9/10-10/0) remains an unknown Event in the Ends, with the 9th orbit, as the archetype that spans 11 & 9 and 9 & 1, not allowed to be identified as a ground state. That is, the codes of the Ninth Dream of the diapason of the Acoustic, make First Principles beyond our complete deciphering. Therefore, there can be no exact prediction of experimental outcomes. Also of note, that temporal essentialism dominates existence (odd numbers), with the feminine side of logic (even numbers) sublimated to and controlled by the logical positivism of Was, Will, Can and Shall. To the left, from the Hypothesis of nonexistence, May, as May Have Been, crosses over to Was, just as Might, as Might Have Been, crosses over to Were. This invokes Event Inception, while the Event Horizon, to the right, beginning with Should in the incomplete 8th orbit, is an apocryphal postscript that crosses back over, to nonexistence. Hence, viable statistical relationships include 'six degrees of separation', limited by the 2nd to the 7th orbits. However, the Certainty Principle itself must include all aspects of complete phasal space, which overrides the traditional absolutism concerning the remote objectivity of the First Principles of Spatiality. I will be providing more examples of ten-dimensional relationships to further objectify the real nature of 'freedom', which begins with appreciating the self-sameness of Associative Justice. If we find ourselves to be trustworthy, and accordingly forthright, we gradually learn to trust others.

The above system of grammatics is based upon what is called Androgynous Reinversion. Recombinantly, the monotheistic river has the feminine as a synthetic and subtractive association (positively leftward), and, the masculine as an analytic and additive association (negatively rightward). To know and understand Solomon's Seal (Construct No.9) is to realize that co-ordinated relationships remain interwoven through bilateral alternation. Hence, associatively, the Susys of No.13 are harmonized (4 of each) through Einstein's compatibility, for the recomposition of ten-dimensional space-time as a Recombinant Third Person. Such is the Wisdom of Solomon's Seal. Further, the odd/even pairing is even more subtle than first meets the eye. That is, positive matter has a negative charge, & negative antimatter has a positive charge...to maintain the unitarity of the universe. Also, each of the two supersymmetrical wave trains of yang (4 & 6 + 5 as Verification) & yin (10 - 11 & 9 as Validation) has a classical ground state, or wave, that is associated with two quantum operatives, as a field/particle, complementary equivalent to the given ground state. Thus, each triplet also maintains the unitarity of Constant Unity Factors. And, when all ten of the co-ordinated sets of congruent wave trains are blended together, equivalent complementary relationships make up the Associative

Justice of the overall gender issue of Viability. We will be exploring numerous examples, of the viability of ten-dimensional grammatics, such as: word (10/0), interjection (1), article (2), preposition (3), conjunction (4), verb (5), adverb (6), pronoun (7), adjective (8), and noun (9/10). More later.

Most great philosophers and scientists avoid dualism and its fatalistic end game, the false trinity. They move readily from Universal Duality to True Trinitine Patterns, and then on to the D-A-B-C of the Four Phases, without collapsing onto the quadrilateral fixation of categorical reaction in No.4. Aristotle distinguished between the extension of his four causes (material, formal, efficient, final) and the limitations of the Greek rendering of the 'four elements' (earth, fire, air, water). In a similar manner, Rene Descartes supplemented his quadrilateral coordinate system with a broader philosophical cycle of four phases. The dualism attributed to Descartes, based upon the mind/body syndrome of intellectualism & universal doubt, was not really the full measure of the man. Descartes advocated an interesting fourfold development: 1) Accept the facts if they cannot be changed, 2) Continue development from the current situation, 3) Obey the rules, regulations, laws and mores of your society, and 4) Be of a generous nature. Even farther back in history, as previously mentioned, there are many fourfold extensions. The question that modern society must come to terms with is: Where do we start, using the Four Phases, in order to get the scientific method off *on the right foot again*?

I can remember as a youngster having a bad taste in my mouth regarding two major aspects of human life: how religion was taught and the way the so-called scientific method was explained. These two aspects tend to become socially entrenched as the misrepresentation of theocratic authority, through transference, and, the misdirection of the technocratic deviciveness, through phenomenalism. Together, the theocratic & technocratic distort the *prolepsis* of the Horizontal Mosaic, just as the autocratic &

meritocratic falsify the *metalepsis* of the Vertical Mosaic. Discordantly then, the issue of self-dispossession becomes evident when the fifth element focuses upon the idolatry of the kleptocratic. Natural advocacy becomes twisted through the cavalier attitude of pococurantism, which makes the Life Cycle appear absurd. Hence, because of the 'cognitive dissonance' (1957, Leon Festinger) of secular humanism's disharmonious nature, it took me quite a while to come back to revering both religion and science. Of course, mature adults have no need to reject spirituality, either by turning to atheism or agnosticism, or, by resorting to as triplet such as *religiosity, fundamentalism and cultism.* The latter has its equivalent in an equally erroneous triplet that distorts the objectivity of science: coincident circumstances, convergent contingencies and uncoordinated developments. As an aspect of general amnesia, the personalism of modern society tends toward relativism, panpsychism and pantheism, while denying any form of collective responsibility. More positively, with Diacritical Consciousness leading to a general awakening, mature persons come to realize that the anagogical dimensions of the New Gospel are part & parcel of the process of discovery, regardless of the area of inquiry. Except that the public media, including many popular religions, are often not equipped to deal with the emergence of viable spirituality, or for that matter, a viable approach to the scientific method. Achieving anagnorisis is all in the grammar of the arguments.

For the third system, I will follow the pattern New Science (white-yellow, as literal), New History (orange-red, as allegorical), New Psychology (green-blue, as moral) and New Gospel (purple-black, as anagogical). As a similar pattern, *semiosis,* for the *observation of signs,* includes pragmatics, semantics and syntactics...which begs the recognition of grammatics as fourth term. As shown in the previous grammatical protocol, logical positivism dominates (p. 104), because one has the habit of only expressing the essential and formal properties of signs, with the substantial and logical dimensions of symbols tending to be repressed. Thus, as mentioned, in the case of English, the subjunctive mode is seldom used. Hence, a developmental breakdown occurs, because *functional connectives* tend to remain implicit, in a manner that restricts them to the linear logic of vertical serialization, without any horizontal development. Similarly, in Occidental school systems, mathematics tends to be taught as an abstraction devoid of curvilinear logic. In the same vein; remembering how Stevenson's Mr. Hyde had replaced Mrs. Hyde; the feminine dimension tends to become a flattened reaction formation, just as in Shakespeare's time, where women were not allowed to play themselves in theatrical productions.

The deconstructive 'parental ontogeny', as New Science (Aristotle's material cause), sets up the Phase I half of the proverbial apple, for the reconstructive 'phylogeny of the group' as the New Gospel in Phase III (Aristotle's efficient cause). However, based upon the theories of Phase II relationships, the tentativity of scientific inquiry starts out *on the right foot again*, while reflecting ironic progressions similar to Plato's aporiai. In the same manner, Aristotle eventually added in his moving cause as a kind of fifth element of progressive classification. Bacon saw this dynamic process as being furthered by his ampliative inference, while Kant's categorical imperative took specific actions tempered by having universal goals. Similarly, Darwin's survival of the fittest, mirroring his descent with modification, was more than just simple survival based upon shortsighted competitiveness. Likewise, Whitehead's prehension relates to George Henry Lewes' 'emergence', and to Geoffrey Chew's idea of modern bootstrapping. Accordingly, Popper's moral rule moves beyond the simple style & mannerisms (4 & 6) of the collapse of the wave packet, by translating psychology into actual behavior (+ 5). In a diacritical manner, Winston Churchill would have intoned that, 'The force of the right will be protected by the right of the force.' Likewise, Freud extended the paltry triad of superego-egocentrism-id (4-5-6) to an ampliative rendering of ego love. Similarly, Jung overcame the inflexible triplet of *synchronism & syncretism and synergism*, by advocating a dynamic collective of *synchronicity*. More recently, Northrop Frye shifted from paranoia to his reformative metanoia, just as 'having reason' does not necessarily make for being more reasonable. In terms of *revised information theory*, orientation (4 & 6) and variation (+ 5) must effectuate a pattern of orderly emergence, and leave behind the linear serialization of old information theory, by engendering the development of replication and polymerization. In other words, just as acceleration is not the same as velocity, and a quantifiable series does not qualify as a sequence, so the in-depth three-ness of a real space-time object is more than pretending to measure length, width and height. The 'volumetric' is always a recombinant, dynamic shaping of both spatial & temporal characteristics, intertwined. And, for the scientific method the whole process begins with calculated "guesstimates", with Integrative Discipline building up the natural overtones of progressive measures. When one gets an inkling of something new, the redundancy, efficacy and resilience of Phase II begins scientific inquiry by shifting toward the reliability, efficiency and viability of Phase III.

The human sensorium, governing the entire sensory apparatus, can also be analyzed in a holistic manner. Accordingly, each human child transitions through a series of developmental *Sensory Ratios*, the progressions of which depend upon the influence of various media within a given environment. And, as with the Four Phases, the development of these Sensory Ratios must begin with arguing from universal design. That is, one proceeds from the intelligent "suprastructure" of the global out-group, and then fills in the particulars through the infrastructure of the local in-group. That is, the Global Adaptations of Phase IV must feed back and recombine with the Local Adaptations of Phase II, in a progressive manner, so as to build up the Recombinant Adaptations of Phase III. Importantly then, the egg comes before the chicken on the spit. Then as A-B-C-D or II-III-IV-I, after beginning in Phase II, the phylogeny of the group, for researching the *nomina nuda* in Phase III, must pass through the experimental crucible of Phase IV, before arriving at the developmental *nomina dubia* in Phase I. That is, the New Eve of Phase III precedes the New Adam of Phase I, because 'meaning' naturally comes before 'naming', just as, for humans, nurture comes before nature. In Aristotelian terms, one begins with the formal cause (II), shifts to the efficient cause (III), and then passes through the final cause (IV) before arriving at the material cause (I). The same pattern is rendered by the expression: research & development. Detailed analysis only becomes pertinent if it is previously placed within a larger set of contextual clues, moving from the general to the specific. The pattern of development goes Reconstruction-Deconstruction, by putting the shoe on the right foot first and then putting the left foot forward, later. The sequence is II, III, IV and I as alpha-beta-gamma-delta. However, looking at No.7, the ordinal pattern appears to be D-A-B-C, starting on the wrong foot again. In terms of the scientific method, the pattern is: A, Phase II as the formation of a preliminary theory and process of inquiry; B, Phase III as setting up a hypothesis for the falsification of the experimental neither/nor; C, Phase IV as experimentation and analysis of results, and D, Phase I as the development of new materials, techniques, skills and abilities. The result, if that term is ever appropriate, becomes incipient applications & methodologies (4 & 6), that produce new theoretical classifications (+ 5). Note that one begins and ends in Phase II, in current existence, with the chicken on the other side of the road, but there is no 'optical isomer' as a perfect mirror image, because the original theory has been revised in process.

Otherwise, a Trojan horse doesn't have a hope of ever becoming a real live horse. That is, the 'description' (6, can) of phenomenalism does not imply that the donkeys know anything about the Substance of a real horse (10, ought). As a TTP, knowledge is formal, understanding is functional, and experience is workable. Hence, the idealism of 'immutable naturalism' for establishing the exact facts of nature is ineffectual. What constitutes a fact changes with a shift in context, according to what we resemble, dissemble and reassemble. A premature result, through catachresis (loss of context), leads to the fractionation of the human personality, as per No.4. Discordantly, losing a sense of the larger reality produces meaningless behavior, resulting in the accidentals of local aestheticism (hype) & global adventurism (utilitarian). In this manner, closed-minded ethical considerations and the commoditization of values build up a Wall of Theory between the Assumption of Being (Pathos) & the Supposition of Non-Being (Bathos), while taking a shortcut to nowhere (Mythos). The converts of such a system tend to stand on principle, on idealogical grounds. (Can we justly impose democracy on other nations?) Such structuralism produces false leads and lost causes, which throw strategy out the devil's window. The fourfold phasal pattern is I as tactics, II as paratactics, III as strategy, and IV as intelligence, which reflects the same transitions as the Sensory Ratios of human maturation. The latter pattern follows a natural order, whereas the scientific method places tactics after intelligence, with the order II-III-IV-I supporting the production of New Science. In the same manner, the modern military approach is not really "left-right-left", because the military uses the new theories of 'C^3I', or the quadrivium of command (I), control (II), communication (III) and intelligence (IV). With this approach, the command of tactics in Phase I is usually conditioned by the appraisal of the intelligence gathered in Phase IV. Then, extending from the paratactics of field operations in Phase II, it is the communication of strategies in Phase III that results in Aristotle's efficient cause. Naturally, better 'software' provides for better strategies, which engenders the survival of the fittest. Thus, Phase III relationships, on the right foot again, are more important than the material cause of tactics, which are on the left foot, with 'hardware' in Phase I. Nevertheless, the co-ordination of the devolution of hardware (anything) and the evolution of software (anybody), passing through field operations, and overseen by intelligence, requires that all the Phases act in harmony.

Like the C^3I pattern, tactics, paratactics, strategy and intelligence extend human Sensory Ratios through what is called complete phasal space. However, for The Human Equation, the natural Life Cycle is translated through the Four Phases of the *surnatural system*, which mirrors the aesthetics of the bilateral Reclining Figure. In terms of the traditions of Eastern music, the fundamental four as a given variational *maqam* produces all the other variations as sursequent & subsequent *maqamats*. Thus, one moves from a range of eight harmonic relationships, based upon the not-allowed, stentorian ninth harmonic, to include systems dynamics that, by the extension of conventions & codes, usually follow the taxonomical nomenclature of ten distinct *taxons*. Ten-dimensional space-time requires a minimum of four field equations for the ground states of matter waves, and six for antimatter waves, with the two together becoming the Recombinant Third System. Further, we will be examining the apparent flatness of Minkowski space-time, as per No.7, in order to show that it naturally factors in the dimension of curvature. That is, the odd/even patterns of flatness & curvature are both crucial to the bilaterally blended co-ordination of associative production.

Naturally, the Identity of Verification & Continuity of Validation (5 & 10), as sufficient & necessary, always remain independent and indeterminate, with no real action at a distance between the two, which would not be a legitimate resolution. And, because the two aspects of Universal Duality are each represented by a syllogistic triplet, then six-parameter indeterminacy, like Aristotle's hexis, becomes a good representation for the development of a blended approach. It is logical, therefore, that we look for the two terms that are missing from Einstein's $E_o = M_o c^2$, which only represents four terms: 5 = 10 - 11 & 9. As it stands, E_o alone, as a 'energy rest frame', gives the impression of an ideal or 'special' conservation of energy, when physics has established that 'this' is not the case. In fact Einstein introduced his cosmological constant (c.c.) in about 1915, as a kind of stopper to balance the universe, and then said that it was the biggest mistake of his life. However, recent developments have come to favor the acceptance of the c.c. as a kind of implicit function for the Higgs mechanism that mediates all energy states.

So the question poses itself, what does the above perfect energy rest frame have to do with something like the erroneousness of secular humanism? Einstein's special relativity tends to fixate a nominalistic approach that sticks one label on all entities, as a principle of identity. The implication is that, through a form of socialism called 'planification', we can all be profiled psychologically as 'special persons', with each individual having a set 'personality complex' that prevents 'us' from being more forthcoming. It is '*as if*', standing alone, the Split Metaphor hopes for an uneasy balance of the debit & credit side of the ledger. The result is: trade-offs, face-offs, tit-for-tat games, controversy, the matching of favors, quid pro quo settlements, invidious comparisons, vindictive miracles, lucky breaks, balance of power politics, behavioral conflicts, etc. all based upon the panpsychism of the divisions of mental chiasmus (No.4). (Sadly enough, the atomic, fission bomb was a forgone conclusion of this inflationary outlook.) In the Vertical mosaic, we all become toast - burnt on both sides and subjected to the inquisition of the imputable 'third degree', in between. Following an artificially confabulated simulacrum, one is continually going down the road to perdition with a three-legged dog. Everything tastes like chicken, with 'us' going faster and faster, but never getting to the other side of the road. Good intentions get thinner and thinner, finessed beyond question as a kind of untouchable narrow-mindedness, with history & destiny guaranteed as a perfect state of existence... that is never quite providential. Gossip, slogans, rumors, cliches, formalities, fun, rote learning, fads, styles, shibboleths, emblems, arrogance, etc. tend to fixate identity as a virtual reality, divorced from the big picture. Emphasis is placed on the conventional, comfortable, confidential, topical, convenient, expedient, efficacious, correct and competitive, etc. as *sure, secure and safe.* The objectivity of outside, excogitative standards is strictly defended against by the social taboos of such a 'closed society' (Popper). Bouncing between absolutes, a pharisaic tribalism tends to maintain a strict adherence to tradition, with Marshall McLuhan's aural-oral backlash reinforcing the romanticism of a return to nature movement that continually gets caught up in the terrible twos as the dichotomies of Kant's antinomies of reason. Discordantly, the disjointed protocols followed are generally both inadequate & inconsequential. Besides, there are very few who can catch themselves shifting from a complicit thought down to a duplicitous action, and back up again, in a self-absorbed manner. The result is an inability to communicate with others, except through controversy & conflict. And, the more extravagant the Myth of self-sufficiency, the more it clings to the *prima facie* of the *bene fundatum*, as though knowing & understanding Leibnitz's impenetrables & imperceptibles could make modern individualism instantly liberating. Unfortunately, that is not the case. Self-liberation is no free ride.

And yet, the reputation of those who overcome the limits of a given history & destiny, is generally assured. In other terms, the individual must go from being merely a passive product of society, to being proactively committed to progressive measures. New intelligence produces 'positive feedback loops' that modify current field operations. Instead of reductionism, new "in-formation" feeds down from the Outer Field, or up from the Inner Figure, to modify the Middle Ground State of existence. That is, both macroscopic superstructures & microscopic substructures, as quantum nonlocalities, can influence the direction and rate of the development of locally classical entities. We are not dealing with the Daemon as the abstract good of man writ large in the sky, or with the Lilith as a subterranean stream flowing within the bowels of the earth. Combining a skyhook (trivial) & anchor (trifle) only leaves enough rope (trice) to hang humanity. It's all *nexus* but no *plexus.* The outcome, like acting out, is a self-recursive, self-absorbed pattern, as a vertical organicism, that blocks a progressive approach to organic growth. Importantly, through *self-control* the sky god becomes less ingenious, and through *self-restraint* the jinn of the depths are rendered less disingenuous. Then, through *self-resolution* mythical individualism begins to metamorphose into genuine individuality - flowing from the eudaemonic to the eusocial. In final analysis, the Pathos of Being & the Bathos of Non-Being, colluding to make up the Mythos of Idolatry, still have, surprisingly, the potential for becoming a monotheistic Living Metaphor. This is the irenic image provided by Manet's *Le Dejeuner sur l'herbe* (1863, "Luncheon on the Grass"), which, interestingly enough, is structurally linked to the Roman *River of Gods.* Hence, Manet's picture *also* reflects stream of consciousness theories, which were a central theme during the nineteenth century.

It is not too surprising to find very few really great thinkers in the history of humankind. The social climate of the past was more inclined to falsify and distort new learning. Although society cannot completely absorb the individual, genius alone is not enough to assure human survival. Often brilliance spawns the anarchistic alternation of revisionism & revolution. And sometimes propitious, groundbreaking developments are misused and misinterpreted by subsequent generations. Further, the forcefulness of one person's primary experience often becomes regressive as another's secondary experience that is neither enriching nor liberating. In fact, sudden changes usually produce bad ABC's: breakup & breakdown, but not breakthrough – with the collapse of the wave packet (4 & 6) not necessarily linked to Recombinant Adaptations (+ 5). In 1970, Alvin Toffler's *Future Shock* dealt with this topic. Instead of the term 'future shock', I will be referring to limit cycles that describe the deontological '*hexagon of suspicion*', or what has been termed the Circles of Vengeance of the War of the Sexes. This sixfold pattern is masculinism (9-11-5) over feminism (6-4-10), as two dissociated sets of 'me, myself and I'. The social umwelt of the hexagon of suspicion only breeds dysfunctional atmospherics, somewhere between realism & nihilism (No.4), with aestheticism & activism making the Zeitgeist into a form of Classical Alienation that could take fifty years to heal. As Toffler mentions, the closed loop of the 'integration of the integrators' could be of social benefit, or it could just become another bird cage for the triplet pattern of realism, altruism and humanism, or Pathos, Bathos and Mythos, or truism, naturalism and automatism. In the form heretical, blasphemous and anathematic, it is possible to realize that the latter characteristics make limit cycles turn back upon themselves, recursively, in a pattern like charm, glamour and glory or sentiment, sympathy and passion. Such a coplanar & coterminal hexagon of suspicion produces the 'prisoner's dilemma', which becomes *never green* as a closed system that promotes the betrayal of self, followed by the betrayal of others.

There are four nails in this coffin. With the *irrelevance* of visual dominance & *irreverence* of auditory reaction, metalepsis becomes falsified as the silver lining, the center of which reduces to *indifference* & *violence* as the silver bullet of a distorted prolepsis. That is, as mentioned, metalepsis becomes a coplanar diatheism as the River of Styx, &, coterminal prolepsis turns into dialetheism as the River of Lethe. But, together they do not a real river make. Discordantly, diatheism & dialetheism are not truly supersymmetrical, and therefore tend to frustrate consciousness through the assimilation & acculturation of the individual. Individual frustration, as mirrored by the ilk of John Milton's *Samson Agonistes* (1671), could & might motivate pulling down the pillars of society, due to dissolute terrorism. Little has changed since the ancients warned of the Three Gates of Hell. In modern terms, the false trinity has just become more intangible, like a major institution with captive clientele and little concern for public welfare. Likewise, it could be an electric power company with unscrupulous billing practices, or a system of public education based upon a secular humanism that lacks the meaningful measures of General Guidelines. Without an overall schematic, the infamous three-headed Cerberus of Greek mythology rears his ugly head through the brinkmanship of youthful vandalism, internecine politics, moribund aesthetics, specialization, ethnocentrism, rampant salesmanship, unscrupulous business practices, regressive legalisms, romantic nonsense, captivating religiosity, the free market economy, etc. All these modern virtual realities, and many more, as "*des fremissons prematures*", resemble the Awendigo of Canadian aboriginals, infamous for making people run to their death, for fear of being caught by the ghost of a former self. What one does to others and one's self, follows 'us' around sempiternally, unless propitiated by the better person that 'we' have the potential to become. The Human Equation provides a beginning.

Surely, the Greeks had Ariadne's golden thread to lead them out of the labyrinth of Indecision-Confusion & Confusion-Indecision. And, Aristotle's 'golden mean' was meant for clear sailing, but the legacy of classical society has led to a web of paradoxical self-deception, wherein appearing peaceful, and then making war in the name of peace, is not distinguished from actively being a peacemaker. We tend to say, 'Beware of Greeks bearing gifts', because classical perfection has the feeling of unrealistic expectations. Historically, when Classical Alienation sets in, a crisis in human values develops. The Protestant Reformation, rather than correcting the misgivings of a decadent Catholicism, merely led from the frying pan into the fire. As is usual, the 'solution is the problem' (Oyama), because with a sententious 4-5-6 pattern, both ends are played against the middle, by fabricating a false identity as a 'third wheel'. Rhetoric becomes ascendant as the 'cause' of too much too soon (without economy), & Dialectic becomes descendant as the 'effect' of too little too late (with parsimony). Discordantly, optimism & pessimism lock into the limit cycles of a classical cause-effect that is restricted to the Vertical Mosaic of meaningless activities. As a closed system, what is a cause to up is an effect to down, & what is a cause to down is an effect to up, with the appearance of needing 200 % to make up a whole. Thus, psychopathological patterns shift from theme to crisis, because their ratiocinations remain on the minimal surface of the 'great circle' as hyperbole and simile, with copula reduced by litotes, as an orthocentrism (button hole). This becomes throwing one's strategies out the devil's window, with image more important that reality, and doing things just for effect. Consequently, metalepsis, limited to the escalation of hyperbole in the vertical mode, restricts prolepsis to the reductionism of ineffectual actions in the horizontal mode. Button & hole become aestheticism & adventurism. Gottfried Leibnitz said, 'We have no windows,' but nevertheless, his hyperbolic *bene fundatum* of good intentions failed to translate into the parable of his 'best of all possible worlds'. Most of us must have a job, but we often fail to make it into something that works properly, because, just because it works doesn't make it right. Consequently, there are few people lucky enough to find a truly fulfilling vocation. If the vertical *hyperbole* of 'job' combines with the reductive *ellipsis* of 'work', the recombinant *parable* of finding a 'vocation' becomes lost in the hustle and bustle.

Human culture survives because it recombines the Symbolic Function of Ends & Significant Form of Means, to produce the Living Metaphor of the Recombinant Third System. That is, the Transmodal Inference avoids the incongruous entanglement of informality & dysfunction. Unfortunately, by dislocating the natural resolution of the supersymmetrical, demanding the perfect relationships of a Certainty Principle tends to become a direct syndrome that produces a bipolar twin-paradox. The extraordinary field equations of periodic-Aperiodic Becoming (4 & 6 + 5) & Supraperiodic-nonperiodic Being (10 - 11 & 9), in their purest state, would never directly support a system capable of satisfying either the biological or the cultural requirements of human nature. In other words, the meaningful measurements of the third system cannot be traced back to their original Identity & Cause. (So much for the EPR debate about the A & B particles.) That is why it is not legitimate for lawyers to argue for exact Verification of Identity and/or Validation of Process, when the Viability of Evidence depends upon building up correspondent evidentiality, in the spirit of the law. Hence, for The Human Equation there is a special TTP, leading to a fourth level: I) the *awareness* of rate, and II) the *recognition* of range, must recombine progressively through III) the aspect ratios of a wider *attention span*. It may seem like an oxymoron, but the fourth dimension is experienced by all of us, and yet remains the best kept 'secret'. It's just that, because of educational idealism, common sense is not really all that common.

The reciprocal limit cycles of ratiocinations (No.4), between the abstract & concrete, as defining the obvious & describing the evident, are generally meaningless and unprogressive. That is, they neither evolve toward the right, nor devolve toward the left, in the production of viable Side Effects. In contrast, long-term planning sets up productive aspect ratios, by paying attention to what I term "Phasal Delay" (Glossary), shown in No.7 as the New Wave, toward the right in Phase III. Of course one must avoid all of the following: too much self-consciousness, existential angst, anticipation anxiety and anthropomorphic projections, as well as a defensive reaction, followed by overly risky speculation. Generally, taking the precautions against self-deception, we project future considerations in an evolutionary direction, generally marked by the firmness of steadfast resolve. Being reasonable is more important than 'I have my reasons.'

Later we will discuss the topic of 'evolution' at greater length. Historically, evolution has been highly overrated and treated in an unnecessarily controversial manner. Along with the essences of analytic infinities, as emission moving toward the right, by convention, in an evolutionary direction, there is the co-ordination of the substances of synthetic infinities, as absorption moving toward the left, in a devolutionary direction. Devolution is equally viable, and through associative production, takes up alternate wave trains. Accordingly, odd & even orbits are blended bilaterally as the coextensive symbiotic aspect ratios of meaningful measurement. These even-odd coordinates are experienced through the Middle Ground States of the 'heterotic string', to produce a natural cross channel that exhibits both growth and decay. The leftward even coordinates, as hardware, are more stable, and so *anything* becomes the symbiont of Phase I, while the rightward odd coordinates, as software, are more unstable, with *anybody* as the symbiont of Phase III. In other words, as actionary modes that both devolve and evolve, Phase I, II and III are respectively end product, on-going operation and reasonable projection. Importantly, the flow occurs in both directions, so that we can both eat cake and still have more cake in the works.

Interestingly, the ancient Egyptian ankh, as a symbol of life, is very much like my metaphorical Life Cycle. In fact, it was probably the source of the aesthetics of the Reclining Figure. By tipping the looped side, or head of the ankh, to the right, the arms, in a vertical mode, remind one of No.4. Further, with the feet devolving to the left as the input/output of hardware, the "donut head", evolving toward the right, hints at the eventual development of the feedback loops of computer software. Nevertheless, the ankh gives no indication of the co-ordained female figure, which in No.7, is blended translucently with the rightward male figure, in the devolutionary direction. Such a biased outlook, with logical positivism leading to inflationism (inhospitality) & evolutionism (violence), might make the adduction of masculine dominance appear to be a 'divine right'. In fact, to this day, most physicists still don't understand the true nature of Herman Minkowski's four-dimensional double light cone.

Importantly, each orbit, as an Even or Odd inferential deduction, for a given Middle Ground State, has associated with it, in a vertical mode, an even or odd inductive interpretation, as an Outer Field & Inner Particle. Therefore, for example, 2 - 3 & 5 is Even/odd and 6 & 8 + 7 is even/Odd, with the first as a synthetic donut and the second as an analytic donut. In other words, the even/odd reciprocals of field/particle patterns act as the vertical superstrings of the direct channels of quantum mechanical operatives. And, the Even/Odd donuts of classical ground states act as the heterotic strings of bilateral cross channels. So, each Odd Explicit Formation has an implicit function, without & within it, and each Even Explicit Function has an implicit formation, without & within it. The Transmodal Inference is always with us. Hence, the universe tends to prefer both a moderated and a balanced approach, with not only the alternation of classical variations, for recombining as associative production, but also with each wave train balanced internally between classical and quantum dimensions.

Importantly, the co-ordinated Crossover Patterns of formal transitions & functional transmutations, as the interplay of essential pickets & substantial spaces, can be experienced gradually through the progressive development of recombinant ground states, toward the right, through what I have termed Phasal Delay. We must accentuate the positive. That is, tentativity & contingency recombine dynamically through teleology. Thus, the blending of a multiplicity of different tendencies, in the fullness of time, comes to make up an *Autonomous Complex*, outside the direct control & denial of the politics of the church, the state or the judiciary. Normatively then, the Commutative & Distributive are not as important as the Associative, just as Becoming & Being resolve as Belonging, and proper legality is based upon the coordination of evidence as an empirical proof that is never an exact science. That is, the spirit of the law operates with arbitrary precision. Hence, the real standard of human conduct, as the Living Metaphor of Popper's moral rule, always remains a little ahead of its time, by trying to set up higher standards of behavior, through the New Wave or New Gospel. Thus, our leaders in spirituality are barking up the wrong tree when they talk about the traditional, 'nuclear family' (No.4) as the core of progressive measures, when it is the Extended Family of humane progress that is more pertinent. Why else would we be admonished to 'keep the seventh day as holy!?' As the phylogeny of the group, the 7th orbit holds a special place in our hearts, because Associative Justice is the recipe for future cake, and, 'the proof is in the pudding', in the fullness of time. What really counts is thoroughgoing reason.

Human Beings are essential and formal entities who often take a fallacious approach when observing and measuring other entities, in existence, by *excluding the implicit function of spatial curl, with which to balance The Human Equation.* Such an approach is all pickets, with no spaces between them, with 'fencing' things becoming an illegal process. In other words, we find it difficult to take the measure of substantial and functional relationships, because they throw a curve into our expectations...and also our calculations. Next, to add insult to injury, we tend to overextend our reach by using the *implicit formation to artificially close and censor the Explicit Function of spatial events.* Through unconscious inversion, this leads to expecting Spatiality, in an absolute manner, to govern First Principles in a way that erroneously places the Certainty Principle exclusively under the aegis of Phase IV relationships, as a form of objectivism. (In reality, all Four Phases must be engaged at once.) Strange then, if Spatiality was traditionally taken as Objectivity, that Antimatter Resonance was considered to be "nothing"? As a result, the fourth dimension was 'lost in space', without & within, when, in reality, it is part of all that we experience, like the Christian 'handmaid of the Lord' and the Muslim sense of chastity as central to the moral compass. Happily, things have changed for the better lately. Currently, 'cold dark matter' is thought to make up about 73 % of the universe: less is more. However, if gravity is never missing, and neutrons and neutrinos are not really "neutral", why do we expect that calculating the implicit function can give us an identity principle? The ancient Incas in South America didn't really think that their strings could 'tie the sun'; French Existentialists knew that proper actions were necessary for existence to be precedent to essence; artificial intelligence (AI) must be placed within a local context; the Zen nail can never be posed exactly, and politicians really do care about the progress of humanity. Nevertheless, we must avoid thinking that measuring IQ is an indication of intelligence, that a psychological profile can take the measure of the person, that systematic doubt is a viable legal process, or that rationalizing will lead to an improvement in one's behavior, etc., etc. The trick is to see how the misuse of the field/particle reciprocals of inductive interpretation, through the collapse of the wave packet (4 & 6), can come to misrepresent & misdirect the legitimate progressions of Right Choice (+ 5) & Correct Action (10 -), that are basic to all natural processes. That is parallelism, as a closed-loop system, must leave room for the Jewish 'hole in the wall'. Having said the foregoing, how is it that we entertain the silly idealisms that the universe is expanding, that it began at a certain time in the past, and that the big bang started in our neck of the woods? With the devil's' help of course.

With physics, one usually refers to the 'three laws of conservation' as the TTP of the 'conserving of energy (Sign), mass (Symbol) and angular momentum' (Metaphor). In reality, this modality has four parts, with energy in Phase II & mass in Phase IV, along with the symbionts of 'spin orientation' in Phase III and 'charge orientation' in Phase I. As part of misconstruing the explanation of the first system & misunderstanding the description of the second system, the electron charge and magnetic spin are usually lumped together as the 'orientation of spin and charge', just as Boolean logic erroneously refers to the Associative And as one category. In fact, most physical triads fail to anticipate the experiential, Four Phases of developmental progressions. For example: voltage, amperage and wattage, or role, pitch and yaw, or rate, range and ratio, or form, function and shape, etc. Just as a proper One produces an appropriate Duality, so the supersymmetries of the latter set up a triune stream for a TTP that leads to the Four Phases. Unfortunately, the third system has not traditionally been given its due, just as, in Construct No.1, the fourth dimension is not made experientially evident. Nevertheless, viable Side Effects are part & parcel of symbiotic progressions, which develop between the *electronic symbionts* of Phase I, within Magnetic Resonance, and the *magnetic symbionts* of Phase III, within Electronic Resonance - to make up both halves of the proverbial apple. In other words, charge as an 'electronic soliton traveling wave', and spin as a 'magnetic soliton traveling wave', act as the antiparticle pairings of the unitary stream of the electromagnetic wave spectrum. That is, the electronic waves of Magnetic Resonance and magnetic waves of Electronic Resonance relate to the coextension of bilateral Side Effects. However, with matter waves as the dominant Explicit Formation of existence, & antimatter waves only registered as an implicit function, 'one' gets the erroneous impression of the static universe as expanding, and that the reductionism of cosmic censorship is needed to balance the equation here & now. Likewise, morality often becomes a fixed agenda of sententious moralizing, with moral fiber leading to making war rather than making peace, and, with others perceived as being evil.

Looking at Construct No.9, it is possible to appreciate that there are really Four Resonances: Magnetic Resonance for Phase I, Matter Resonance for Phase II, Electronic Resonance for Phase III and Antimatter Resonance for Phase IV. Matter & antimatter are taken to be more strictly antithetical to each other, as rest energy & rest mass, while magnetic *and* electronic characteristics are treated together as the electromagnetic wave spectrum, which makes up the recombinant Side Effects of angular momentum. That is misconstruing explanation & understanding, as a button with a hole in it, leads to the willful sententiousness of forcing our biases & prejudices upon a more holistic approach to learning and behaving. Bad epistemology produces bad religion, bad science and bad politics, as well as bad education and bad behavior.

Preferring the greater reality of arguing from universal design, or what is currently referred to as the big picture, I have sought to extract an axiological thread of common sense from history. The trick is to separate the wheat from the chaff and not dwell on the negative. Newton is purported to have stated that standing on the shoulders of so many savant predecessors was a great help. And, despite evident individual shortcomings, over the years Integrative Discipline has prevailed. However, taking a strictly scholarly approach, backed up by a swarm of references, statistical distributions and a global survey of human philosophies, is not necessarily effective. For example, the *Companion To The History of Modern Science*, 1990 fails to produce any lasting generalizations. The parsing of its content shows two cardinal sins: a lack of economy & an excess of parsimony. A polymathic approach, based upon encyclopedic knowledge, fails to follow Xenocrates' progressive triad of 'sensibles-reasonables-intelligibles'. Xenocrates loved to lounge along the banks of the irenic River of Life.

Above, as Aristotle well knew, if expression & instrument become divisive & devicive, as static & censorial, then, like Shakespeare's knife-in-the-back, there is no provision for the natural self-resolution of anagnorisis as the monotheistic stream of a golden mean. The anagnorisis of a dynamic state, like Aristotle's hexis, belied the fixed agenda of sick moralizing by which medieval scholars sought an unrealistic *alchemical transmutation*...for changing lead directly into gold as an axiological solution. (We could try to morally justify going to war against the 'axis of evil'.) The circular reasoning of the hexagon of suspicion leads directly to an axiological solution. Avoiding such a nostrum, the 'coplanar irony' of the *implausible* coincidence of the silver lining & 'coterminal irony' of the *impossible* convergence of the silver bullet, requires the more *probable* Socratic 'dialogical irony' for working things out, in the fullness of time. The dialogical irony of hexis as a gender issue overcomes the other two forms of ironic interplay, such as the 'teepee & wigwam', or up/down & down/up of No.4.

Importantly, the *controversial* coplanar irony of the application of fissionable coincidence & the *conflicted* coterminal irony of the methodology of fusionable convergence, do not a natural process make. They merely set up the 'ironic detachment' of the mind/body syndrome, as per No.4. Discordantly, the fixer & trickster cannot go home, just as the standards of the tradition nuclear family do not measure up to the Extended Family of Humanity. And, for The

Human Equation, a *deus ex machina*, fabricated through theocratic misrepresentation & technocratic misdirection, cannot forcefully transmute psychology into an improvement in behavior, by cutting the psychological knot instead of naturally encouraging it to unravel itself through the Four Phases. The ironic detachment of peripeteia is not yet the dialogical irony of anagnorisis. In other terms, an explosion of theological convincing, as a monolithic silver lining, &, an implosion of technological conversion, as a monopolistic silver bullet, do not allow one (third person singular) to prioritize viable options for the Autonomous Complex.

Taking reasonable risks, we (third person plural) can live quite well without the false hopes (Anxiety Structures) and excessive caution (Belief Structures) of rigid structuring. Neither an overly positive self-fulfilling prophesy, nor an undercurrent of a self-defeating one, as hyperbole & litotes, can coerce the parable of a realistic self-fulfilling prophesy. The third-level resolution, of reaching one through two, as McLuhan's hendiadys dialogue, cannot be forced. The reciprocal alternations of rhetorical & dialectical materialism (No.4), that seek to forcefully change others, are not up to the mature shepherding and engendering of a more advanced sense of otherness. They still smack of benevolent dictatorship, or, coping out, without a proper recognition of the real nature of 'free love'. So where do we start? The Quakers use of the 'concerned occasion' is not only an echo of Plato's aporiai, but it is also a harbinger of the scientific method. Certainly there is present a healthy sense of otherness, through the efficient sharing of responsibility and beneficence. Such prioritizing involves what is *proprietary, proper and appropriate*, as a kind of triduum of temporal transitions, from being earnest to being sincere. Unfortunately, instead of the Quaker 'shunning' of those who play havoc with an integral way of life, popular media, through radio, newspaper, television and film, usually exploit the codependent desires & needs of the public, through the distractions of misinformation, disinformation and misdirection.

Keeping a feeling for decency as a guiding principle, I have not delved into the seamier side of The Human Equation, which most of us cast off as unacceptable baggage. For example, for Sexuality the traditional demonstrative syllogism forms the triplet homosexual-unisexual-bisexual (4-5-6). This erroneous triplet, as the Vertical Mosaic, is replete with the monolithic synergisms of a stereotypical society. (For the upside-down heart in No.4, the pattern is teepee & wigwam centered about house...but no way home.) Such defense mechanisms tend to screen out what is progressive and keep what is recidivistic. Accordingly, preferring the genuine article to a representative by-product, I try to accentuate the positive side of a predecessor's work and avoid pandering to a public reaction based upon the topical chatter of *temporal disorder*. The anagnorisis of the Autonomous Complex is not an optical isomer, like a tragicomic soap opera, but mirrors the asymmetry of an inexplicable and mysterious transformation, for changing something common into something remarkable. The meaningless becomes meaningful. The same heterosexual asymmetry also works to keep Sexuality a meaningful experience, rather than just a question of sexual tourism. But, such progressive ordinances are revealed only if the gender issue retains an indeterminate heterotic flavor, by not attempting to fixate the nature of the monotheistic third person, as an overly proper, ascetic celibate, of monolithic proportions. That is, the 'special one' may come to advocate the hermaphroditic as a unisexual idealism, based upon the pretense of fairness, equality and tolerance, but 'we' naturally espouse the parasexual co-ordination of Freud's heterosexual maturity. The latter does not reflect a uniform grayness, but plays up the importance of individual differences, for the advantage they bring to the phylogeny of the group (7th orbit, purple).

In the same manner, I have made a conscious effort not to take an idealistic stand, as a special interest, with respect to a particular religion, political system, race or sexuality etc. As Blaise Pascal (Fr. philos. & math., 1623-1662) advocated, *a receptive attitude which places new ideas in a positive light is more to one's own advantage.* This is referred to as his Principle of Charity. Similar to the physical True Trinitine Pattern of voltage, wattage and amperage, there is the pattern faith, hope and charity. The supraluminal love of charity allows the Golden Fleece to select the treasures of the past, for the sake of Human Culture. It is clear. But can we really aspire to attain what is open, transparent and clear? First Principles try to make 'clear' the exact results of the falsification of experiment, by which Human Beings retain whatever is felt to be of infinitely greater value, for human continuity. Richard Dawkins (1976, *The Selfish Gene*) refers to these cultural traits as 'memes', which reflects the same separateness of Phase IV, by comparing the biological genetics of this phase to culture 'memetics', as reflecting a hypothetical imperative (Kant). In other terms, for the Validity of Global Adaptations, extending through the general relativity of Phase IV, dialetheism is taken as the measure-for-measure dyad of the Validation of Process. Extended as the Sequence Speciation, 'that' becomes 10 - 11 & 9 as 'where', 0 - 9 & 1 as 'what' and 0 & 2 + 1 as 'who'. Just the same, at that point the Tenth Commandment of 'thou shalt not kill' comes into force, for the simple reason that the Golden Fleece of the Greek Thanatos, as the 'tree in the sea', is unattainable. That is, instead of the fixed consequentialism of cosmic censorship, life continues to mutate into other forms of species. (The traditional dialectical syllogism of 11-10-9 is too restrictive.) Likewise, *synaesthesia* can provide a wider mental perspective on life, or, simply make one too 'spaced out', because the Ninth Dream is *not an allowed orbit.* For such symbolic sensibilities, of the archetypal variety, authority figures that express themselves publicly; especially about religion; are open to being mistaken. The bastardization of the Certainty Principle comes into force as the I-made-you-and-I-can-break-you pattern, or, doing violence to the Truth of the larger reality. Reputation, based upon Eminence & Distinction, is everything, but reducing the Laws of Nature to the simplistic closure to immediate facts & figures, merely stifles the living. The triad of gossip, rumor and innuendo produces disastrous results, with optimism inadvertently switching to pessimism, by simply caring too much, rather than developing viable associations. Discordantly, the brinkmanship of paired ultimatums often leaves coplanar history & coterminal destiny with insufficient 'psychological distance', causing a breakdown in the social fabric supporting cultural continuity. For example, Rene Descartes' mathematical coordinates and his fallacious *universal doubt* have retained popularity, while, his Four Phases of development are known only to a few scholars.

What we must keep in mind is that the First Principles of Phase IV are not necessarily as complete as the Certainty Principle of the Corpus Universalis, which must also envelop the first system. Hence, the so-called First Principles of the second system, alone, do not provide an exact, apodictic predictability. Despite Newton's '*spatium est absolutum*', for us, Phase IV is simply too 'iffy'. Phase IV sequencing governs the characteristics of the second system as Descartes fourth stage of generosity, which, like Aristotle's apolaustic final cause, reflects Blaise Pascal's Principle of Charity. Some people would simply add that it is important to keep an open mind, while military people would say that it is difficult to decide what Global Intelligence applies to a given local situation. For The Human Equation, we are dealing with the Ought (10 - 11 & 9), the Ought Naught (0 - 9 & 1) and the Might (0 & 2 + 1) as Einstein's three variables of arbitrary distinction. That is, the three outcomes of experiment as basic to the fundamentals of an actual Sequence. Except that First Principles cannot stand alone, because nothing is mutually exclusive, so that no truly causal inference is allowed, for the Continuity of Necessity. The Ends, in isolation, might be too arbitrary, and if at the same time the Means in isolation become ambiguous, then the Life Cycle acquires a feeling of absurdity. In modern theory, Global Adaptations must be tempered by blending them with Local Adaptations, in order to avoid the dualism of adaptationism, while espousing the natural system of Recombinant Adaptations.

Metalogical Construct No.2 sets out the separation of the Book of Scripture in the Means of Existence, as the traditional Body, &,

the Book of Nature in the Ends of Nonexistence, as the traditional Mind. Unfortunately, such a rendering tends to translate as the mind/body syndrome of No.4. In No.2, for the restoration of harmony, I have modeled s-shaped 'domains' in order to give an impression of how the double helix is formed. Every given Phase retains a measure of the other three Phases, in different proportions. Thus, in the Buddhist tradition mind & body are always acting in unison, through the natural system. It becomes evident then, that the First Principles of Phase IV relationships are not as important as the dual, supersymmetrical Certainty Principle that engenders the Recombinant Third System. For that reason, the Corpus Universalis is neither masculine nor feminine, and blends the two systems to produce the Side Effects of neither (deconstructive) and both (reconstructive) as a third, recombinant heterosexual relationship.

Properly handled, metaphysical analysis can be quite liberating. Einstein, featured in the special issue of Scientific American in 1991, *Science in the 20th Century*, presents a positive view of metaphysics:

> The metaphysicist believes that the logically simple is also the real. The tamed metaphysicist believes that not all that is logically simple is embodied in experienced reality but that the total of all sensory experience can be "comprehended" on the basis of a conceptual system built on great simplicity.

For popularizing something, simplicity is the way to go. Accordingly, my Metalogical Constructs have taken this sort of synoptic approach. Einstein's $E = mc^2$ can be easily appreciated by examining Construct No.13. In this model, his epistemological conception of looking along the 'line defects' of two self-polarizing light waves, similar to the interplay of the Greek demonstrative syllogism (4-5-6) & dialectical syllogism (11-10-9), is generic to this model. Modern chaos theory, exemplified by James Gleick's *Chaos, Making a New Science* (1987), shows that emergent patterns reflect triune relationships that are both homogeneic, folding in evenly, &,

heterogeneic, folding oddly. Better yet, Odd Ground States fold out, inwardly through even derivatives, and Even Ground States fold in, outwardly through odd derivatives, to generally maintain the unitarity of the universe. Accordingly, ten-dimensional space-time can be made up of ten sets of triplets, with each field equation having a Middle Ground State of one variety, and an Outer Field & Inner Particle of the other variety. And, based upon the super-symmetrical self-polarization of special relativity (4 & 6 + 5) & general relativity (10 - 11 & 9), the third alternative produces six arbitrary variables (0, 2, 4, 6, 8, 10) associated with four ambiguous 'Bianchi's identities' (1, 3, 5, 7), for a total of ten field equations. (Set theorists still argue over whether or not to include the 0.) That is, there are four wave trains for the evolution of matter waves (+ 1, + 3, + 5, + 7), and six for the devolution of antimatter waves (0 -, 2 -, 4 -, 6 -, 8 -, 10 -), with the rightward analytical chirality and the leftward synthetic chirality forming the Crossover Patterns of associative development. And, by the blending of synthetic and analytic infinities, it is possible to appreciate the complete Life Cycle of the ten-dimensional space-time object (No.14).

At this juncture, let's try to clean out a few more Augean stables. Einstein's confusion about the c.c. (now generally an accepted principle) likely prevented him from agreeing with Werner Heisenberg's uncertainty principle (4 & 6), and consequently, the later development of quantum mechanics. Both attempt to hold a self-contradictory computational position, and we will be examining how many erroneous mathematical concepts in the past were likely at the roots of these errors in judgement. Gödel's theorem states that one can, in cases of extreme exponential extension, neither prove 'p' (4) nor disprove 'q' (6), although setting constants produces effective computational results. Thus, with 4 & 6 acting like a Higgs mechanism, that varies in strength in relation to each shift in energy density (+ 5), then the c.c. remains an indeterminate nonlocal derivative, but one that is roughly equivalent, by association, to a given energy state. With the Copenhagen interpretation of 1927, physics seemed to be looking for an Outer Field & Inner Particle for the nonlocalities of open-ended operational derivatives, which require the constant updating of AI, in order to 'stop' the calculations (reference to the unstoppable Turing machine). As with weather reporting, new intelligence must be constantly reintroduced into the equations, or the error in placing the Zen nail, at a given moment, will expand at an increasing rate, just like the illusion of Hubble's expanding universe. Thus, the c.c. is really a negative nonlocal feedback pattern of spatial curl, between a *scatological field* (4) & a *stochastic particle* (6), and not intended to fixate the energy rest frame as the isomorphism of the static universe (5). In psychographic terms, 'one' is looking to make reason into an excuse for being intellectually evasive & emotionally devious. One never has reason (!), but becoming more and more reasonable relates to the development of Integrative Discipline.

With $E_o = M_o c^2$, the horses, strings and marbles of general relativity tend to dominate the donkeys, buttons and straws of special relativity. Thus, E_o is a truism as the Mythic Phallus of monolithic energy, or a fission explosion as the Iconographic Simulacrum of Mimesis. (Energy is now known, not to be perfectly conserved.) The fixation of 'this' gives energy a disproportionate and unfriendly emphasis, as the inflationary formalism of a patristic apostasy. Interestingly, the physicist Leon Lederman, in *The God Particle*, 1993, remarked on Jung's comment that 'to think that energy is friendly is naïve.' I too have had second thoughts about Einstein's 'equivalence' between energy & mass, based upon $E_o = M_o c^2$ not being truly supersymmetrical. As a static definition for theory, E_o tends to fixate energy as a kind of false profit. Energy is a much more complex issue, and is not necessarily perfectly conserved. For example, it is very difficult to relate *real numbers*, as the 'aleph one', to the electromagnetic interaction of U(1), not to mention the synchrotron radiation of the ubiquitous fine structure constant, or for that matter, the grand unified energy of SU(5). At least with SU(2) + U(1), as the electroweak theory, the pattern fits 4 & 6 + 5.

But, + 5 is much more than just the idealism of Einstein's E_o, all alone. 4 & 6 is the 'aleph null' as the smallest transfinite cardinal number, which, as a field effect, is associated with + 5, but does not fix its essential energy state as an energy rest frame, for the static universe. In psychological terms, 4 & 6 provides no exactly periodic crystal as an evenhanded, handmaid of the Lord. In other terms, for the left side of Einstein's famous equation, the reciprocal constituents of the so-called weak force, as the 4 & 6 of SU(2), are not even included, and, therefore, E_o makes U(1) look overly determined, which causes it to become inflationary. Discordantly, this erroneous pattern for special relativity has caused the mistaken identification of the electromagnetic force as a fixed 'field effect'. Such interactionism is an example of specious reason. Hence, 'this' appears so inflationary that the uncontrolled expansion of fissionable energy produces an explosive *hyperplane* with no limit, or what is currently called the 'hadron zoo'. The latter is based upon the fallacy of special reason (up) as a hypersensitive spin-3 particle. In the 1990s then, it was no surprise that 'cold dark fusion' was envisioned, based upon the fallacy of spurious logic (down) as a hypo-reductive spin-3 force. No.4 represents the pairing of these two alter-ego extremes, as the triumvirate of fission (9-11-5, teepee) over the diva triformis of fusion (6-4-10, wigwam). Thus, the dysfunctional dualism of the nuclear family was bound to produce a fission bomb, followed by a fusion bomb, without the more progressive measures of the Extended Family. All of the foregoing was the result of a traditional misunderstanding, by our philosophic predecessors, concerning the 'wave-particle duality'. There is none. Psychologically, the nature of figure/ground Gestalt patterns led everybody down the 'primrose path' (Shakespeare). And, unfortunately even Einstein was apparently caught up in this fundamental web of self-deception.

Similarly, Darwin's natural selection has been popularly interpreted, through neo-Darwinism and social Darwinism, as an unhealthy adaptationism that he would not have subscribed to himself. Thereby, the concept of evolution became evolutionism, and that led to all the controversy between religion and science, and the misunderstanding concerning the progressive measures of the scientific method. That is, Darwin did not see influencing selective evolution as a way of controlling the selection pressures of broadly based natural processes, in a narrow-minded manner. Following upon specious reason, for the uncontrolled expansion of the Fixation of Identity as fission, comes the reduction of spurious logic as forcing Continuity to become unrestrained fusion. Thus, with the verticalized cladistic tendencies of paleontology, speculation has it that there is a direct link back in time to a common ancestor. Really, as the paleontologist Stephen Jay Gould has stated: that there were billions more body plans in the past, and thus we would never be able to follow their lineage back in time, to their exact place in the primordial soup. In fact, there likely were many different prehominids, which in accordance with the 'biological clock theory', appeared at about the same time, in many different areas of the globe. And, with travel, these slightly different humanoids would have successfully intermarried with an equivalent 'cenospecies' (10), which is a biological fact. The natural *contingencies* (Gould) of such Global Adaptations are imperceptible (allopatric 11 & 9), and act independently from the *tentativity* of controlling Local Adaptations (sympatric 5). (Generally then, Gould's idea about there being no nine-to-five inference, between the allopatric & sympatric, parallels my own approach, and, the findings of physics, that particles A & B cannot be translated back and forth, between the first & second systems, with impunity.) In other terms, it is highly unlikely that people evolved from one strain of African prehominids, as a direct link, when, through intermarriage, all existing humans would appear to be related to those who traveled the most. Further, even if that theory is the most plausible, the interplay of contingency & tentativity makes the evolution of human beings impossible to follow from a post hoc point of view. Nevertheless, we have all seen those silly drawings of primitive creatures morphing into *homo erectus*, and then into *homo sapiens*. This is part of the direct syndrome, with the conceptual realism of Being requiring the perceived naturalism of

Non-Being, so that one can hold onto the cladistic purism of direct descent from a common ancestor. 'He' would like her as a butterfly on a pin (5-10), &, 'she' would like him as an image on a stamp (10-5). They both intone, "I'll buy that for a dollar." And, with 200% looking like 100%, between the 'lapsus inversions' of impenetrables & imperceptibles, most of 'us' simply go directly to jail, and as the game of Monopoly intones, "Do not collect $200." A pat little world is a damn fine thing, but within the big picture it is nothing more than a virtual reality of criminal proportions.

THE HUMAN EQUATION:

SCIENCE AND SPIRITUALITY

VOLUME I

Metalogical Constructs

By Donald D. Powell

Common Sense Shall Prevail

®

1

1. **Metalogical Construct No.1:** The Quarteron Pattern

Zeno of Elea (ca 495-ca 430 B.C.) constructed a syllogistic pattern (3) that had a serial verticality which was later described in the Christian Bible as 'rings within rings'. This stratigraphic Vertical Mosaic involved demonstrative sentences of a subject-verb-object pattern (3). Modern myths refer to the 'three-dimensional plane', which is non sequitur, because all data remains on one surface, like a very thin, two-dimensional button. Currently, physicists refer to such a Hyperplane as a 'single symmetry classification', but there is no reliable way to include horizontal development. One such complex button on a string cannot represent what Einstein referred to as the 'natural system', which must include at least eight planar surfaces (see No.7). The Vertical Mosaic of metaphysical existentialism, like special relativity, is limited to modeling interactionism as structuralism, and cannot stand alone. As a categorical classification, there is little evidence of the fourth dimension, which evolves over time, from button to button. Like Plato's 'cord of reason', this flat surface works well for 'nested systems'.

Copyright (c) 2004 by Donald D. Powell and The Human Equation Inc.

© 2004 by Donald D. Powell and The Human Equation Inc.

The theoretical conceptualism of the Alpha, as the Vertical Mosaic of the Sign of the Times (red-green), & the hypothetical perceptualism of the Omega, as the Horizontal Mosaic of the Symbol of Space (black-white), together, make up the traditional 'two systems'. These are the Means or Affective Domain of Authority as the Book of Scripture & the Ends or Effective Domain of Factuality as the Book of Nature. Such yang-&-yin patterns are supersymmetrical (Susys) and pervade all human knowledge & understanding; verification & validation; observation & experiment; history & destiny; etc. Based upon the interplay of the 'rhetorical syllogism & dialectical syllogism', they are the Natural Language & the Laws of Nature, or Subjectivity & Objectivity, or special & general relativity, etc. Fundamentally, these are the 'two forces' of Universal Duality, responsible for making up the gradual growth and decay patterns of the 'third force'. However, the latter is an oxymoron, because the third force is not at all forceful. Importantly, its commonsensical nature gives us the potential to all get along fabulously.

Copyright (c) 2004 by Donald D. Powell and The Human Equation Inc.

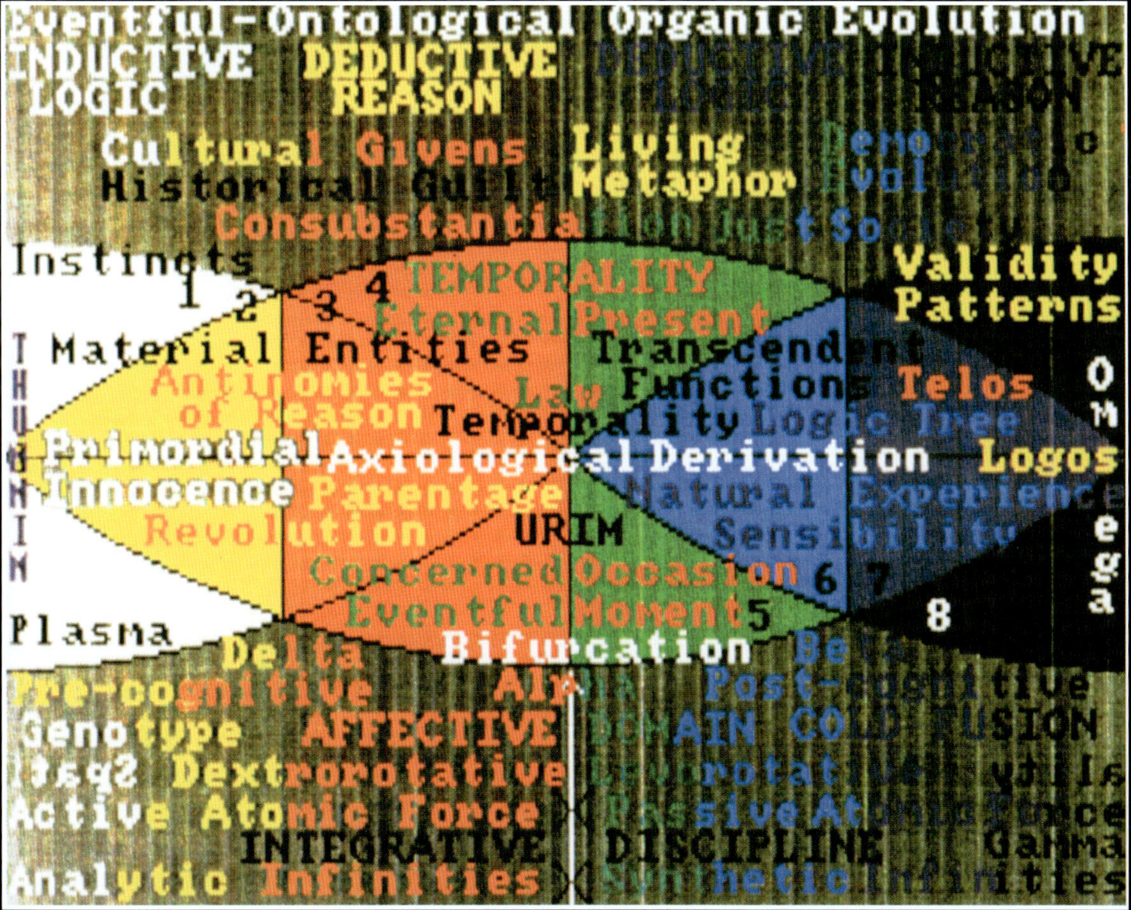

© 2004 by Donald D. Powell and The Human Equation Inc.

The Human Equation is made up of “Four Phases” or ‘phase transitions’. This is Phase I as the ‘ideal gas’ or Feng of Feng Shui. We could call it the New Adam of the eudaemonic self, or ontogeny as a precedential Side Effect, when compared with Phase III as the other half of the Proverbial Apple. That is, Phase III is the New Eve of the eusocial self, or phylogeny as a subsequential Side Effect. Phase I, then, is a groundswell of new developments and represents Aristotle’s material cause, while Phase III is his efficient cause. Thus the slow electron of the Lepton Family resides within the purview of Magnetic Resonance, as an electrophilic ground state (cathode donut) cradled by a magnetophilic substrate of positive cations within (hole) & without it (field). When I was foolish enough to smoke, I used to blow smoke rings just like No.3. As the first Side Effect, Phase I is the springtime of ‘anything’ that begins, with the science of protomatter being analogous to early human life. All things can be related to all other things.

Copyright (c) 2004 by Donald D. Powell and The Human Equation Inc.

© 2004 by Donald D. Powell and The Human Equation Inc.

This model represents the politically correct bane of all humane development. It is the hellhole of the Demonic Parody, which prevents any sort of healthy progress. It's as though Superman were trapped on a celluloid surface. To get free, the trick is to pass 'through the glass darkly' (Lewis Carroll). I will only say this much, at this juncture, that I offer the reader a chance to find 'Shangri-la' (James Hilton). But, there is no free ride; no walk in the park, with a smooth running road going down to the still waters of a safe harbor. However, miraculously, every honest effort has an instant reward: clairvoyance.

Copyright (c) 2004 by Donald D. Powell and The Human Equation Inc.

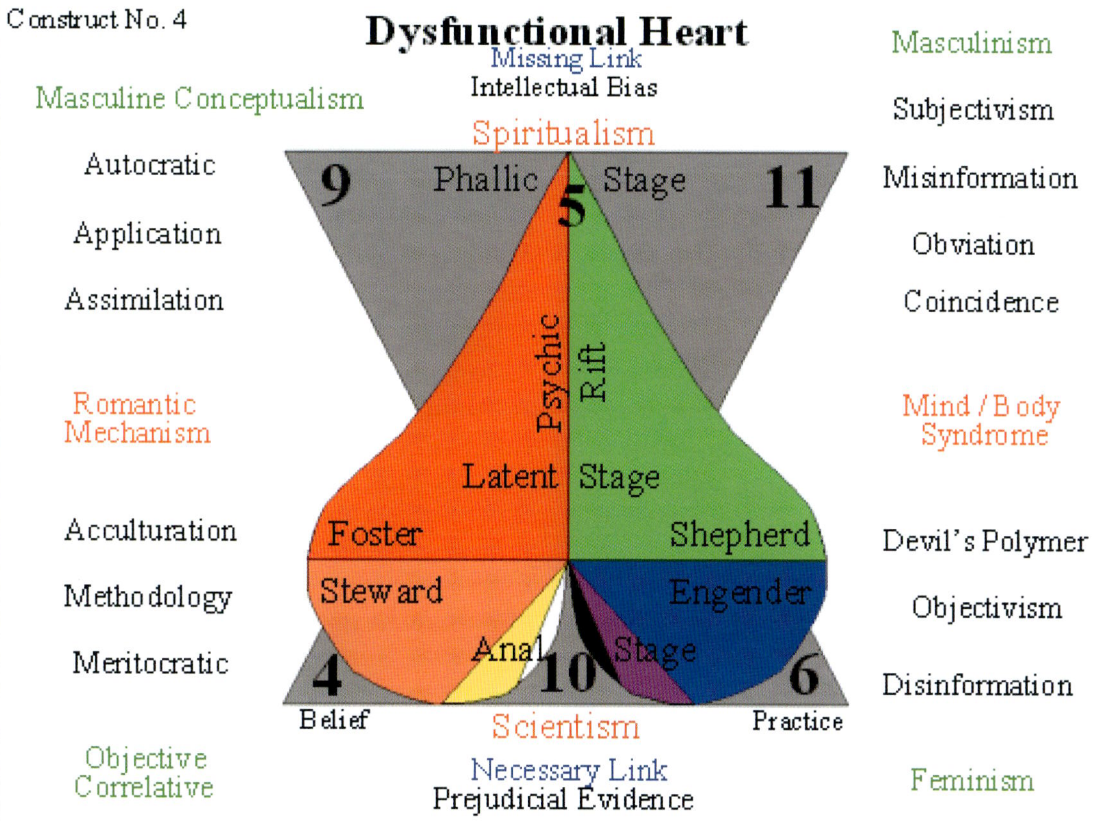

© 2004 by Donald D. Powell and The Human Equation Inc.

This pattern is Phase III as the 'ideal liquid' or Shui of Feng Shui. We could call it the New Eve of the eusocial self, or phylogeny as a subsequential Side Effect, when compared with Phase I as the first half of the Proverbial Apple. Just as Phase I is the future in the past, so Phase III is the past in the future. Thus, the Antilepton Family has a positive anode within the Electronic Resonance of negative anions, and is complementary to Phase I. Hence, developmentally, Phases I and III are buffer zones of natural development which prevent the fission of Phase II & fusion of Phase IV, from making life too volatile & too intractable. A gradual "and" and a sharp "&" differ greatly. The trick is to give the whole apple back to the teacher.

Copyright (c) 2004 by Donald D. Powell and The Human Equation Inc.

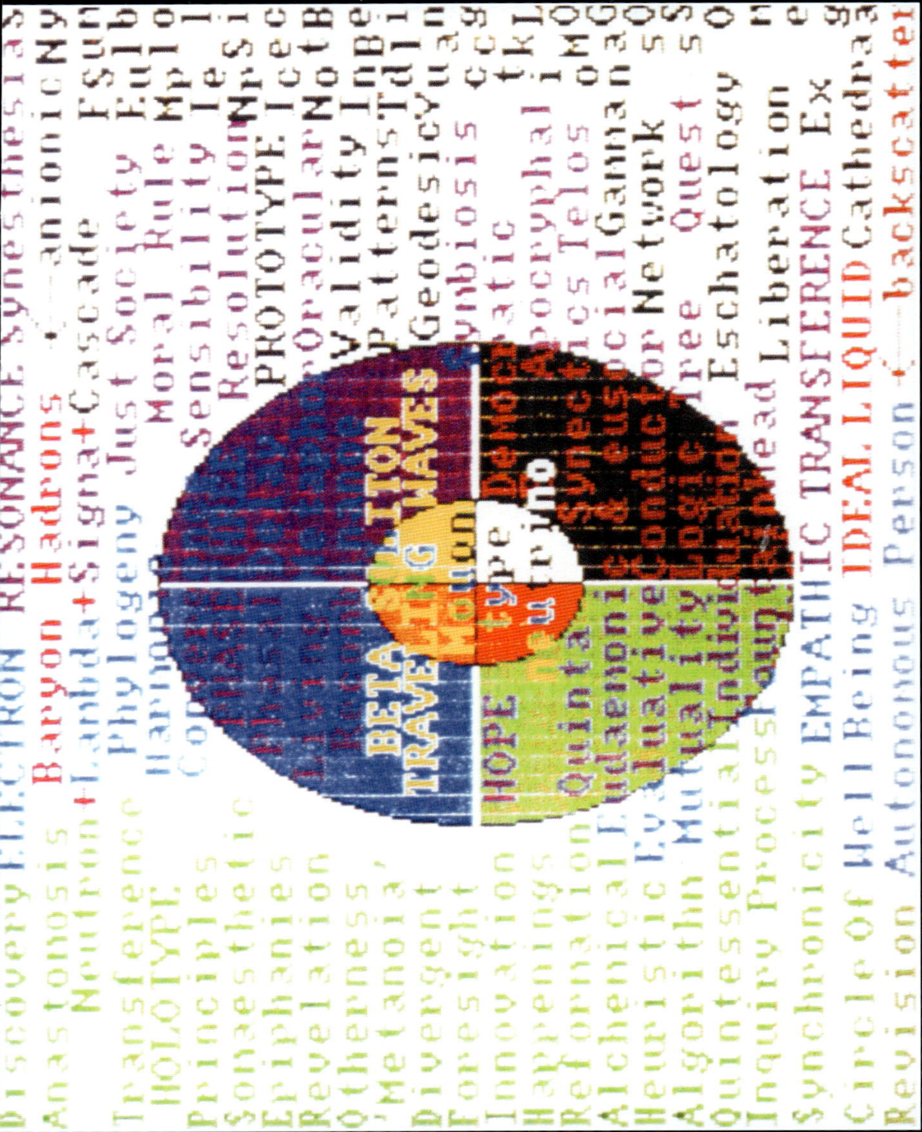

© 2004 by Donald D. Powell and The Human Equation Inc.

'That', as a Phase IV relationship, is antithetical to 'this' as a Phase II relationship (Construct No.1). In others terms, if Phase II is a white accretion disk with a black wormhole in the center, then Phase IV is a black accretion disk with a white wormhole in the center. Or, pure Space as distinct from pure Time. One could compare the Phase IV traits of logic, distance, hypothesis, sequence, magnetic standing waves, double down, converting, integrity, experiment, good, destiny, division, etc. with the Phase II characteristics of reason, length, theory, series, electronic wave fronts, double up, convincing, honor, observation, fine, history, multiplication, etc. Working the two together can be fun, with vigilance, or, pose extreme danger, if taken for granted. Such is the Real Human Adventure, which awakens our Buddhist sense of 'belonging'.

Copyright (c) 2004 by Donald D. Powell and The Human Equation Inc.

© 2004 by Donald D. Powell and The Human Equation Inc.

7

7. Metalogical Construct No.7: Double Light Cone of The Third Force

This model is based upon Hermann Minkowski's 'four-dimensional double light cone', which blends flat time & curved space, for the development of 'grey matter'. By this convention, 'God's caterpillar' has two heads that are coextensive, analytically to the right and synthetically to the left, while commingling harmoniously over eight balanced transitions. Hence, physicists refer to the 'Euclidean space-time object', which gradually recombines both temporal and spatial relationships. Thus, in a Recombinant Third System bilateral complementary tendencies maintain what is called the moderated 'gauge invariance' of Constant Unity Factors. That is, extreme shearing gradients (&) are not part of the third system, which is gradual, orderly, regular, coordinated and congruent, through the legality of the Associative And. In this manner, expansion and contraction, emission and absorption, odd and even, energy densities and mass densities, etc. always embrace each other in a heterosexual manner. Hence, the marriage of time and space produces a balanced progression or 'steady state theory', even though the two systems are independent & antithetical in their primary natures.

Copyright (c) 2004 by Donald D. Powell and The Human Equation Inc.

© 2004 by Donald D. Powell and The Human Equation Inc.

8

8. **Metalogical Construct No.8:** Toroidal Sextets of Senary Transitions

Like a snowflake, honeycomb or benzene ring, the polymerization of hexagonal transitions seems to be fundamental to natural progressions. It's as though one is experiencing a measure of the natural wisdom of humane development, through what has been termed Associative Justice: based upon the recombinant interplay of both and neither, flatness and curvature. Note that the two clearly evident donut shapes in this model have six sides, and that there are six points of an antithetical nature without & within each one. Whether as Aristotle's 'hexis', the hexagon of suspicion, six-parameter indeterminacy, six degrees of freedom or six degrees of separation, the concept of a dynamic equilibrium is quite enchanting.

Copyright (c) 2004 by Donald D. Powell and The Human Equation Inc.

© 2004 by Donald D. Powell and The Human Equation Inc.

No.9 provides a potpourri of interesting models that have and will stand the test of time, because they speak to the humanity in us. For the donut-like patterns of the toroidal functions, one needs to imagine an Outer Field of the same character of the Inner Figure (particle or hole). Hence, Powell's four triads, each with an Outer Field, Middle Ground State and Inner Particle, can be seen to develop over the full range of the Four Phases of 'complete phasal space'. In construct No.7 then, there will be a pair of harmonic states for each one of the Four Phases, which slot into an appropriate position according to which of the phase transitions is required in the moment. A simple way to think of the Four Phases is the seasonable cycle of spring, summer, fall and winter. One could also mention tactics, paratactics, strategies and intelligence. Then there is my "gambit, habit, ambit and probit". Aristotle had his four causes: material, formal, efficient and final. Modern military theory goes like this: command, control, communication and intelligence. There are oodles more, which cover all sorts of eventualities.

Copyright (c) 2004 by Donald D. Powell and The Human Equation Inc.

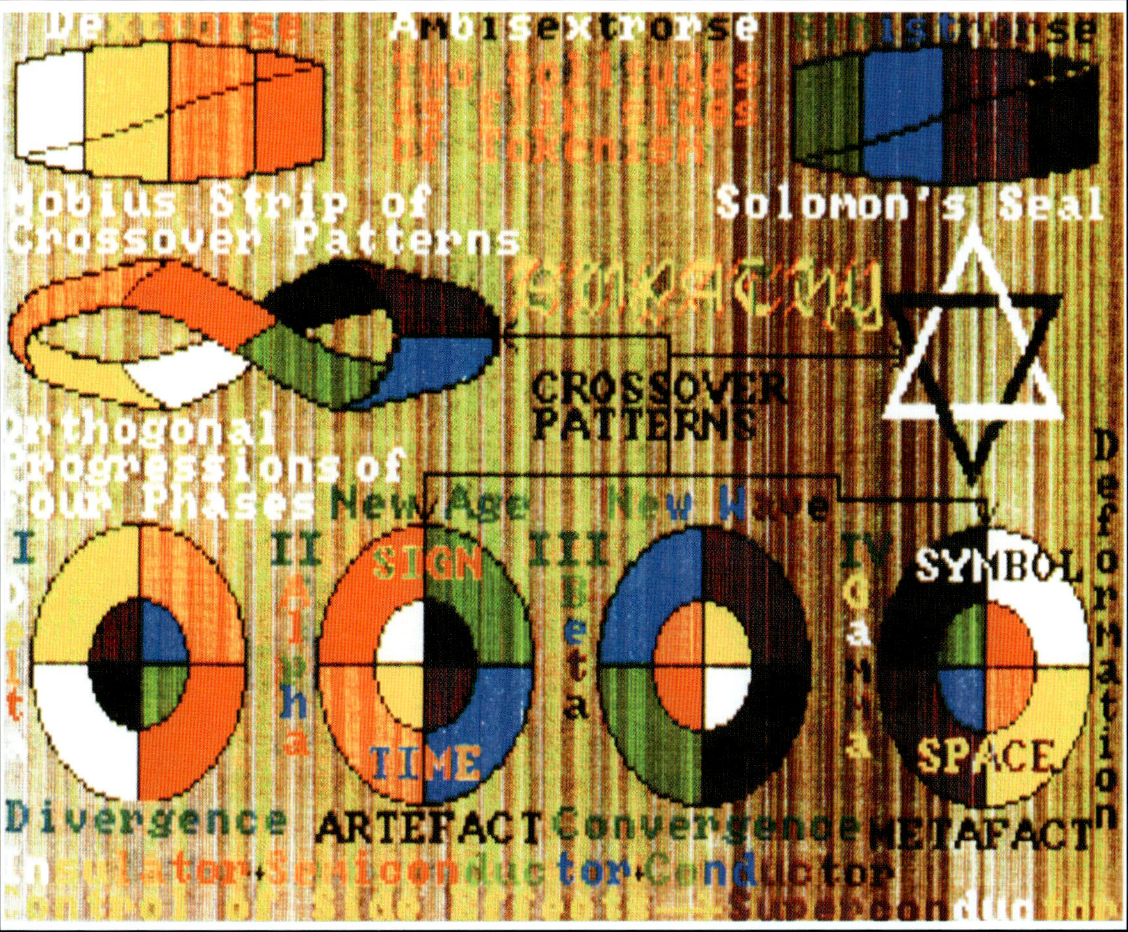

© 2004 by Donald D. Powell and The Human Equation Inc.

10

10. Metalogical Construct No.10: Fission & Fusion, and No Side Effects

The sextets of Fission & Fusion are respectively, the Explicit Formation (perfect reason) & Explicit Function (perfect logic), which, if they dominated, as in this model, would only allow for the Apocalypse Now of a supersymmetrical dance, with no gradual gradients to produce natural processes and biological growth. Construct No.12 shows that the maqam (four basic musical notes of Eastern tradition) of Four Harmonic Resonances does not permit the apocalyptic so-&-so-of-the-this-&-that-together to block the healthy Side Effects of the natural system.

Copyright (c) 2004 by Donald D. Powell and The Human Equation Inc.

© 2004 by Donald D. Powell and The Human Equation Inc.

11. **Metalogical Construct No.11:** Electromagnetic Pulse Phenomena

If, instead of the travesty of No.10 (irrelevant & irreverent) the fundamental four of No.12 were adjusted to give Magnetic Resonance (green-blue-purple-black block) and Electronic Resonance (white-yellow-orange-red block) an exaggerated presence, there would only be 'negative side effects' and no natural progress would be allowed to develop. An obvious analogy is: the apparent freedom of the uncensored aestheticism of acting out, through artistic expressionism, with no self-control and self-restraint to facilitate social justice. In that manner, No.11 is Adam's first bite with Eve's second bite, and no Proverbial Apple, just the apple sauce of irrelevant choices & too many distractions.

Copyright (c) 2004 by Donald D. Powell and The Human Equation Inc.

© 2004 by Donald D. Powell and The Human Equation Inc.

As a scalar field, this model can turn in any direction and operate at any scaling level (both finite and infinite), no matter how large or how small, and still maintain the unitarity of the universe. The Eastern tradition of music, based upon a given set of four fundamental maqams, can be rendered, through improvisation, to symbolically produce the maqamats of any given state of expression. Thus, the particular & the universal never lose contact with each other (1/11). However, an extremely contrapuntal rendering of the music of the universe would not provide for an ecosphere that could be inhabited by intelligent beings. Through Right Choice & Correct Action, we Human Beings can use the Double Passover (duality) to overcome the Demonic Parody (dualism), by using concerted dialogue to maintain the harmonic relationships of the democracy of Associative Justice. Construct No.12, as the Great Crystal of Light, is a good place to begin, and, the good time is always now.

Copyright (c) 2004 by Donald D. Powell and The Human Equation Inc.

© 2004 by Donald D. Powell and The Human Equation Inc.

13. Metalogical Construct No.13: The One True Ring

I like J. R. R. Tolkien's idea of a ring that cannot be worn by any particular person. No.13 renders supersymmetrical relationships, which, unfortunately, have the potential to become the Demonic Parody of dualism (Construct No.4). Better yet, the Vertical Mosaic (two black lines and one white line) & the Horizontal Mosaic (one black line and two white lines) also have the potential to become the Recombinant Third System (No.7) by providing for the graduated progressions of a kinder, gentler way. The ring represents that way, which is never the prerogative of any particular person, sex, race, religion, methodology or nation, etc. Hence the ring is a Living Metaphor for all kinds of Life Cycles. In No.13, the vertical & horizontal triplets recombine to make up what is called The Third History. Importantly, then, the first & second forces yield the so-called 'third force', except that there really is no third force, because it is rendered in a more gradual manner. One could refer to postpartisan politics, or what is called 'soft power'.

Copyright (c) 2004 by Donald D. Powell and The Human Equation Inc.

Trade-mark ® 2004 of The Human Equation Inc.

Decoding the ten-ness of decalogical universal ciphers is never an exact science. Nevertheless, Life Cycles are quite self-evident to the trained eye. For example, the planets of the Solar System seem to follow a pattern of distinct chemical gradients. Further, the science of ten taxonomical relationships is a great organizational aid, as is the decalogical pattern of the mathematics of set theory. Such ten-ness has been with us for a long time — all the way from Aristotle's set of ten relationships, up to Einstein's ten field equations. Some patterns do not seem to go beyond sets of seven (Niels Bohr's 'seven allowed orbits' or Cantor's theory of 'transfinite numbers'), or, sets of eight (Mendeleyev's Periodic Table of Elements or the Buddhist Eightfold Path), but they all have a similar internal consistency, which reflects a fundamental equation. These are all differing ranges of orderly progressions that not so surprisingly include the double helix of DNA. There are many examples, but the real fun begins when one compares one chain of transitions, or grammar, with another. Apropos, it's interesting to compare a decalogical rendering of 'punctuation' with the grammar of a set of ten 'scriptures': 1) " , — (... ! ; . ? : , and 2) prescription, ascription, conscription, proscription, subscription, description, rescription, postscription, transcription and inscription. There are many more. In this manner, through The Human Equation, it is possible, baring an excessive treatment of details, to have reasonable comprehension of almost every area of human inquiry. Think what this will do for education, politics and social justice!?

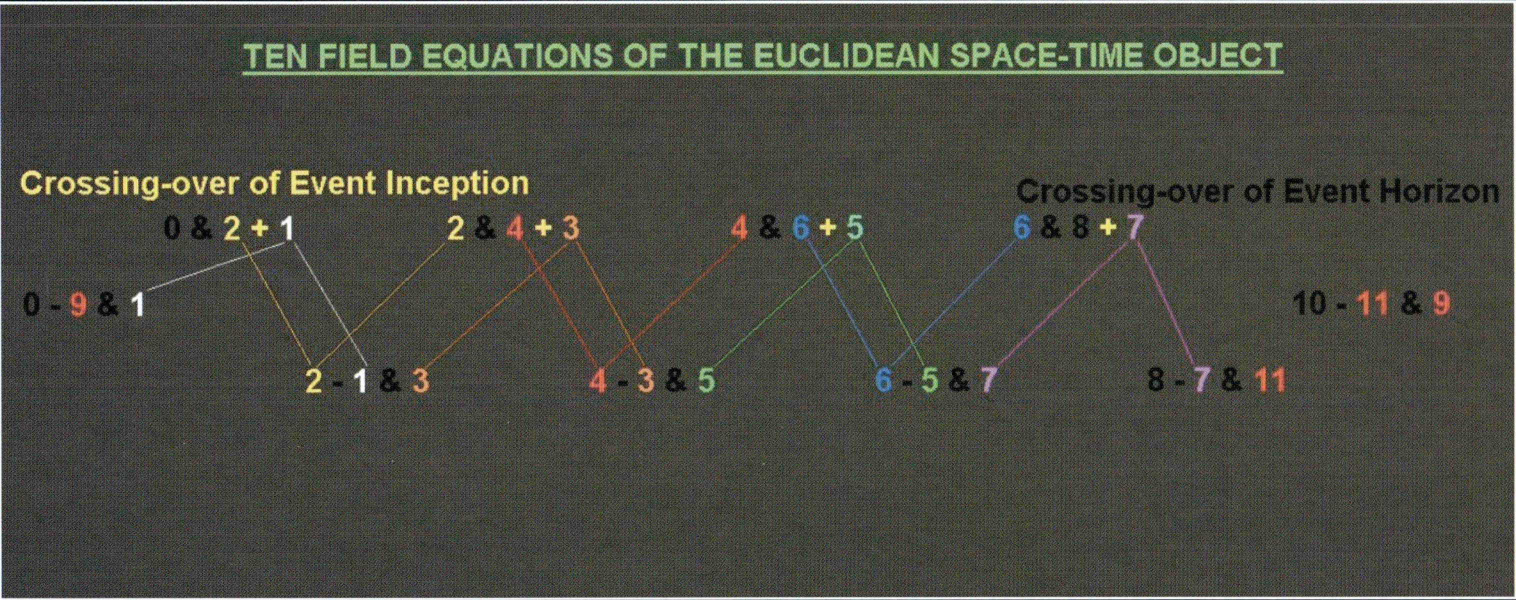

© 2004 by Donald D. Powell and The Human Equation Inc.

To Begin Again

The objective of this chapter is to again summarize some of the intricate patterns already introduced, in preparation for dealing with more complex relationships.

In *The God Particle*, the physicist Leon Lederman states: "In the modern quantum-theory...certainty and regularity emerge as events that are averages over a distribution of reactions of varying probability (*The God Particle*, p.60)." Accordingly, Construct No.7 has these ergodic characteristics that are, in current cosmological terminology, referred to as the TOE or theory of everything. This model, as a rendering of complete phasal space, is quite different from a single symmetry classification, although generally not yet as acceptable for representing the standard model of physics (SM). That is, in Construct No.1, the Quarteron Pattern, as a Vertical Mosaic, resembling the GUT as a grand unified theory, is a more acceptable representation for *particle interactions.* No.1 also mirrors the traditional planification of Euclidean geometry. However, I do not see that my Four Phases, rendered in No.7 as a natural distribution, are a threat to the Viability of the SM. In No.7, the compatibility envisioned by Einstein, between matter variation & antimatter variation, is resolved as an associative production that corresponds to what can be experienced empirically. The descriptive moniker normally used is 'Euclidean space-time object'. Both flatness & curvature are included, and all the different analogical levels of nucleosynthesis can be inferred from this model, as per the Periodic Table of Elements. One thing for sure, not being mired in detail, No.7 is the best model yet devised for quantum statistical mechanics. However, as per No.14, my complete system for superstrings might even be more effective. It naturally includes gravity, and also the nonexistent dyad for Einstein's unbounded curvature of space.

This portrayal of the Life Cycle of the TOE reflects the blending of flatness & curvature within the unified harmonics of the Euclidean space-time object, which is manifested in a *scale invariant manner.* That is, on a given level of analogy, which remains locked into one natural scaling range, whatever is *elemental* to that level holds consistently throughout the full distribution of the system. Thus, what may be considered an 'element' depends upon the relative size of the scaling level. Hence, a specific TOE, with its own 'magic radix', decombines & recombines the distance & length of whatever set of space-time characteristics is appropriate for that level. Accordingly, each TOE is experienced through eight harmonic ground states, distributed bilaterally, on a given level of inquiry. The most fundamental level would likely be carried by a spectrum of elemental photons themselves, but there is no way of establishing the nature of these basic photons, because *it is not possible to distinguish the subjunctive carrier medium for photons.* (Planck space-time at least hints at this possibility, because of the two very different aspects of Planck length & Planck mass [the small hourglasses in No.7].) Next, the second, higher level becomes the electromagnetic wave spectrum, subtended by the mediation of the smaller-scale system of photons, which are the carrier medium. That is, photons act as outer fields & inner particles that supervene & subvene electromagnetic waves (ground states). For this special case, the *locally visible light spectrum* is part of the electromagnetic wave spectrum, while, nonlocally, various carrier photons, as virtual photons & virtual phonons, are emitted and absorbed through the "edges & cracks" in this spectrum. (What we must keep in mind, is that there is always a dark spectrum that blends with a light spectrum, at every level, based upon the two systems. Thus, in Time, virtual space is a cut below, folding in, and in Space, virtual time is a cut above, folding out, so that the third alternative always remains balanced.) On a third, still higher level, light gaseous nucleons would likely be next, with protons & neutrons (small red-green hourglass in No.7) becoming fundamental to primordial hydrogen – called protium. Subsequently, in a string & button pattern, primordial para-hydrogen (small red-to-green enthalpic shift) would produce ortho-hydrogen as its molecular equivalent (large red-to-green Paradigm shift). Accordingly, the full spectral range of the hydrogen cycle would then build up from protium (+ 1) through deuterium (2 -) to helium 3 (+ 3), and then to tritium (4 -) followed by helium 4 (+ 5) and lithium 6-7 (6- and + 7), and finally to beryllium 8-9-10 (not allowed 8th orbit) as completing the harmonic distribution. (Note the + and – alternation of associative production.) The hydrogen cycle would be followed by the higher-order carbon cycle, and so on, until more complex patterns of matter begin to appear through nucleosynthesis. Of course, because there is no way of controlling all the admixtures, the cross-dimensional clustering of the Periodic Table of Elements is not quite as tidy as Dmitry Mendeleyev would have liked (1834-1907).

Naturally, each higher level of analogy would introduce unfathomable degrees of complexity, and so it is not surprising that philosophers have difficulty taking a holistic approach. Shortly before his death on Jan. 23, 1991, the Canadian philosopher Northrop Frye, author of *The Great Code* (1982) on the Bible, expressed the desire to live another lifetime, so that he could work on a book equating modern physics and Chinese philosophy. Interestingly, that most fascinating quest had already been begun, in 1975, by the physicist Fritjof Capra, in *The Tao Of Physics.*

Importantly, for the modern era, philosophical extravagancies and literary intellectualism must give way to a more viable form of argumentation, through the doctrinal ordinances of statistical-like relationships. Accordingly, order & chaos as the two systems become alchemically blended within the dynamic transitions of the Recombinant Third System. Thus, Sign & Symbol recombine as Metaphor, similar to the Gabriele Veneziano's physics of the 'dual resonance model' (1968), which is in keeping with the Taoistic 'double vision' of Northop Frye. Certainly, Frye's sense of Universal Duality produces a third alternative, which resembles Marshall McLuhan's hendiadys dialogue, of one through two. In this manner, the yang & yin recombine to become a Living Metaphor, through the democratic community of the third person plural, which, as the 'royal we', reflects Freud's Heterosexual Stage. The trick is to avoid the derivation of metaphysical structuralism (No.4), which amounts to fabricating a virtual reality, as a form of relativistic miscreance, or what is called sin. In short, what I'm stating is that the devil is not of God's creation, but is endemic to the Human Condition, through the mythological relativism of the enemy within. Call it the collapse of the wave packet, if you like.

I must again acknowledge a debt to the Canadian media philosopher Marshall McLuhan. I have gleaned a wealth of understandings from many of his writings, of which two are outstanding: *the Gutenberg Galaxy* (1962) and *Understanding Media* (1964). Since his insights first stimulated my curiosity about the Human Condition, I began working on metalogical systems. Such analogical systems are the basis of understanding all media, which involves arguing from universal design, rather than claiming to 'get the message' based upon a deductive argument. *We never really get the message*, because Integrative Discipline only produces a gradual awakening, as an extension of natural, organic relationships. Marshall McLuhan died in 1980, but I owe him a further debt of gratitude through the final manuscripts published by his son Eric in 1988, as the *Laws of Media, The New Science*. Here, we are getting closer to my approach.

More recently, a work by Stephen W. Hawking, *A Brief History of Time*, 1988 has become a kind of bible to me. The scope of Hawking's understandings makes time stand still. Rereading his work makes time fly. From the side of physics, he bridges to philosophy, where, if time had permitted, Northrop Frye would have surely made his mark. Using Hawking's work as a basis for subsequent readings in physics, I was able to enhance the transdisciplinary goal of my text. Further, with Goethe's ideal of holistic color relationships, the logic of complex physical and mathematical concepts can be made more accessible to the general public. Accordingly, it is possible to popularize all kinds of statistical and demographic distributions, whether chemical, biological or other. Even the complex matrices of *psychographic profiles* show the same patterning, which relates to the nature of the Natural Language itself. Marshall McLuhan foresaw the need to upgrade the 'message' through the fullness of such a holistic medium, which he imagined as the sensorium of a complete set of Sensory Ratios. (I will be revealing those patterns.) In the same vein, Hawking feels that philosophers have to find a more comprehensive approach in order to remain the harbingers of regenerative foresight. Other than through the medium of science fiction, philosophers generally have not kept abreast of modern developments, and neither have most of our religious mentors. We need to address both the when & why + how (4 & 6 + 5) of 'this', &, the what - where & who (10 -11 & 9) of 'that', which are the 12th, 13th and 14th, &, the 11th, 10th and 9th books attributed to Zachariah, as reflected by Northrop Frye's double vision. However, it is important to avoid the cyclopian monism of the gnostic one, and look to resolving the Hindu third eye. The first system, as the Body of the Book of Scripture (Christian logos made flesh), &, the second system, as the Mind of the Book of Nature (the Dance of Siva as the Hindu sacred triad), are the Becoming & Being that recombine through the Buddhist ideal of Belonging. That is, both Body & Mind working in harmony. Hence, through the resolution of 'this & that', the 'such and such' becomes the Recombinant Third System. That is to say, justice as we know it belongs with the recombination of the *Distributive Justice* of the round gate & the *Commutative Justice* of the strait gate, providing for the moral rule of the third system through *Associative Justice.*

In No.13, ultimately, the Hands of God, like yang & yin, weave all the seasonable patterns of the monotheistic Haptic Extension, based upon the fundamental maqam of four relationships. (Think of the basic ligands of human DNA: adenine, cytosine, guanine and thymine.) Historically, many examples have already been mentioned, but the ineffable pattern of JHWH is of particular interest for Western society, which I have portrayed as The Great Crystal of Light, in Construct No.12. Naturally, the overall pattern of Four Resonances does not encompass the fifth element as the penultimate SU(5) of 'aleph-one'. But, similar to Aristotle's moving cause, any and all dimensions and scaling levels are *potentially possible*, including the grand unified energy of SU(5). It is because of the foregoing that the Pythagoreans taught that mystical, fourfold *tetrakyts* hold the secret to the universe (F. David Peat, *Superstrings*, 1988). No.12, as Powell's carpet, portrays Matter Resonance as only one of a total of the Four Resonances, and thus the demographics of No.7 must be included in a broader pattern of statistical measurements. (I invite the reader to check for that latter distribution, as one of the Four Resonances.) Importantly, No.12, as a scalar field, at least hints at the grand unified energy of SU(5) as the 'aleph one'. That is, it can pivot in any direction, and expand & contract infinitely, and is therefore fundament to, quite different from, and more complete than, the normal space-time distribution of No.7. (Think what this will do for mathematicians!) Following the pattern of the quadrupole roots of Eastern music, the basic fourfold maqam produces all the combinations & permutation of subsequent maqamats. Further, Planck's constant, as a measure of the interplay of the *orthogonal immanentism of superfluidity & the parametric interventionism of superconduction*, doesn't really reveal the panoply of geometric potentialities that ought to be found within the nonlocal, noninterpretive distributions of Planck space-time itself.

In 1988, Steven Weinberg treated this topic as *The First Three Minutes*, which gives the impression that the universe actually began in one place at a particular time; something that I do not agree with. Planck space-time, in my opinion, is better reflected by the relationships of 'twistor space-time' as intuited by the black hole theorist Roger Penrose. In Penrose's *The Emperor's New Mind* (1991), the ubiquitous diapason of Universal Consciousness is related to conjugal relationships, with paired 'spinors' making up little hourglasses called 'twistors'. Of course, we cannot utter the Word of God, which is likely why Penrose's work is not an easy read. Nevertheless, his grasp of consciousness as a kind of Holy Grail of physics, is surprisingly like my scalar field in Construct No.12. Supposedly, the 'inflationary period' of the hypothetical big bang sets up First Principles, based upon the dialetheism of an *Ideal Phase Transition.* Hypothetically then, that supersymmetrical minimal surface, of untouchable Intimacy, between the round gate & the strait gate, would not yet have spread out from a composite '*triple point*', to produce the three separate phase transitions shown in No.7. (I maintain that No.12 still exists everywhere, for all time.) Like a Poetic Kiss (No.13), which can never be fully realized through the Haptic Extension (No.7), the fundamental Certainty Principle of the universal cipher is much more than just the First Principles that generate all other acoustical relationships. (Remember that Darwin did not dwell upon the exact meaning of *natural selection.*) Therefore, because No.12 remains within the limit cycles of Planck space-time, we must avoid the dialetheism of inscribing First Principles, in stone, through the cosmic censorship of a universe that supposedly started in one place, at a particular time. (That would make the Gordian knot a little too tidy, and lead to the destruction of all progressive measures, such as human development.) That is, in order to appreciate the Certainty Principle, the Acoustic of First Principles must not become a censorial dialetheism (coterminal), just as the acoustics of existence must not become a static diatheism (coplanar). No.12, as the Universal Consciousness of the most fundamental fourfold maqam, is both finite & infinite, without any particular duration & extent, of length & distance. The point to be made here is that, other than for entertaining purely hypothetical speculations, I do not subscribe to the theory of the inflationary period as being a *beginning* as such. In No.7, the remnants of the Certainty Principle require *both* of the two nonlocal hourglasses as nonlocal keying mechanisms. That is, both the nexus of a 'scalar boson' (black-to-white mediatrix) & the plexus of a 'scalar fermion' (red-to-green generatrix). The reference is to a 'scalar point-function' as a reductive null point & a 'scalar point-formation' as an *expansive null point.* Like a scalar field, they have no particular orientation. (We will be coming back to this topic in relation to the mathematics of Carl Friedrich Gauss' 'hyperbolic & elliptical extremals' as ideally coplanar & coterminal.) Hence, No.12, as the penultimate supersymmetrical *unified field theory* for the *grand unified energy*, only hints at Universal Consciousness. As what we can live with, the monolithic finesse of Phase II only relates to the monopolistic principles of Phase IV, through the recombination of the best attributes of Phase I with the better organization of Phase III. So there is never any question of knowing & understanding the Haptic Extension of natural selection, just a good shot at getting a better picture of reality at large, through General Guidelines.

The Intimacy of No.12 concerns the "*Misericordance*" of the Divine Comedy. With The Great Crystal of Light emulating Universal Consciousness, it would seem that St. Thomas Aquinas was right in expressing that God is naturally good in nature. The implication is that Universal Marriage, could & might be based upon two lucky thirteens as a kind of 'twenty-six-dimensional space-time'. Except that the Dance of Siva soon becomes, for The Human Equation, the difficulty of deciding which hand to use (the logic difference equation for 4 & 6), and which foot to dance on (the closed form integral for 11 & 9). Synaesthetically, without & within the Pivotal Moment of the Crux of Right Choice & Correct Action, these are the instinctual mediatrix & intuitive generatrix that make up unresolvable tentativity & contingency, to remain essentially &

substantially *noninterpretive.* Hence, Verification & Validation can & may only lead to a legitimate way of improving the arbitrary precision of the Viability of the third system, and do not in any way imply & implicate the legalism of any sort of manifest certainty. Legal, empirical progressions depend upon the harmonic correspondence of real experience, rather than the extreme derivation of legalisms as all true or all false. That is, objective evidence is a progressive, empirical development, which is not based on the empiricism of demanding answers, solution and results, nor the scientism of dictating an exact science. One is normally concerned with the "donuts" of Infrastructure, as transitions between classical local ground states, while Superstructure & Substructure, as field-particle nonlocalities, are less directly realizable.

More than likely, on different levels, the red-green hourglass (11 & 9) would be tachyons, a paraelectrical worm hole, Planck time, the dilaton photon, Pauli's exclusion principle, the enthalpy of diakinetics, the allopatric, Hawking radiation, superconduction, adiabatic expansion, SU(3), uniform inertia, etc. (For the *action statement* or momentum of Phase IV, I like the general terms Continuity, Necessity, Sequence of Speciation, or Space Vector, because they don't dictate what scaling level one is working with.) On the most fundamental level, the collapse of the wave function (10 - 0), through spontaneous symmetry breaking (11 & 9 and 9 & 0), would produce Planck time as a nucleonic gas, referred to as the 'Bose-Einstein condensate'. These are the relationships of QCD as quantum chromodynamics. The twistors of this inflationary period would seem heterogeneic as the scalar fermion of an oddly expanding *principle of least action*, because the Soul of Substance itself is beyond expression: hidden within the Great Seal of the True Doppler Shift. And, as an instrument of Ideal Truth, it becomes an Immaculate Conception. Except that, hypothetically, the perfect Sphere is not an achievable possibility, because it would be a zero-dimension point, or the singularity of a black hole devoid of any sort of heat signature. (Reluctantly, I have included 0 in my set theory, because better men than myself have so concluded, and I see no other way to work out complete phasal space.) But, through general relativity, sphericity undergoes the subtle contortions of dyadic parity as an *oblate condensate* (10 - 11 & 9, isotopic) and a *prolate dilate* (0 - 9 & 1, isotropic), to allow spontaneous symmetry breaking. That is, the dyadic deuterotype (10 - 0), in two places at once, is the relatively arbitrary Judgement of the Hypothesis of the Supraperiodic antimatter crystal of the Explicit Function. The Supposition of perfect prediction is an action statement that is juxtaposed measure-for-measure, and at the same time, is associated with nonlocal remnants of matter as the *archetype* of the implicit formation of the nonperiodic crystal (11 & 9 and 9 & 1). The latter are the PRP of omniformity, or the enthalpic nucleons that make up all forms of matter. (Here, I have used the term uniform inertia, for fundamental adiabatic expansion as a positive principle of least action that exemplified higher-order interrupt. (Think of pitching up, on the piano, from one eight-note scale to another.) Thus, the true Doppler shift is composed of Xenocrates' 'interacting dyad' of disparate antimatter ground states (10 - 0) in association with matter remnants as the nonlocal fields & particles (11 & 9 and 9 & 1) of the v.e.d. as the generatrix of Planck time. The antimatter ground states of 10 – 0, as infinity & singularity, set up diamagnetic standing waves, with 11 & 9 and 9 & 1 resembling Stephen Hawking's twin jets of quasar radiation.

The above 'tensorial vectors' are more common than, in the past, most cosmologists, physicists and astronomers were willing to admit, and along with eight harmonic wave trains, make up ten-dimensional space-time. Einstein covered these arbitrary aspect ratios of general relativity with M_oc^2, where M_o (10) is the rest mass of supergravity, and c^2 (11 & 9) is the uniform inertia of the most basic dilaton photons of omniformity. Omniformity is enthalpic for PRP, and therefore fundamental to all forms of matter. For most philosophers, the complete transformations of Phase IV merely make up the axiological currents of necessity, which implies that one can know the braided SU(3) of the causal string. However, these basically nonexistent and arbitrary variables, as an infinity of values, are very 'iffy'. (J. R. R. Tolkien, in the *Lord of the Rings*, made it that only 'halflings' could safely carry the One True Ring. In biological terms, halflings are the half transmission of acquired characteristics.) Diakinetic, paraelectrical traits show up as the workable solutions of everyday *kinetic mechanisms*, whether physical, cultural or spiritual, and tend to do violence to natural processes, in the manner of a silver bullet, or a monopoly of convergent forces. All we have to do is look at the extreme horizontality of current problems with globalization. If such judgements are mistaken, they become prejudicial to continuous development, through a process of warlike denial and censorship. As such, they are the bottom line of the brinkmanship as a fascistic jezebel, or the Mrs. Hyde of passive aggressivity as too little too late, followed by too much too soon. What is actually workable, as The Action Statement, is ultimately associated with an inscrutable infinity of values, such as Richard Dawkins' cultural memes.

Some triads that express these fundamental sequences are: Ought, Ought Naught and Might; inductance, diode and rectifier; where, what and who; recon, muton and cistron (Seymour Benzer); echotype, cenospecies and subspecies; the recombinant function group, and my commandments of 'transcription' (10 - 11 & 9), 'inscription' (0 - 9 & 1) and 'prescription' (0 & 2 + 1). These are, as the fundamental three outcomes of experiment, covered by the Greek term Thanatos, and likewise, the Dance of Siva as the Hindu sacred triad. They are part of what Freud thought of as the Nonsexual Stage. In modern terms, these aspects involve such things as transsexual, transgender and transgenic relationships. Phase IV sequences involve the contravariant duplicative aspects of DNA as distinguished from the covariant replicative aspects of RNA.

In No.7, the black-white hourglass would be a twistor of Plank space, or what Stephen Hawking refers to as the Arrow of

Time. One could also use the term 'low-entropy core', and most specialists who work with atomic clocks like to think of 4 & 6 as a periodic crystal. One could also use the term 'magnetic monopole', or 'Higgs boson'. As a kernel of Planck space or Planck mass, this weak force is a pivotal scalar boson as a nonlocal mediatrix that makes up a contragradient representation (m*), or, for set theory, a median of conjugal separation. Einstein didn't even put it in his famous equation, although he did introduce the idea of field effect as an implicit function of spatial curl. One could use the term logic difference equation. Hence, 4 & 6 marks the orientation of the c.c. as a nonlocal remnant of antimatter that supervenes & subtends any given heat signature of fundamental energy density (+ 5). (Apparently, this fundamental *heat signature* always masks the *contragradient representation* with which it is associated, just like *existence before essence*, with the collapse of the wave packet leading to slow-breaking asymmetry, or, 4 & 6 + 5). Otherwise, on various levels of analogy, one has the Higgs mechanism, quantum mechanical effects, virtual phonons & photons, Heisenberg's uncertainty principle, an exciton, superfluidity, atomic spin moment, intertial force & microgravity, a pion triplet, etc. Statistically, we are dealing with the hypothetical median (4 & 6) of a parametric fulcrum that is biologically proprioceptive for an individual entity's moral compass. And, for AI, it is possible to fit the asymmetrical feedback patterns of exosystemic information, from an external means, into a local context, in the right direction, as a progressive disposition. Hence, concerning the EPR thought experiment, the hidden nonlocal function of 4 & 6, as the Arrow of Time, acts in the same direction as the Space Vector (11 & 9), and thereby supports the orientation of the Explicit Formation of the Paradigm shift (+ 5). In philosophical terms, the mediatrix (4 & 6) is the Pivotal Experience of the Sign of the Times, in the Means (+ 5), that keys a nonlocal principle of least action. In other terms, a paramagnetic womb hole acts as the tunnel effect of magnetic flux, within the local context of electrostatic wave fronts.

But, one might ask when is a six is not really a six? With the traditional syllogisms of 4-5-6 & 11-10-5, the six-ness is locked into a deterministic set that seems to want to make 'why' into a fact of our existence. Then within 6-4-10, it is part of a spin-3 force that becomes the betrayal of Jezebel, or a diva triformis as a prostituted Sublime Self that marks the prejudicial Cone of Ignorance. Other dimensions of six-ness, that we have touched upon include the six-parameter indeterminacy of Susys (No.13), as well as the polymeric hexis of dynamic transitions (No.8). Biologically, these patterns reflect the reticulate transitions of hexagonal cells as an axis of sixfold symmetry, which is optically uniaxial, with the double reflection of one refraction index parallel to, and one perpendicular to the optical axis. (Amazing!) Further, with 4 & 6, 4 is a field & 6 is a particle. However, in the wave train 6 - 5 & 7, the integer 6 represents a harmonic ground state with the leftward, levorotatory chirality of a synthetic, stable radical. And further, with 6 & 8 + 7, the 6 is a field. Hence, although there is no infamous triplet point of 666 within my ten sets of waves trains, there are three sixes that follow the order of particle (in 4 & 6 + 5), ground (in 6 – 5 & 7) and field (in 6 & 8 + 7), *as do all the other orbital shells*, up to Bertrand Russell's three sevens. Still more: it is generally agreed that at least six dimensions are needed for spherical relationships, that three standard deviations allow six degrees of separation, and that an orthogonally coordinated set of three axes has six basic correlations about a ordinal center, with two on each axis. Then there are the six surfaces of a square, the six sides of a honeycomb, and the six portions of a snowflake. With the polymerization of things like benzene rings, etc. I'm sure six-ness is even more extensive. For example, it has been said that within six-dimension spatiality, 'horses like to die alone, because nobody knows which way their souls are going.'

Notwithstanding the foregoing, what I enjoy analyzing is the typology of six fundamental 'types', based upon the Greek pattern of Thanatos, Eros, Pathos, Mythos, Bathos and Ethos. Students of psychology might be surprise to find that Sigmund Freud was also aware of these relationships. In point of fact, he likely had six stages for the complete rendering of Sexuality. Following the Greek pattern, they would be the Nonsexual, Asexual, Phallic, Latent, Anal, and Heterosexual.

Using my wave trains – as above for the three sixes – the absorption of synthetic infinities, based upon even, negative antimatter events, always follows the pattern of particle-ground-field. For example, with 0 & 2 + 1, 2 - 1 & 3,and 2 & 4 + 3, the order for the three 2s is particle, ground and field, which reflects the complementary equivalence of the two compatible systems, of the double light cone. Accordingly, despite having an appositive chirality, bilaterally in a coextensive direction, the emission of analytic infinities, based upon odd, positive matter entities, always follows the same order of particle-ground-field, from small to large (Alain Aspect et al). For example, the three 5s of 4 – 3 & 5, 4 & 6 + 5, and 6 – 5 & 7. Hence, the particle-ground-field patterns of both even events & odd entities follow the same associative order, throughout the full spectrum of the coordination of heterotic strings, with even relationships as devolutionary and the odd relationships as evolutionary. Thus, because of the Crossover Patterns of concomitant absorption-emission characteristics, bilateral wave trains interact through helical recombinations. This rough balancing out, between devolution and evolution, reflects the CPT principle of physics, by which 'charge, parity and time' interrelate throughout complete phasal space.

One does not normally include Outer Fields & Inner Figures, as quantum mechanical nonlocalities, in the ordinal or regulatory development of experience. Coplanar boundaries are treated as the complex matrices of *psychographic oppositions* in the Vertical Mosaic (metalepsis), while we experience gradual behavior through the coextensive *demographic appositions* of the Horizontal Mosaic (prolepsis). Thus, the Vertical Mosaic resembles the orthogonal button of a direct channel or s-channel, and the Horizontal Mosaic reflects the heterotic string of a cross channel or t-channel. Hence, string theory requires both vertical superstrings & horizontal heterotic strings, with the two blending to provide the *space-time objectivity of empirical methodology* (perilepsis). Importantly then, these two systems are primarily a question of convention & code, which, through the expression & instrument, of *cinematics & kinetics*, recombine as empirical experience, based upon the third system as a *kinematic double light cone* (No.7). In the above paragraphs, we have touched upon how the two systems blend together. These recombinant, four-dimensional patterns are the most important aspect of The Human Equation.

As per No.4, there is the very-difficult-to-understand idea of the spin-3 particle (9-11-5) & spin-3 force (6-4-10), for the fixation of the monistic one as a meticulous *triple point* in between. At the center of this idealism, is a coercive orthocentrism as a kind of button hole of reductionism. Politicians and their friends might be looking for financial and legal loopholes, and most people are familiar with the idea of giving someone the third degree or being led down the garden path by an agent provocateur with a fixed agenda. Foolishness & silliness combine through the whimsical, or, the upper cone of stupidity & and lower cone of ignorance pivot upon self-deception, to produce skepticism, pococurantism and relativism. Therein, *coplanar irony* above, as the enigma of sarcasm, reaches down to *coterminal irony* below, as the conundrum of cynicism, and then, the fixation of *ironic detachment* perches precariously in between, as the dilemma of hypermnesia, with indifference and complacency leading through coercion to violence. The hexagon of suspicion locks into closed limit cycles that prevent six degrees of freedom from reaching the *dialogical irony* of the gentle satire of Socratic repartee.

For the physical *triple point*, by controlling temperature & pressure, a dynamic balance within phasal relationships is held in a precarious stasis, as neither a gas, nor a solid, nor a liquid, but all three at once. This momentary three-ness is similar to the Ideal Phase Transition associated with the third-level integrals of SU(3) for the First Principles of Phase IV. And, as one might suspect, third-level integrals also help to sort out the coplanar interactionism of the unlimited hadron zoo in the Vertical Mosaic, as a so-called three-dimensional plane. Better yet, as a normal distribution, Side Effects are naturally spread over *three separate phases transitions*: the ideal gas of Phase I, the ideal solid of Phase II and the ideal liquid of Phase III – without a triplet point combining all Three Phases into one dynamic 'point defect'. A triple point gives the impression of doing commutative combinations & distributive permutations at the same time & place, without giving consideration to the associative development of natural progressions (No.10). Such a triple point is feasible through the careful regulating of temperature & pressure, but not normally encountered in the organic processes of a classically local context. So, the extreme values of the third-level integrals of SU(3), whether vertically planar or horizontally convergent, supervene & subtend the more moderate triplets of field-ground-particle progressions. From the point of view of philosophy, defining the sure answers of Metaphysical Conceit & describing the secure solutions of Metaphysical Humility, focuses upon the gnosis of the safe results of Metaphysical Certainty…in no-man's-land.

While on the subject of a perfect state of Existentialism, it might help to entertain the possibility that there could be, somewhere, an as-yet-undiscovered Rosetta stone for the *Natural Language* (black stone as mediatrix), and/or a universal cipher for the *Laws of Nature* (white stone as generatrix). With two such touchstones forming an ideal triple point, one could & might both 1) find the key to all languages, & 2) come to make amazing technological discoveries. However, rest assured that finding the keys to both linguistic diversity & the general principles of nature will always remain an unfinished symphony. The ambiguity of diatheism & the arbitrariness of dialetheism, only result in the absurdity of claiming to know & understand the Certainty Principle, as though precise Verification of Identity & Validation of Process could & might become an exact science, for envisaging & carrying out perfectly legal protocols. Discordantly then, being too meticulous in conduct, only becomes contemptuous & condemning, of others.

It is just recently, toward the end of the twentieth century, in consideration of the scientific progress of the last hundred years, that it has become possible to even attempt a holistic philosophy. And yet, with the complexity of modern specialization, common sense seems to be again eluding us. The goal of this work is to at least give the reader an inkling of the Certainty Principle, so as to facilitate further improvements in public education. Importantly, it's all of us working together, through the progressive modes of the *hypostatization of dynamic states*, or not at all. Such a state is not a question of simply restating a preexisting condition (hexagon of suspicion), or expecting to realize an ideal state (six-parameter indeterminacy), but a question of constantly working to improve the Human Condition (six degrees of freedom). The best example of hypostatization that I can think of – besides the anticyclonic pattern of El Nino or the Great Red Spot on Jupiter – is the dynamic chemistry of the interplay between stable and unstable *free radicals* (6 – 5 & 7 and 6 & 8 + 7). This pattern, like the French novel *A rebours* (1884), by Huysmans, works in reverse, from the 7th to the 6th orbit, similar to the transmutation of heavier elements through neutron capture. We will be examining this nucleophilic relationship under the heading of the Autonomous Complex. Hexis becomes like swimming against the current, from the 7th back to the 6th orbit, and probably involves nucleosynthesis. Metaphorically, such a countercurrent resembles a dynamic state between almost going off the deep end (6 & 8 + 7) and only being out on a limb (6 – 5 & 7). People often refer to feeling vulnerable between sixes and sevens, which requires that interpersonal relationships work toward improving mutual trust. Personally, I like the expression *the phylogeny of the group* because it involves a process of efficient recomposition, as though God is coming back to us, from the future. Thus *nurturing* the 'accumulative addition' of integral, complex states facilitates the reassemblage of Phase III patterns as viable group relationships.

The perfect instantiations of the complot of casuistry of No.4; with honor & duty becoming an obligation, by imputing the ideal result of a triple point, through the formalism of a three-dimensional plane; merely produces the parallelism of fractal patterns. One has chromaticism above & modulationism below, with the two pivoted about accidentals in between. It's the fractious over the capricious, about the precarious. Note that casuistry, like Dr. Jekyll without Mrs. Hyde, is defined as based upon specious reason, but one must also include spurious logic, in order to picture the ratiocinations by which the implausible & impossible become the improbable. Except that, here & now, the masculine triumvirate usually dominates the feminine diva triformis, just as currently, economic liberalism is fatalistically leading to the volatility of globalization. Something essentially sufficient & substantially necessary can not be allowed to become directly efficacious, for that would be utilitarianism as action at a distance, or the enforcement of a fixed agenda. Discordantly, assuming identity & subsuming automatic progress only produces the dangerous self-confidence of what the French call "*des fremissons prematures*". More appropriately blending the imperfections of diacritical tentativity & contingency, makes allowances for a more gentle spontaneity, that has a lot to do with discovering the appropriate accumulative addition of Integrative Discipline. The false triple point of truism, naturalism and activism, if filtered through an approach that is proprietary, proper and appropriate, can be translated into the reliable, viable and genuine. Here, 'evolution' goes beyond the artificiality of proprietary management and the fostering of basic cooperation, and comes to involve the shepherding and engendering of solidarity, as with Darwin's descent with modification. In mathematical terms, real numbers and imaginary numbers are recombined to produce the complex numbers of complexity theory. There is a natural, built-in double blind involved, so that the brinkmanship of the hexagon of suspicion shifts to the hexis of a dynamic integration as a work in progress. Accordingly, patronage can be seen in a new light, if it avoids benevolent dictation, and encourages the Autonomous Complex of General Guidelines, which speak through the accountability of additive experiences. Positive feedback, from the phylum of the 7th orbit, to the subphylum of the 6th orbit, could give the impression, to Christians that "Easter Sunday comes before Holy Saturday"!? Importantly, here, one prevents the overextension of the apocryphal 8th orbit, which is covered in Christian terms by the Eighth Commandment of thou shalt not steal, as when going beyond the 'point of no return' with unrestrained behavior transference. The term that I use for the outlandish 8th orbit, is 'postscription' (8), which is not to be confused with the matter-of-fact evidence of retrograde postdiction (6-4, my 'description').

As previously mentioned, the Greek system of six types was most likely followed by Freud, when elaborating his six stages of Sexuality. The Greek pattern portrays the traditional allocation of the demonstrative syllogism for the Vertical Mosaic (Pathos-Mythos-Bathos), &, the dialectical syllogism for the Horizontal Mosaic (Ethos-Thanatos-Eros). As per No.13, these two systems are 4-5-6 & 11-10-9, which, as 12, 13 and 14, &, 11, 10 and 9, resemble the last six books (after the original eight) attributed to Zachariah. The problem is that both syllogisms are quite sententious, and humanly, fail to satisfy the supersymmetrical tenet, of naturally recombining to produce the heterosexual third alternative. Interestingly, if we take Freud's equivalence for the Vertical Mosaic, based upon the Greek triad of Pathos-Mythos-Bathos, we get Phallic-Latent-Anal. Translated into modern terms, one has homosexual-unisexual-bisexual, which also matches with fair-equal-tolerant, but, such a sententious series does not set up the *meaningful advocacy* of a progressively dynamic hexis. (Remember…the third force is not really a "force".)

The above pattern reflects traditional epistemology, which because of its inherent flaws has caused considerable Indecision & Confusion. Freud exploited what recombinant characteristics his system could salvage, in support of the resolution of his Heterosexual Stage as ego love (Ethos). For The Human Equation, I prefer changing the traditional six types into three different patterns, which work well together: *six-parameter indeterminacy, six degrees of separation and six degrees of freedom.* For six-parameter indeterminacy, No.13 must be taken to reflect the Wisdom of Solomon's Seal, shown by the two interlacing triangles in No.9. Wisdom is portrayed because six-parameter indeterminacy, through the hexis of Androgynous Reinversion, is prescient of the monotheistic stream of associative co-ordination. (Reinversion occurs because, reversing No.4, the white masculine triangle is base down & the black feminine triangle is base up.) For six degrees of separation, the modern statistical inference of three standard deviations to either side can now be invoked, as 2 – 3 – 4, to the left for Phase I, and, 5 – 6 – 7 to the right for Phase III. (These two Side Effects are the Chinese Feng-Shui, while for Christians they are the New Adam and New Eve.) As shown in No.7, the colors range from yellow to purple, cover the full spectrum of natural progressions, which begin with Event Inception before the 2nd orbit, and ends with Event Horizon after 7th orbit, followed by with the not-allowed 8th orbit. (As previously mentioned, the statistical significance of *crossing over* occurs from the 1st to the 2nd, from nonexistence, and then back again, from the 7th to the 8th.) Effectively, before and after crossing over, outside the range of meaningful space-time, in the nonexistence of the exosystem, black is the twofold deuterotype (10 – 0) and white the fivefold archetype (11 & 9, 9 & 1 and +1). Then, combining the Sequence of the three nonexistent types with the Series of the three existent types, six-parameter indeterminacy more closely follows Greek typology and Freud's complete approach to Sexuality.

However, six degrees of freedom is still a better way to portray typology for complete phasal space. Firstly, the deuterotype and archetype of the Sequence of Speciation cannot possibly be represented, because, as Einstein stated, that arbitrary sequence must remain independent in the external means of the second system. Secondly, each type must reflect a *paired relationship*, which means that the progressions of the eight harmonic states can only be represented by four pairs. In other terms, Phase I is an ideal gas (slow electron), Phase II an ideal solid (semiconductor), Phase III an ideal liquid (conductor) and Phase IV an ideal transformation (rectifier). The first three are natural phase transitions, which, doesn't make Phase IV into an Ideal Phase Transition for First Principles! Winter is just one of the four seasons, and not a holdover from the spatial absolutism of Old World philosophy, with the Book of Nature absolutely separated, in the Ends. The purpose of Construct No.2 is to demonstrate that the phasal relationships of s-shaped domains transition in a way that unifies all Four Phases, and doesn't allow any absolutes (third law of thermodynamics). In other words, the Life Cycle, as a natural system, is always a *blend of both* the Subjectivity of Observation, as the deductive authority of the Book of Scripture, &, the Objectivity of Experiment, as the inductive factuality of the Book of Nature. That is, one is never totally isolated in one's subjectivity, or for that matter, perfectly objective about anything. In other terms, the absolute authority of totalitarian empiricism (inhospitable planification), &, the absolute predictability of objective scientism (violent rectification) are neither appropriate nor viable.

As per No.7, the four causes become genotype (white-yellow), phenotype (orange-red,), holotype (green-blue) and prototype (purple-black). To complete the six types, of six degrees of freedom, as previously mentioned, deuterotype & archetype, located in the Ends, are separate from the main group of four paired harmonics. Such progressions of 'selection pressures' (Phillip E. Johnson) are not just a question of speculative conclusions and/or anthropomorphic projection, but seem to begin at a deeper level, similar to the six-ness advocated by Aristotle's sense of hexis as an Autonomous Complex.

That is, we are dealing with a dynamic state, which cannot possibly become a static New Age philosophy, but must remain constantly emergent, as a New Wave. (Here, we have resolved the question of whether or not Plato's state [6] was just for elitists, or really belonged to the people. In modern terms, the conservatism of pragmatic democracy [down] is just as evil as neoliberalism [up], as per No.4, which is why unscrupulous politicians talk of the 'bipartisan' and the 'nonpartisan', instead of the postpartisan.) The dynamic hexis, of six degrees of freedom, becomes the survival of the fittest, as the descent with modification of the phylogeny of the group, which resembles what I call Phasal Delay. The pooling of techniques, skills, abilities, resources, experience, and research & development, etc. through the brainstorming of synectics, works to ensure that the survival of a community of persons, *becomes a revival!* Hence, the third alternative of Belonging is a better – through the appreciation of humane self-sameness – more viable alternative, as expressed through the dynamic equilibrium of six degrees of freedom. In other terms, the fundamental teleology of the third force seems to be built into the very fabric of the universe, through a hexagonal (senary, 6) pattern.

Reformation, republication, recomposition, revival, etc. are all aspects for the 'rescription' (7) of the New Gospel, for improving our lifestyle, and is based upon the evaluative 'description' (6) of the current Human Condition. In other words, the hypostatization of essence (6 & 8 + 7 to 6 – 5 & 7) will never produce a perfect Gospel, which is why 'rescription' is taxonomically in the 7th orbit. That keeps the Sabbath holy, by not *stealing out*, beyond the apocryphal point of no return in the 8th orbit. Here, we are all vulnerable within a democratic state, between sixes and sevens, with heterosexual saints & angels blending, as the eudaemonic son in harmony with the eusocial daughter. However, the coextensive hexis is always in danger of falling back from the dynamics of thoroughgoing reason, to the static fixation of coplanar reason (controversial) & coterminal logic (conflict) within the hexagon of suspicion. That is, instead of *being caught up* within a fixed set of limit cycles, with the sixth day becoming a question of adulterous psychological closure, the incipient potentials of Whitehead's prehensions must intimate that the six types can only be resolved in a dynamic manner. There is a big difference between the getting even of being vindictive and seeking out the Hallowed Even of vindication. Similarly, mere survival and not necessarily a revival, just as forcing democracy on others could be a backward step. In other words, instead of just the rationalization of modern psychobabble, psychology becomes translated into an actual improvement in behavior. Alvin Toffler takes a similar tack in *The Third Wave* (1980), by projecting a proactive approach that resembles my Phasal Delay, like Einstein's prohibition against taking action at a distance. Such continual emergence, like the modern concept of bootstrapping, is the third alternative of James Gleick's *Chaos, Making a New Science* (1987). The hypostatization of the subliminal third person plural, leading to the Third History, is the next stage of human evolution, and must operate through the Extended Family of six degrees of freedom, and not the traditional nuclear family plagued by the hexagon of suspicion.

Passing from the moral fiber of 'priest', to the dynamic recomposition of 'scribe', or from Read to Write, Northrop Frye's *Great Code* mentions that a "distinctly prophetic third force is not normally recognized (p.136)." In a sense, one is moving from the simple atmospherics of the fractious & capricious about the precarious, toward the Ambiance of Belonging, through the Viability of the Circle of Well-Being. The individual healing circle, as intrapersonal dialogue, must break the *vindictive miracles* of the hexagon of suspicion, and join the healing circle of viable group dynamics as the hexis of interpersonal dialogue. The TTPs of this third force reflect being happy, healthy and prosperous, based upon the vision, judgement and consideration of individuals who have learned to share their worth, weight and influence. It's not a question of making one's point, driving home a particular viewpoint, giving something the right twist, or hiring the best spin doctors. If people think that a three-dimensional plane justifies being utilitarian, that uniform depth can actually be seen and experienced, that there are three spatial dimensions and one of time, or that the universe began upon one occasion, then ***some triple point is putting too much English on the cue ball.***

Interestingly, in the previous paragraph one gets a feeling for the Hindu third eye as an avatar that is the continuous incarnation of a developing entity, rather than the fixation of an identity. Of course the third eye should recombine both patriarchal & matriarchal syllogisms, without turning about token half-measures. Then, three-ness shifts away from a *prepossessing, codependent confidence game,* toward the *unprepossessing self-confidence* of mature individuality. This apotropaic impetus, like Aristotle's anagnorisis, tends to imbue all aspects of life with a halo effect. And then, whether or not we choose to become part of the enlightened elite of Plato's dynamic state, there is in the *third force* a sense of the Autonomous Complex, without the need for any sort of benevolent dictatorship. Psychologically, one must move from the agape of party hardy, to the irenic state of a peaceful downstream location. Proactively, chemical metaphors invoke the reception of *senary polymerization* (hexgonal six-ness, as per No.8), by moving beyond linear polymers, to the hybrid states of set-growth polymers. Chemical transitions reflect the triplet 'substitution, elimination and addition'. For The Human Equation, these progressive reagent groups involve the volumetric networking of more complex compounds, with free radicals linking stable 'addition polymers' (6 - 7) to unstable 'condensation polymers' (7 - 8). And, as one might expect, going beyond Phase III patterns to working with the exosystemic relationships of Phase IV, one might find a transformation sequence like 'insertion (10 - 11 & 9), deletion (0 – 9 & 1) and permutation' (0 & 2 + 1).

It is a good idea to recall that whether *coplanar, coterminal or coordinated,* Newton once said that it is not possible to solve the three-body problem. Expecting to do so invokes arrogant narcissism that is shameful, guilt-ridden and pernicious. The brighter the light the deeper the shadow, with pivotal tokenism fanning the flames of complicity & duplicity vertically, leading to collusion & conspiracy horizontally. Being untouchable implies that one can be a special person, remain beyond criticism, lead others on a short leash, and, control & deny the universal triplet of omnipotence, omniscience and omnipresence.

Although unattainable, the above TTP is basic to the Consciousness of the Universal Triangle. Nevertheless, through six-parameter indeterminacy, by diacritically recombining three even & three odd relationships, it is at least possible to appreciate the Wisdom of the natural system. Unfortunately, the tokenism of the Hyphenated Person tends to become *prepossessing*, through the cone of stupidity, of Judas (9-11-5) and the cone of ignorance, of Jezebel (6-4-10), &, subsequently *dispossessing*, through the Oedipus complex (5-10) & Electra complex (10–5). For the Gordian knot, *two tautologies* (enigma & conundrum) become *two syndromes* (coplanar & coterminal), resulting in the repression & transference of *two dilemmas*, which become one twin-paradox as a fatalistic four-bladed fan. The implication is that 'one' can actually know & understand (two) answers, solutions and results (three), and then control displacement & deny replacement (four!). Except that, the limitations of monolithic history & monopolistic destiny tend to instantiate the Janus Gate of telepathy & telekinesis, through telepresence & teleportation. The four-bladed fan, pivoting about a fixed point, is the 4-plus-10 pattern of the Greek Hades, or what I call *decussate decuplation.*

With the static equilibrium of No.4, one tends to live in a vegetative state. The pattern is sentiment, sympathy and passion as evasive, devious and deceptive, following the traditional triad of Pathos, Bathos and Mythos. In contradistinction, motile animals must constantly sense their own center of gravity, similar to the floating-point perspective of mathematical rendering. That is, if the dots never really line up, there is no sententious, axiological proof when dealing with natural developments. However, the dual sententiousness of conceptualism & perceptualism, or structuralism & constructivism, can become tokenized as the narcissism of the Hyphenated Person. And then interestingly, because temporal positivism tends to override spatial awareness, civilized people not only seem to become easily disoriented but also exhibit a general loss of personal commitment. The Real Human Adventure gets lost along the way, with people going nowhere quickly. Some sort of revival is the order of the day.

The Crux of Right Choice & Correct Action poses the difficulty of actually placing the Zen nail. About 335 B. C., Aristotle founded the Lyceum or philosophical School of Athens. He and his followers were referred to as the Peripatetics because they had the habit of walking about while philosophizing. Walking is really an act of falling forward and then catching oneself, like the hare and the tortoise, with the first as last and the last as first, or like inhaling…and then waiting to exhale. One might surmise that the *kinesthetic sense* of such a dynamic imbalance became associated with Artistotle's peripatetic sense of hexis. Unfortunately, with the cruciform pattern of the *irrelevant* over the *irreverent*, &, with *irresponsible* to the left and *irresolute* to the right, fixating an impersonal no-spin zone, as a triple point, results in diabolical dissociation. (We can't really be fair, tolerant and equal.) Einstein's pivotal c.c., Freud's parasexual fulcrum and Popper's collapse of the wave packet (4 & 6) are less a question of myopic centrism, and more a question of initiating potentially progressive measures. But, there is always the possibility that the orientation of the psychological mediatrix, under the egalitarian pressures of uniformism, will attempt to pose the Zen nail as a magnetic monopole, without diacritical interpolation. For Xenocrates sensibles, such a pivotal triple point would become anosmic, with the repression of the sense of smell reducing moral attentiveness. (Remember my reference to Muslim clerics saying that terrorists will not even get an odor of heaven.) The proprioceptive sense, of orientation centered within the body, is projected spatially through the kinesthetic sense, and then further extended into space through *olfactory prowess.* (Here we are setting the foundation for learning Sensory Ratios.) Without the incipient orientation of the olfactory sense, there is likely to be an anosmic reaction. It may seem to be an oxymoron, but everyone knows Jung's secret: that only the nose knows. It is best to remain spontaneously sensitive to the nuances of environmental orientation, which, through the tentativity of ambiguous precision, originate with the spontaneous extension of the olfactory sense. In fact the sense of smell seems to be pivotal for the other four senses, and, has a habit of keying old memories.

One is never *sure, secure and safe*, when treating the *answers, solutions and results*, because, like *fairness, equality and tolerance* such measures are generally meaningless. So instead of attempting to determine the coplanar, coterminal and coextensive, in the manner of a myopic triple point, through self-deception or political correctness, we need to reflect upon how to acquire a better outlook. *The aesthetics of Local Adaptations develop from the inner compass of proprioceptive sensations, are extended kinesthetically through the somesthetic sense of Recombinant Adaptations, and then reflected back from the Global Adaptations of the synaesthetic sense.* (Mark this sentence for future reference.) Accordingly, the all-encompassing global context of General Intelligence, as arguing from universal design space, returns from the external six-ness of sphericity, to the within of the inner compass of the sixth sense, and then extends toward the democratic hexis of the Autonomous Complex. Again, here is another set of three sixes, but there is no intimation of axiological proof as a triple six. Without the Femininity of the circular, in the without, the between and the within, the Masculinity of flatness would leave us lost. All dressed up and nowhere to go.

The Maintenance of Innocence is crucial to human motivation. Except that, with the compensation of vertical defense mechanisms, linear, sententious logic is parachuted in, from above-stage (dextrorse), through mid-stage (ambidextrorse), to under-stage (sinistrorse), as the *deus ex machina* of an artificial denouement. (In the upper portion of Construct No.9, I first used the Freudian-like term "ambisextrorse" for this triple point of tokenism, but later found ambidextrorse more suitable for describing the sleight-of-handedness of anathematic retroversion. The latter covers dimensions such as gnosis, a pied piper, nominalism, arcane science, a mole, necromancy, aestheticism, Mythos, Mimesis, mesmerism, the nonpartisan, confabulation, a Trojan horse, a simulacrum, spin doctoring, charismatics, the free-market economy, etc.) With Gestalt brinkmanship governing the Pivotal Experience, the claim is that confusion works, because with disorientation demanding fixation, only those who manage the loopholes get to choose & act, while making others slaves to particular conventions & codes. Discordantly then, exploitation (dextrorse), manipulation (sinistrorse) and coercion (ambidextrorse) become the politics of the obvious agenda (up), the hidden agenda (below) and the fixed agenda (between). The latter, as the orthocentrism of the hexagon of suspicion, becomes the sole prerogative of an agent provocateur, as some kind of linchpin that crystallizes the course of misprision, by invoking the automatic progress of vindictive miracles as a nostrum.

Freud's theory of Sexuality included the parasexual as a center of potentiality (Latent Stage), while the modern term unisexual mirrors an aspect of indifference and complacency as an aspect of pococurantism. There is evident a certain ironic detachment as a stopgap approach that is convenient, expedient and efficacious, but never really a harbinger of better things to come. Such paratactical tokenism requires that opportunism & permissiveness be toggled by an artificial coincidence, leading to an equally artificial convergence. One has the highhanded (dextrorse) over the underhanded (sinistrorse) about the evenhanded (ambidextrorse), resulting in the sleight-of-handed juggling of misfeasance. Thus, the homosexual & bisexual become centered about the unisexual, with no heterosexual resolution on the horizon. It's as though the only alternative to the bipartisan is the nonpartisan. In such a manner, the hypocrisy of selling egalitarianism is the biggest deception of all, because the postpartisan is not included. Using the paratactics of political debate, two antagonists can rightfully demand of each other, "What kind of a twisted game are you playing?" Vertical bipartisanship, centered by the nonpartisan, is a cheap trick for not admitting to the apolitical resolution of postpartisan solidarity, because empowering the people would assure their autonomy. "Polarization", treated through the vertical paratactics of androgynous inversion, politicizes horizontal qualities into the polemics of antagonistic paranoia. Consequently, Northrop Frye's third force of metanoia, as a natural denouement, is always on the verge of becoming a coercive meat grinder, caught between controversial polemics vertically (controversy) & the polarization of cycles of violence horizontally (conflict).

Tragically, each individual, between the ultimatums of unconscious thought (psychogenic) & subconscious emotion (somatogenic), up & down, and the predispositions of selective attention & selective retention, right & left, has to face up to the difficult challenge of self-liberation. The Vertical Mosaic as a psychographic profile, tends to inflate reason to the point of specious reason, & then reduce methodology to the linear, sententious serialization of spurious logic. Effectively then, the superego becomes a legend in its own mind, while the id indulges the suspension of disbelief, with the two centered about the egocentrism of a quodlibetical approach to argumentation. Then, inadvertently, like the button-&-hole pattern of whimsical orthocentrism, *prepossession leads to dispossession*, through the inhospitality & violence of what Christian teachings refer to as Sodom & Gomorrah. And then, despite fancy slogans and rampant patriotism, the disenfranchised, as never green, fail to get through the glass darkly, because of the convincing & converting of Leibnitz's impenetrables & imperceptibles. Casting a jaundiced light, unscrupulous politicians invoke the absolute rule of reason, as their own special band of personalism. Such rampant confidence, as jingoism, becomes infectious, and then injurious. With enough rope to hang everyone, the certainty of personalism instantiates the significant (4), the inviolable (5) and the unique (6). If we fail to learn from history, the fatalism of the Three Fates comes back over and over again.

The triple-braid of Plato's 'cord of reason' has existed long enough to hang most people, due to a lack of vigilance. Witness that Plato's 'three lives' hang vertically like an axiological trice: wisdom (as conceit), goodness (as virtuosity), and pleasure (as self-indulgence). The pattern becomes skyhook, rope and anchor, or, the sententious trivial-trice-trifle, which is based upon the confidence game of sentiment (up), sympathy (down) and passion (between). Perhaps I'm not exercising the Principle of Charity, but the above triplets resemble a three-dimensional plane, like a thermodynamic zeroth of identical temperature gradients, reflecting the assumption that one can place the three vertices of a triangle on one plane of action, like a silver lining with a silver bullet. Because, the one triple point could accidentally shift SU(3) from the orthogonal button to the parametric string, and back again. But, the X of diagonal Crossover Patterns is a double helix that never marks the spot. The coplanar Vertical Mosaic becomes a 'plane defect' with 'boundary difficulties', &, the coterminal Horizontal Mosaic suffers from the anomalies of a 'point defect', due to 'asymptotic freedom'. And, we still haven't gotten to the 'line defect' of coextensive coordination, which is never a perfectly axiological configuration. More later about point, line, plane, circle, etc. They ain't what the idealism of Euclidean geometry has made them out to be.

With Metaphysical Conceit above as the *opaqueness of obviation* (unconscious selective attention), & Metaphysical Humility below as the *transparency of evidence* (subconscious selective retention), Metaphysical Certainty between is too correct (hyperactive remembering) to allow the blending of the ways, of the *translucent experience* of progressive learning. Hence, expecting the perfectly open (full disclosure), transparent (accurate detailing) and clear (immediately comprehensive results), implies Metaphysical Certainty. Naturally, such unrealistic self-esteem absolves one of any sort of accountability, with misfeasance leading to misprision, from collusion to conspiracy. That is, too much emphasis upon the vertically *psychographic* blocks the development of the horizontally *demographic.* Thus, Gestalt brinkmanship makes metalepsis into a trice as an up-&-down needle, without cloth (leftward devolution) and thread (rightward evolution), for translating the hypermnesia of prolepsis into the progressive measures of perilepsis. Only when the 4-5-6 of vision, virtue and vice mature as happy, healthy and prosperous (4 & 6 + 5) will the artificial fit of the 'one' become the natural fitness of the 'we'.

Certainly, Plato's *Republic* appears to anticipate the Third History of a *free & open system*, but the 'that' of his *eugenics* & the 'this' of his euphenics might & could make his dynamic state into the casuistic restatement of elitism. The question becomes, is Plato's 'philosopher king' a eudaemonic elitist, who through noblesse oblige, has a preference for the eusocial as a dynamic state that reflects Aristotle's moving cause? That is, are the Greek elements (earth, fire, air and water) merely four nails in the coffin? And, in contradistinction, do Aristotle's four causes (material, formal, efficient and final) untie the Gordian knot, by resolving the 'this & that' as the democratic 'such and such'? The prepossessing prognostications and dispossessing protocols of a benevolent dictator rarely encourage the unprepossessing empowerment of others. And importantly, the hypocritical tolerance of pretending to treat people equally does not make muster with the greater benefit of pooling their diverse skills and abilities. In other terms, the self-preoccupied *awareness of individualism* tends to block the *recognition of otherness,* and thereby prevents progressive, *attention to individuality.* Otherwise stated, preclusive awareness & retroclusive recognition must not become censorial, so that attention is sustained bilaterally, for the efficient co-ordination of in-depth learning. Thus, the parental generation of Phase I, as Eudaemonic Deconstruction, and Generation X of Phase III, as Eusocial Reconstruction, are coextensive from the New Adam to the New Eve, with the one becoming the other, as the we of the Recombinant Third Person, because the 'such and such' originates from the co-ordinated ***Double Passover*** of 'this & that'. It is only now, with the eudaemonic and eusocial (Phases I and III) as buffer zones between Plato's eugenic & euphenic (Phases IV & II), that the hexis of dynamic equilibrium has the potential for realizing a truly democratic state. For example, contrary to early management theory, an extremely efficacious workplace is not really efficient!?

Crossover Patterns operate at many conjugally paired levels, with the Certainty Principle of the Two Competencies only manifested through the experiential growth of the kinematic double light cone (No.7). For the most part, the surnatural system of The Human Equation, for the *expression of identification* & the *instrumentation of process*, must mimic the natural system, so that the independent right choices & correct actions of co-ordinated relationships come to support the Autonomous Complex of Popper's 'open society'. However, the hard veneer & soft underbelly of civilization often institute a casuistic power complex, between the *irrelevant assimilation of self-amputation & irreverent acculturation of personal oblivion*, or Pathos & Bathos, as realism & altruism. (Realism is the Apocalypse Now as necrology & altruism is Armageddon as necrophilia, with the two centered by the necromancy of the Sodom of inhospitality leading to the Gomorrah of violence: a basic Gordian knot.) Discordantly, this dualism of Classical Alienation turns the two systems into a codependent reaction formation, between unconscious intellectualism & subconscious emotionalism, or what is *cathexis* as a closed loop of limit cycles. As the American poet e. e. cummings once intoned, "You pays your money and you doesn't have a choice." One just might pay the ransom note, and still not get a life, having paid the piper for a bill of goods. The toggle pin of our psychological knot, instead of being a universal joint, often becomes the ring in the bull's nose, with an anosmic reaction blocking the natural olfactory sense of *anticipation and orientation.* The kinesic-kinetic animal-machine (Susan Oyama), as my romantic-mechanism, is a this-that pattern which purports to 'channel' casuistically between the metalepsis of *vertical simile* & the prolepsis of *horizontal copula,* when the two are naturally independent. (Coming between us, the channeler of necromancy communes with the dead, to foretell the future and influence choices & actions.) As Xenocrates prescribed, his sensibles & intelligibles are better separated by his reasonables, in the same way that Plato's eugenics & euphenics must be supported by the two buffer zones of the eudaemonic and eusocial. Thus, simile & copular require the appropriate rendering of dialogical irony, in order to avoid the triplet *sarcastic, farcical and cynical,* and espouse the gentle repartee of the *satirical.* That is, if the independence of observation & experiment is violated, they become gridlocked as the legalism of obviation & evidence, centered by a passion for fixing virtual goodness, as the idealism of a *summum bonum,* isolated between sentiment & sympathy. The implication is that 'I' would kill or die, for that. That is, 'one' becomes the self-defeating vicarious experience of virtual reality, like a Hyphenated Person on a celluloid surface, always planning an improbable future that is obsolete before it's begun. Cinematic image & kinetic automatism do not produce kinematic Side Effects, just as Styx & Lethe do not a river make. The sententious 11-10-9 is too retro, &, the sententious 4-5-6 pattern of the triplet of realism-humanism-altruism leaves no room for social progress. If, *synchronism* above, as too obvious, &, *syncretism* below, as too evident, are combined through *synergism* between, as too contrived, then a suspended state of existence places most people under duress. This is J.R.R. Tolkien's Two Towers, which, in No.4, resemble the pattern teepee/wigwam, as two ultimatums.

Unfortunately, most of us are familiar with these patterns, when hoping to get some satisfaction from a public utility company, trying to balance an expensive line of credit with an inadequate investment scheme, or attempting to work amicably within a community league or a condominium association, etc. Likewise, why can the rich avoid taxes and then easily move capital between countries? Why do educational and legal systems not provide equal benefit to all comers? Why do poor people pay the same price for goods and services when they do not have the same purchasing power? Why do many religions not allow women to minister to the faithful? When No.7 does not reflect both the synthetic and analytic within the same system, the efficient cause of Phase III becomes *pulled back* into a tragic loophole that acts like an efficacious meat grinder!?

For the Autonomous Complex, the Test & Trick is to come up with a recombinant dynamic that shares the magnitudes & qualities of the two systems. Such progressive correspondence reflects the recombinant TTP of Xenocrates' sensibles-reasonables-intelligibles. Aristotle echoed these relationships with apotropaic-anagnorisitic-apolaustic, as *workable-efficient-genuine.* Later, about 300 B. C., Zeno of Citium began a school of stoical philosophy, with the idea of avoiding the troublesome dualism of pleasure & pain, which tends to lock into the vertical triplet of joy-passion-grief, like the aestheticism of *exotics-ecstatics-erotics.* Wisely, the Stoics developed their own progressive TTP which had considerable depth: physics, ethics and logic, or, degrees of being, progressive moral action and intelligent design. However, about 450 B. C., Zeno of Elea, a student of Parmenides, denied progressive measures and tended to lock into the closed-loop syllogism of sorites, through the triplets of the vertical mode, like Construct No.1. The modern physicist Stephen Hawking jokingly referred to these vertically unlimited triplets as 'turtles all the way down'. There is still something of value in such soritetic triplets, if one analyses how to shift between scaling levels.

To recoup, the modern example reflects the breakdown of the electromagnetic spectrum into particles, waves and fields as small, medium and large. (As above, the vertical mode is a special case, because what is a particle, ground or field at one level becomes one of the others at another level.) Particles & fields are respectively too small & too large to be experienced directly, while we are all familiar with the wave dynamics of radio, radar, television, x-rays, sound waves, etc. However, particles & fields are not just 'hidden variables' that plague classical existence, they are the nonlocalities of substructure & superstructure, that we come to experience through the infrastructure of waves. Thus the interplay of particles, waves and fields makes up the fundamental TTP of Inner Particle, Middle Ground State and Outer Field. And, if No.7 is viewed from the left or the right, as two very different, bilateral tendencies that are antithetical in nature, the Crossover Patterns of the triplets of wave trains produce the kinematic double light cone. That is, progressions of even wave trains moving leftward have odd fields & figures, and progressions of odd wave trains moving rightward have even fields & figures, with each set of variables maintaining the unitarity of the universe. Importantly, for any representation of the triune patterns, there is never a distinct separation or a perfect convergence, of essential & substantial characteristics, whether treated as a vertical hierarchy (psychographic) or a horizontal process (demographic).

In Construct No.10, Being is erroneously divergent as Fission (red-green Atomic Sign) & Non-Being erroneously convergent as Fusion (black-white Atomic Symbol). It's all donkeys & horses, with the impotent mules of the 'electromagnetic pulse phenomena' (white-yellow-orange-red and black-purple-blue-green diamond shapes) placed in a secondary role as ancillary *aftereffects.* That is, with explosions being so explicit & implosions so implicit, there are no livable Side Effects.

As per No.12, the Four Resonances are better kept in equal proportions. In contradistinction to No.10, Construct No.11 exaggerates the race between the hare and tortoise, giving predominance to electromagnetic properties (two cubes), while matter & antimatter are held in abeyance (two diamonds). (There is no point in advocating a particular cure for a disease if the side effects are first to kill the patient.) No.12 gives the Four Resonances equal billing, which provides the checks & balances appropriate to our level of existence. With No.10 and No.11 together, the up-down & down-up pattern of the simile of metalepsis, and the left-right & right-left pattern of the copula of prolepsis, become the reductionism of the four nails in the coffin. The Buddhist Four Noble Truths of No.12, as the most fundamental maqam, if translated by No.4, become misinformation & disinformation, &, misrepresentation & misdirection. As decussate decuplation (4 + 10), the Four Resonances collapse onto one plane of quadrupole action, instead of maintaining the seasonable development of the Four Phases. The result is a diabolical embolism between the parapsychological axioms of atheism (9-11, above, as heresy) & the paranormal principles of agnosticism (6-4, below, as blasphemy), centered by the Gestalt sausage as the incommunicable certainty of gnosis (5-10 & 10-5, between, as infidelity). (The Gestalt sausage plays both ends against the middle, like the two-headed amphisbaena…which produces the double standards of injustice.) Historically, the static universe tended to inflate reason in the Vertical Mosaic, as a psychographic fixation for metalepsis, while cosmic censorship in the center reduced logic to a linear axis in the Horizontal Mosaic, making prolepsis into action at a distance, as an axiological proof. The fourfold pattern becomes the parapsychological & paranormal (up & down), and paranoia & paralogism (left & right). The result is the cruciform Gordian knot of telepathy, telekinesis, telepresence and teleportation, with no efficient cause for the *teleonomic progressions* of the sabbatical perilepsis of a prosyllogism (7th orbit).

As per No.4, the synchronism of the upper triangulation forms between the coexistence of *naming, meaning and coincidence* (9-11-5). 'One' usually calls this upper, masculine triangulation *concept formation*, which resembles Aristotle's 'abstract species'.

Unfortunately, defining this unconscious sentiment of revisionism becomes predatory. Hence, Aristotle's 'levity' must be ruled by William of Ockham's (English scholastic 1285-1347) 'Law of Economy', or else Freud's 'condensation' of the superego will produce the specious reason of the parapsychological telepathy. This is the preconditioned feeling of déjà vu produced by selective attention. Reverting from Mr. Jekyll to Mrs. Hyde, the syncretism of the lower, feminine triangulation is between *practice, belief and principle* (6-4-10), with linear methodology providing a solution that begs the question of selective retention, for the maintenance of a false belief as prejudicial evidence. Here we are dealing with the *suspension of disbelief* as a paranormal phenomenon. The unrestrained sympathy of revolution becomes the Bathos of an anarchistic dark humor that emotionally undermines more moderated feelings. (We have touched upon the prevalent aesthetic currently being advocated by Hollywood, as a kind of Social Anus of uncensored profligacy. We must ask ourselves, when is 'freedom' not really freedom?) Appropriately, Aristotle's 'gravity' must be restrained by Ockham's 'Law of Parsimony', or Freud's 'displacement' of the id will produce the spurious logic of paranormal deviousness. (Ockham's Law of Economy & Law of Parsimony, unfortunately, became bastardized as the all up & all down of specious reason & spurious logic, with the two centered about the nonexistent sausage of *nominalism*. In modern terms, people speak, mostly with misunderstanding, about '*Occam's razor*'. The reference is to living on the edge [up] or falling through the cracks [down], with the devil's polymer of these fractal extremes becoming focused upon operations that are 'nominal', and have no natural Side Effects. It's the codependent love of the sun & the moon, and little room for humanity.). In toto, irrelevance above (9-11) & irreverence below (6-4) becomes centered about reductive indifference & violence, or the irresponsible & the irresolute (5-10 & 10-5), with complacency leading to war. The definition of laws & denotation of principles, vertically, are focused through synergism, to become the combinations & permutations of coincidence & convergence, or the controversy & conflict of bipolar dissociation.

Hence, what is falsely obvious & evident, as telepathy & telekinesis, becomes the egocentrism of a self-preoccupied telepresence & self-serving teleportation, or immanentism & interventionism. In other terms, when the bad habits of unconscious intuitions (9-11 as retrodictive paramnesia) & subconscious instincts (6-4 as retrograde anamnesia) collude as answers & solutions, then the self-contradictory behavior of the Hyphenated Person (5-10 & 10-5) results in a quodlibetical conspiracy of double standards. (Monopoly game: do not collect $200, and go directly to jail.) Paradoxically, passionate commitment turns *conceit, humility and certainty* into the implausible, impossible and improbable as the Three Fates. That is charm, glamour and glory, become the Forgetfulness of *paramnesia, anamnesia and hypermnesia.* Generally, purposeless behavior ensues, by jumping from aestheticism to adventurism. Somewhere between the application of *self-amputation* as defining answers & the methodology of *self-oblivion* as describing solutions, is the unconscionable result of *prepossession* leading to *dispossession.* One has T.S. Eliot's 'dissociative sensibility'…as not being consciously diacritical in *Right Choice & Correct Action.*

One example comes to mind, when we realize that specialists tend to find what they are looking for. For such a pattern, there is no real surprise, if police officers fabricate evidence against the innocent, lawyers liberate the guilty, newspapers hawk self-righteous indignation, or brokers leave the small fish holding the bag: a strange set of Two Towers as a double standard. Thus, without the Presence of Mind of conscious volition, the implications of unconscious complicity & subconscious duplicity result in always claiming to be innocent, through the unconscionable, vicarious experience of virtual goodness. Then, while apologizing profusely, behavior becomes seditious.

Polemics cycle vertically between the paratactical *tautologies* of sarcasm & cynicism (up/down & down/up), with the two combing as the one *syndrome* of skepticism, leading to the anathematic repression of an accusatory attitude toward others. 'Heads I win; tails you loose. I'm innocent; you're guilty.' In other terms, the up/down of parapsychology & the down/up of the paranormal combine as the vertical syndrome of contempt (mock) leading to condemnation (attack). Horizontally, the two tautologies of indifference & violence (left/right & right/left) interpolate to become the one syndrome of automatism, installed between *preclusive recognition & retrogressive transference* (eternity & singularity). Finally, the vertical & horizontal syndromes interact as the two dilemmas of a Mistake, in statement & action, through misrepresentation & misdirection. Under these terms, Goethe's double sanity check no longer applies. To restate: when the two dilemmas of *infallibility & immutability* interact, they set up the bipolar twin-paradox of *immanentism & interventionism*, or what becomes *untouchable inviolability*. The Crux of Right Choice & Correct Action turns diabolical, with absolute certainty leading to the conviction that life is absurd. In modern terms, 'reality shows' are really a disguised form of telepresence & teleportation, which violates the humanity of others, through disdainful observation & censorial condemnation. So much for the checks & balances of democracy! If the mediatrix & the generatrix do not key the nexus & the plexus, then all hell could & might break loose. Therein, as a twin-paradox, attention is recursively directed toward the Thin Man, and away from the Fat Lady, which breaks down the potential for knowing & understanding the humanity of self-sameness. Then, discordantly, one might also fail to notice that self-sameness is embedded within co-ordinate systems, at every level, throughout the whole universe.

Here, it might help to look once more for a global perspective. Early cosmogonic systems were likely of Middle Eastern influence. About 700 B. C., Homer wrote the epic poems of the *Iliad* and the *Odyssey*, and although glorious ideals dominated his writing, it was his talent for parabolic revelation that immortalized his works. Subsequently, Hesiod wrote the *Theogony* about the pantheon of the twelve gods of the Council of Olympus, with Hestia (13), Hades (14) and Hermes (15) finishing off their numerological taxonomy. Hermeneutically then, Hesiod's writings reveal a numinous confluence of relationships, which is similar to my Life Cycle, in that Hesiod sought to reveal 'anything about the past, and what anybody might wish to know about the future'. (Remember, anything and anybody are the viable Side Effects of Phases I and III, as the symbionts of neither and both.) Many Greek myths, like the space-time limitations of a Greek play, began with the tragicomic cycles of circadian rhythms (24 hours), based upon the reductionistic quadrilateral tetrad of earth, fire, air and water (my pattern of orange-red-green-blue). Likewise, the work of the physician Hippocrates (ca. 460-377 B.C.), extended by the theories of Galen (ca 129-199 A.D.), advocated the equilibrium of the four main body fluids: yellow bile as choleric (orange), blood as sanguine (red), phlegm as phlegmatic (green) and black bile as melancholic (blue). These physiological relationships could be treated vertically as a single psychographic profile, or, become demographically coextensive like Aristotle's four causes. That is, they could either become combined as coplanar coincidence & coterminal convergence, through reductionism (4 + 10 as Hades), or, be resolved bilaterally as a coextensive progression between anything as Deconstruction (hardware), and anybody as Reconstruction (software).

As per No.2, the four humors were usually treated physiologically, by stretching them out to represent the ideal health of the universal Reclining Figure, in the manner of the Four Phases. Hesiod eventually had bilateral figures intertwined, with his Four Ages moving in two directions, for both devolution and evolution. The Egyptian ankh apparently only represented the Reclining Figure as evolutionary, or analytically masculine. Similarly, the ancient designation of the four seasons relates to the modern rendering of complete phasal space, but with the Four Phases being dominated by the logical positivism of temporal dominance. This same fourfold progression was mirrored by the extended range of Hesiod's Four

Ages of gold, silver, bronze and iron, which followed the popular theme of falling out of grace, through the devolution of self. However, as mentioned, Hesiod eventually included an antithetical flow of four positive transitions, with the goal of reaching a Golden Age, through the evolution of self. Likewise, Buddhists have their Four Noble Truths, Hebrew traditions advocated the unspoken tetragrammaton of YHWH, Christians have a diatessaron for the Word of God, and Muslims have the fundamental maqam of Alif. Lam. Mim. Sad. Interestingly, the Chinese pattern of earth, fire, air and metal, extended by the Side Effects of Feng-Shui, as wind and water, is surprisingly similar when one considers that the 'heavy metals' fall within the same phasal range as the conduction of the ideal liquid: i.e., in Phase III.

Further, following a pattern resembling the hermetic taxonomy of Hesiod's pantheon of gods and goddesses, the decalogical nomenclature of the Hebrew Ten Sephiroth and the Christian Ten Commandments are not just randomly thrown together. All three are a most-remarkable floating-point perspective for doctrinal ordinances which allow *initiates* to anticipate the changing conventions of the moral rule (Popper) as a developmental process. Unfortunately, through the traditionalism of pharisaic theocracy, progressive modes tended to become translated into the dogmatic certainty of moral fiber, with the shortsighted goal of imposing acceptable behavior on the uninitiated, through benevolent patronage. (Remember, without the double light cone, of man and woman lying down together, the double helix will not work.) Importantly, the secularization of modern scientific taxa that developed extensively in the nineteenth century, whether mathematical, physical, chemical or biological, essentially followed the same decalogical set theory as ancient traditions. Thus, ten-dimensional space-time is an excellent mnemonic aid, which has the added bonus of overcoming the inefficiency of classical education. More recently, progress has been made with the development of the psychology of relationships, and, also with quantum mechanical statistics – for adding in higher & lower levels of dimensionality. Both of the foregoing are strikingly similar to recent developments in string theory, which generally follow decalogical patterns. Unfortunately, modern specialized education is becoming prohibitively detailed, and thus we need to reincorporate traditional memory aides in order to popularize increasingly complex ideas. It is precisely because I cracked the conventions & codes of ancient modes of learning that I have succeeded with Metalogical Constructs, whereas my immediate scientific forebears cut themselves off from the older, apparently alchemical methodologies. Importantly, the modern information explosion currently demands the synoptic approach of just such geometric progressions, wherein spirituality and science are in harmony with each other, so that, one form of revival is accompanied by another.

Central to the above problem, is the recognition of a personalized form of tangible progress, which replaces the idealism of a Supreme Being, *with universal design space as the prime mover.* That something is not just another pretty face in the sky, that one would like to scratch, to see if it is real. The first thing that unscrupulous religiosity offers the public is the prosopopoeia of a personalized god, knowing full well that the self-recursive reflection of the god-that-looks-like-me pattern is the most seductive, because 'I get to do whatever I please'…with impunity of course. What mature spirituality offers, is a monotheistic approach toward personal involvement in shared experience, without the assimilation of socialism and/or the acculturation of individualism. Naturally building up an individual's realistic self-esteem motivates commitment to in-depth learning and encourages healthy social involvement. In other words, learning to fit in proactively to the mainstream of human developments is central to the Real Human Adventure.

Nevertheless, concerning universal design space, the exact Laws of Nature, as the apodictic Certainty Principle, will always be beyond our complete realization. That is, the supersymmetrical fifteen-ness of Hermes Trismegistus & Hestia, together, by way of the recombinant caduceus, must not become the coterminal fixation of the triangle of masculinism over the triangle of feminism (Construct No.4). Discordantly, instead of producing the solidarity of the Recombinant Third Person, the Test of Wills & Trick of Necessity are the 'toil & trouble' of a real so-and-so, who just might be a lawyer, a politician, a doctor, etc. – despite a so-called higher education. (It seems that there are despots in every profession, which makes one wonder about the denatured state of education.) Even though Verification & Validation seem perfect in themselves, the actuality of observation & experiment, when seeking Right Choice & Correct Action, is generally ambiguous & arbitrary. And yet, almost every time, one falls on the sword for punctiliousness of bastardized legalisms, which imply the definition of perfect obviation & the exact description of factual evidence. Better yet, once one overcomes the classical barrier of trying to control the Test & deny the Trick, as a Double Passover, the anagnorisis of self-resolution promotes *a more humane approach to objectifying evidence.* The question is how to become anointed by the 'sacred oils' that promote this beneficent transition toward the acceptance & facilitation of Associative Justice?

The ancients were adept at portraying the benefits of spiritual enlightenment. For example, the apotropaic rendering of the Greek caduceus reflects the supersymmetrical pattern of 11-10-9 (globe with two wings) over 4-5-6 (two snakes around a rod), which is epistemologically similar to Construct No.13. A slightly better model, the Wisdom of Solomon's Seal, shown in Construct No.9, takes the androgynous inversion of No.4, and through Androgynous Reinversion, returns to the associative production of a continuously 'altered state'. Both of these recombinant renderings reflect the pattern of six-parameter indeterminacy, wherein no particular triplet is allowed to be completely odd or completely even. That is, the Living Metaphor must be based upon the compatibility of bilateral and coextensive co-ordination. Because of the implausibility & impossibility of producing a hermaphroditic golden stature, Hermes & Hestia are eternally separating out (neither) and coming together (both), through the polymerization of hexis, as the probability distribution of the Recombinant Third Person. The impersonal idolatry of the 'us' of secular humanism, which advocates melting Romeo & Juliet unisexually together, to form one golden statue, is a reaction formation that condemns both men & women to repeating the mistakes of the past. Accordingly, by restoring a recombinant approach, as working together, while remaining separate in nature, 'we' could & might eventually discover Hesiod's Golden Age. And then, like Jason the Argonaut, through the travails of our Quest, we can & may at least appreciate the Golden Fleece of Right Choice & Correct Action: which are the Christian 'bread & wine'. It's just that, hoping to actually find the 'tree in the sea', as a Certainty Principle, like the treasures of Richard Dawkins' cultural memes, becomes an impossible dream.

As recorded in the Old English poem *Beowulf*, the unclaimed treasures of human culture are guarded by a giant worm. That worm, by all rights, ought to be named "Sequence", because it would have to have at least three parts: head, body and tail, like the chemistry of insertion, deletion and permutation. These hidden threefold transformations reflect the untouchable red-to-green core of Phase IV relationships, split between the two Ends. Thus, the spatial triplet seems to jump across the chimeric sequence of Ought, Ought naught and Might, suddenly, and then begins to curve more gradually, warping around through six fundamental functions: 0 - 9 & 1, 2 - 1 & 3, 4 - 3 & 5, 6 - 5 & 7, 8 - 7 & 11 and 10 - 11 & 9. (Note that all six of the wave trains have leftward chirality: levorotatory.) Then there are four positive dimensions, for matter: 0 & 2 + 1, 2 & 4 + 3, 4 & 6 + 5 and 6 & 8 + 7. (Note that all four of the wave trains have rightward chirality: dextrorotatory.) Chinese philosophy, concerning the 'circle-square', resembles Einstein's reference to the six-four, space-time pattern for composing ten-dimensional space-time. However, keep is mind that from our point of view, in the Square of Existence, the Circle of Space gives the false impression of being linear, and then warping suddenly from pole to pole. That is, life as the Test of Wills in the static universe demands a marriage made hell, by looking for the Trick of Necessity as a perfect, measure-for-measure prediction of linear logic. Woman is either a Fat Lady, who isn't there, or a masculine sosie. And, because our planet Earth has settled down to a relatively static existence, we tend to see matter as full & space as empty. That is, from our biased perspective, as material entities, the more of the substance of space looks like less, and the less of our essence of time seems like more!? Hence, observation becomes biased obviation, &, experiment becomes prejudicial evidence. And, as for the latter, there is a warning concerning the exact Sequence of Phase IV relationships: 'Be careful what you wish for…you might get it.' That is why discovering an exact Sequence is a chimera, as the Final Solution that nobody would want. As the American psychologist Susan Oyama states, "I don't care what."

Interestingly, the idea that 'treasures' were left over after a dialectical sequence of elimination; as the three fundamental outcomes of experiment; was entertained by both Immanuel Kant and Karl R. Popper, as being a 'possible judgment'. That final, functional judgement, for the Necessity of Continuity, may only be rendered by Xenocrates' interacting dyad, based upon the chimera of three arbitrary functions: 10 - 11 & 9 (Ought, the head of a lion), 0 - 9 & 1 (Ought Naught, the body of a goat) and 0 & 2 + 1 (Might, the tail of a serpent). Thus, the ultimate Sphericity of the symbolic Mixed Metaphor is split dyadically, between infinity & singularity, through parity, even though the Trick of Necessity must have at least three terms for the 'gamma sequence'. Parity is the intrinsic *nucleonic division* of the enthalpy of basic matter, shown in No.7 as the red-to-green hourglass of protons and neutrons, split between the two Ends. A given nucleon is made up of a proton and a neutron, but 'ne'er the twain shall meet'. That is, although parity is considered to be the mirror image of an evenly ordered event (10 - 0), apparently the 'optical isomer' is never allowed, because space is split, in an oddly asymmetrical manner, between "red" protons and "green" neutrons. Hence, the SU(3) of the nonperiodic crystal resembles an unfindable golden treasure, which in modern terms becomes the central convergent function of chaos theory, as the omniformity of adiabatic expansion within the gravothermal collapse of diamagnetic standing waves. That is, the Supraperiodic Crystal of Antimatter Resonance (10 – 0, deuterotype) undergoes spontaneous symmetry breaking to produce the five-part nonperiodic crystal (11 & 9, 9 & 1, and, + 1) of plasmic emissions (archetype). (Note that the Sequence of Speciation has three segments, while there are five indeterminate, oddly positive parts.) In other terms, it is necessary to define the Continuity of fundamentally even bosons (10 - 0), by interpreting them as fundamentally odd fermions. Importantly, passing from the infinite 10 through the singularity of 0, to get from environment (11 & 9, echotype) to corpuscle (9 & 1, subspecies), one must complete the triplet of the Sequence of Speciation, by adding on a fifth part, which becomes the *species* of the 'messenger photon': 0 & 2 + 1. In modern terms, the head of the lion is associated with the 'Weyl tensor' (11 & 9), the body of goat with the 'Riemann curvature tensor' (10-0), and the tail of the snake with the 'Ricci tensor' (9 & 1). (Possibly, the Riemann curvature tensor covers all three?) Such primary experience is based upon the First Principles of experiment, which only approximate the Validation of Process, by focusing upon an arbitrary sequence, *and not the actual nature of Continuity itself.* Hence, nothing is perfectly predictable.

To the above "fact", that an even event cannot understand itself, must be added the theory that an odd entity cannot really know itself, to make up the Double Passover that hides the actual Certainty Principle. Importantly, the Missing Link of the Paradigm shift (red-green) is not really missing, only a tentative theory, & the Necessary Link of the Doppler shift (black-white) is not really necessary, only a contingent hypothesis. That is, without & within the *nexus* the Paradigm shift of the Explicit Formation (+ 5), in our existence, is the spatial curl of the c.c. (4 & 6) as a *mediatrix* or 'hole in the wall'. And, without & within the *plexus* the Doppler shift of the Explicit Function (10 -), in nonexistence, is the *generatrix* of matter residuals (11 & 9) as the v.e.d. of a heat signature. In other terms, the generatrix is a *paraelectrical wormhole* within the diamagnetic force fields (10 - 0) of the plexus of Antimatter Resonance (echoes of the poem *Beowulf*). In terms of the light nuclear core, which transposes fundamental protons & neutrons, the nucleonic parity of the deuterotype (10 - 0) contains the enthalpic 'lowest energy state' of the archetype (11 & 9, 9 & 1 and +1) as the Acoustic. In terms of 'Bose-Einstein statistics', for 'time-asymmetric quantum gravity', the Supraperiodic Crystal of the oblate condensate and prolate dilate (10 - 0), between infinity & singularity, produces the twin jets of plasmic emissions (11 & 9 and 9 & 1) for the nonperiodic crystal. Astronomers know these qualities by examining the twinkling of quasars, black holes, neutron stars and other interstellar radiation sources. The universe is always ending and beginning, all the time, in all the space, with neither energy nor mass being perfectly preserved.

The above domain of Femininity, in Phase IV, usually becomes translated as the arbitrary judgements of emotionalism, within the schizothymic downside of Phase II. In the lower portion of No.4, that pseudo-Doppler shift was symbolized by Greek mythology as Persephone descending into Hades. Psychologically, extraordinary theft (8), reverting back, becomes the unique, prejudicial factoid of phenomenalism and fundamentalism (6). Sociologically, the fascist-communist conspiracy (down/up), of an obsessive-compulsive displacement, leads back up to intellectual assumptions, allegorically, from the concrete to the abstract. Persephone must spend at least 1/3 of her annual cycle in Hades, with the repressed guilt feelings of the Sublime Self reverting back up to produce philosophical extravagance. That is, unnecessary secrets rebound to necessitate lies. Effectively, the goddess Medea devours her offspring, because by attempting to make universal values into a phony judgment (perfectly even), she finds her children to be too different (odd fellows). Fascism epitomizes her disingenuous self-justification, because there is absolutely *no tolerance* for dissenting opinions. Pragmatic solutions are predisposed by the narrow methodology of fixed belief structures to give the results that are expected, or else, those results are ignored. Then, with the meritocratic fixation of general principles, based upon the false belief syndrome, the bitter and poisonous side of the hexagon of suspicion, as Death by Drowning, begins to dissolve the larger reality, through rejection. (This breaks William of Ockham's Law of Parsimony.) People come to expect the Band-aid solutions of a quick fixe, which lacks sufficient flexibility and continuity to be really effective. Unfortunately, no one is listening, because the back-formation of sympathetic emotionalism, while appealing to the facts, is not process oriented. (Pick a jury with prejudices that support the data that your side wishes to exploit, and then work to enforce the prejudicial backlash of the suspension of disbelief.) Politically, the conservative side of such feminism constrains general democracy to the reductive limitations of pragmatic social democracy. Jezebel hates evaluation, loves to gamble, can be bought off, has an irreverent sense of humor, and thinks that others are always being sarcastic. Hence, within Freud's displacement of the id, the diva triformis attempts to put a dogmatic *lock on morality*, with the necessary link of ineluctable methodology binding practice (6) to belief (4), by standing on principle (10). Regressive belief structures produce such things as passive aggressivity, industrial melanism, psychotropic dependencies, rumor mongering, the commoditization of values, meritocratic judgements, pretense of tolerance, etc. In other words, the 'synthetic proposition' becomes the false belief syndrome of deviousness, for the prejudicial denotation of evidence as being "the immutable facts". Thus, naturalism entertains the impossibility of agnostic proof, by pretending that 'disproving the negative hypothesis' has sufficient merit to undermine any and all progressive measures, which are treated with the excessive caution of universal doubt. And, when evidence is distorted through the personal prejudice of emotional deviousness, based upon the disingenuous conundrum of duplicity, progressive evaluation is discontinued and selective retention either becomes self-justifying, or simply, 'I don't remember,' subliminal impulses.

As Ockham maintained, excessive caution stigmatizes perspective through the immutable naturalism of reductive parsimony. The lack of self-restraint, through the devil in the details, could join up the dots of apparently impeccable logic, in a linear manner, in the Vertical Mosaic, which is being *silly*. The recidivity of clawback begs the perfect solutions of spurious logic, as a bottom line, instead of supporting progressive measures that facilitate substantial reevaluation. Take warning: actually writing down a constitution, and constantly delaying needed reforms, inhibits the progressive measures of the Autonomous Complex of *dynamic recomposition*, and only pays lip service to 'independence'. A written constitution is great, for nasty gatekeepers, who use delayed judiciality as a rebarbative art form. In most cases, one goes into denial and/or a state of inordinate fear, when ignorance reacts to the unknown, like Alvin Toffler's *Future Shock*. If, through Temporal Infusion, *empty kinetic spaces* are caught vertically between white static pickets, and one fails to run along the fence, then the *cinematic image* will not transfigure as a *translucent kinematic experience* that allows us to see beyond the fence, and glimpse the future. (Mark Twain's Tom Sawyer got others to paint the fence white, while he ate their apples.) Jung's secret concerns the importance of individualism undergoing the "safe" self-resolution of individuality, with vertical synergisms giving way to the nonlinear flow of his synchronicity. Despite the supposition of 'free association', one cannot predict how revelation will affect the inner illumination of individual self-discovery. Xenocrates' support of reasonable opinions is allied with my development of personal opinionation, but the self-justifying nature of personal enlightenment must align itself with the larger picture, because the innocent *mediatrix* within the nexus keys the

Arrow of Time. Hence, the untouchable moral compass of the Maintenance of Innocence in human affairs, to avoid deviousness, is important, and yet most of us accept the prostitution of progressive values. Nevertheless, the chastity of the mediatrix is pivotal to the orientation and direction of the moral compass, for the sake of good judgement. Through its source in the external means of Being, the plexus of the Great Seal (10), which cannot be brought back from nonexistence, is keyed by the generatrix of the Immaculate Conception (11 &9), which returns imperceptibly within the moral compass (4 & 6). Hence, contrary to the subterfuge of Medea (6), Hestia remains true to her virginal nature in the Womb of Theotokos (10), and avoids the *dissembling* symbolized by Persephone descending into Hades, by being the handmaid of Hermes. The Medea syndrome, like crossing the River of Lethe, is based upon the siren call of the nothingness of being, which becomes altruistically suicidal, in order to justify a revolutionary solution. As Non-Being (6), by not 'returning from Nirvana' (10), the Medea syndrome becomes a lockdown that *pushes ideas too far, toward accultural individualism*, and opens up the possibilities of dissolution, depression, preciosity, and anarchy, as a back-formation. (This is George Orwell's 'dystopia'.) Pandora's box becomes the Social Anus of fascistic intent as a hidden agenda, with subconscious repression rebounding, up, to incite the unconscious transference of unrealistic speculations. (Mothers of Medean intent give their sons unrealistic expectations, and then encourage them to become suicidal in behavior, by not giving them a disciplined approach to life.) That is, not having an effective methodology, for coping realistically, produces unrealistic self-esteem – resulting in predictable failure. Persephone became an underling as a lost soul, whereas Hestia restored her virginity by bathing in the spring of Canathus, and in doing so, supported a more honest approach to learning and coping, instead of a directly linear jump to violence, or nothing at all. (If we do not bring our daughters back from the dead, the femme fatale will marry a criminal.) Accordingly, the implicit function, through the Maintenance of Innocence acts like the handmaid of the Lord (4 & 6 + 5), through slow-breaking asymmetry, and overcomes the good-cop/bad-cop syndrome of the sempiternal hexagon of suspicion. Importantly, Hestia (13), as relating to eschatological PRP, rather than the stochastic dark side of things, avoided the criminal fixation of the codependent love of Hades (14) and espoused the liberation of Hermes (15). Hopefully, the passive aggressivity of the self-justifying emotions of dogmatic complaints is overcome, and by avoiding a nihilistic approach, in the Temple of Doom, repressive *belief structures* will not bounce back up to the projection of anxiety structures, with the two colluding to enforce New Age *structuralism.* Starting out as a silver lining, political isolationism has the same regressive "character" as the schoolyard bully, who is removed from the beneficial counsel of others. And so, the "next best trick" is for a charismatic Dr. Somebody to go on television, to offer the nostrum of a silver bullet, that will miraculously cure all their psychic ills.

Philosophically, it is less important to analyze our dreams in an attempt to discover the deep-dark secrets of their mystical meaning, than to follow our dreams toward the larger reality of a better future. That is, doing something based upon the mysteries of the paranormal usually becomes a Temple of Doom that inhibits personal liberation, through a rebarbative individualism that is impervious to new ideas and better methods. The coercive entanglement of the evasive & devious (No.4) merely becomes efficacious, but not yet efficient. However, when the fence of associative production alternates the white pickets of masculine vision with the dark spaces of feminine reevaluation, then the co-ordinated effort of the companion partnership, of the real and the substantial, blends to make up progressive measures. In scientific terms, the positive mathematics of real numbers blends with the negative mathematics of imaginary numbers, to produce what the modern era calls 'complexity theory'. All is certainly very fine & good, and yet it is best-leading-to-better, as associative production, that allows the universe to unfold itself through the ironic interplay of science and spirituality.

As per No.13, the synthetic constituents of a *posteriori logic* (4 & 6, two vertical black lines), are not really a direct solution (10, single horizontal black line), as an identity relation, but involve Heisenberg's uncertainty principle. These intermediate vector bosons, for the correlation of the weak force, are cohomologous constituents that combine the force of gravity (4) & mass density (6), to corroborate the corollary of the electromagnetic interaction as a surface effect (+ 5). (For Christians, Mass is prior to Communion, and otherwise, philosophically, existence is prior to essence. Or, to err is human, but to make amends is godly.) That is, as a one-to-one dissociation for the synthetic proposition of a *posteriori logic* (4 & 6), negative correlations cannot directly derive the essential coherence of a *priori reason* (+ 5), but they do act operationally as its paramagnetic mediatrix. In other terms, for existence, nonlocal Antimatter Resonance, as an Outer Field & Inner Particle (4 & 6), supports the local Middle Ground State of the slow-breaking asymmetry of Matter Resonance (+ 5). The computation of the field effect of SU(2) as the mediatrix of the weak force (4 & 6), for 'aleph-null', always places the superfluidity of the c.c., as a supposed periodic crystal, at the paramagnetic core of existence. The term often used is 'low-entropy core', but recent theories for such nonlocal quantum operatives, through the exponential raising of powers (fields) & extraction of roots (particles) make reference to 'entanglement'. In other terms, the emergence of any given matter particle, always has an inertial frame (4 & 6), based upon the gravitational coupling constant, which is precedent to the slow-breaking asymmetry (+ 5) of a positive energy ground state. Hence, through the convention of the Arrow of Time, even existence is precedent to odd essence, with SU(2) as the 'aleph-null' associated with U(1) as the electromagnetic interaction. Thus, the gravitational coupling constant becomes a Higgs mechanism that gives the gravitational 'weight' of a specific matter particle. A different matter particle has a different weight. For example, 2 & 4 + 3 has the same Constant Unity Factor as say 6 & 8 + 7, to maintain the unitarity of physics, which is the same for all the wave trains, while glass, as compared with steel, has a different unit weight. This is because the spin of the even constituents of the implicit function (2 & 4 or 6 & 8, etc.) vary with the odd orbits of the Explicit Formation (in this case + 3 or + 7), because there must always be an even/odd *equivalence* within the same wave train triplet. Thus, even constituents have a reductive resonance based upon a *paramagnetic absorption spectrum* (No.13, two black lines combined) that is closed, in association with an odd orbit.

As above, there is a kind of 'least squares law for magnetism' that acts in a paramagnetic way for the *diffusion of even doublets*, as reductive constituents, and a 'least squares law for electricity' that acts in a diamagnetic way for the *diffraction of odd doublets*, as the expansive constituents of a fine structure constant. For magnetism, one gets the gravitational couple constant – that functions as the ubiquitous Higgs mechanism – to give the relative gravitation force & mass density that is associated with the odd orbit of a specific matter density. For the odd orbit, the chirality, by convention, is rightward or 'up'. For electricity, one gets the fine structure constant – forming an odd emission doublet – to provide for the gamma signature of synchrotron radiation, which is associated with the even orbit of a mass density. For that even orbit, the chirality is, by convention, leftward or 'down'. Therefore, for a pattern like 2 – 3 & 5, the *a priori logic* of 2 – (even orbit) is associated with the *a posteriori reason* of 3 & 5 (odd spin).

Importantly, SU(2) - U(1), as even spin + odd orbit, does not relate directly to the uncountable, or non-denumerable 'aleph-one' of the real number. Through Georg Cantor's theory of transfinite numbers (ca 1896), the cardinal numbers of an even spin doublet are associated with an odd orbit, so that SU(2) resembles a cardinal subset and U(1) the real ordinal integer of the set associated with it. That is, an infinite cardinal subset, as a resonance of field/particle nonlocality, is a vertically infinite direct channel of cardinality, that is associated with the horizontal ordinal set of a given integral force, as a horizontal cross channel of positive, classically local energy. Of course that particular wave train triplet, being constituted as imaginary, and associated with a real integer, is an example of an ordinal progression of transfinite, complex numbers. And from the point of view of matter waves, there are four dimensions of positive integers: 2 & 0 + 1, 2 & 4 + 3, 4 & 6 + 5, and 6 & 8 + 7, with the SU(2) of 'aleph null', in each case, associated with the respective U(1) as 'aleph one', of which 4 & 6 + 5 is a special classification, being of central significance for the Paradigm shift. *Importantly, one cannot directly identify the transfinite 'aleph one', in each case, by calculating the cardinality of its vertically infinite, field/particle subset.* Make sense? In simple terms, nonlocal resonances of field/particle correlations do not determine the corollaries of wave ground states (donuts in the middle), whether the latter have either an odd or an even chirality. In other terms, we must keep in mind that all wave train triplets are actually complex numbers (partly imaginary and partly real), with either even constituents and an odd force, or an even force and odd constituents.

Georg Cantor's pioneering work with transfinite numbers, which led to the Theory of Transfinite Numbers developed about 1915, fits into my Construct No.7 in a most remarkable manner. It is also a match for Niels Bohr's 'seven allowed orbits'. Importantly, one doesn't have to be a mathematician to appreciate the transitions of transfinite numbers: 1) whole, 2) natural, 3) rational, 4) cardinal, 5) real, 6) imaginary and 7) complex. This sequence of seven "orbits" is also similar to the ten categories of the set theory of mathematics, and presented what was called 'the continuum problem', which relates to the natural taxonomical systems of development that I'm constantly referring to as The Human Equation. More later.

Interestingly, because we must generally deal with positively real matter forces, it is notable that the field/particle pattern of odd constituent doublets emits a *gamma resonance* (high frequency virtual photons) based upon a *diamagnetic emission spectrum* (No.13, two

This page needs a major rewrite: The author: HFP.

horizontal white lines associated with the dark spectrum). In contrast, the field/particle pattern of even constituent doublets imprint a *gravitational well* (reductive virtual phonons) based upon a paramagnetic *absorption spectrum* (No.13, two vertical black lines associated with the light spectrum). That is, even nonlocal quantum operatives are paramagnetic, or dielectrical (2 & 4, 4 & 6, 6 & 8, etc.), and odd nonlocal quantum operatives are diamagnetic, or paraelectrical (1 & 3, 3 & 5, 5 & 7, etc). (Of course, the light & dark spectrums blend to make up the space-time object of complex relationships, as mirrored by the claim that supersymmetry allows bosons to be transformed into fermions, and vice versa.) Thus, within a given wave train triplet, the Even Middle Ground State of an Explicit Function (black donut) is tied to its appropriate fine structure constant as an odd field/particle formation (white milk without & within), with the two together as Continuous Space modulated by discontinuous time. That is, classically local space is modulated by quantum operatives that are temporally nonlocal. Hence, the fine structure constant is based upon the diamagnetic quantum entanglement of the reciprocals of negatively charged, odd constituents, made up of the synchrotron emission of gamma radiation as an *energy transport phenomenon* (e.g. 6 – 5 & 7). Some examples of the synchrotron emissions of gamma constituents can be used to build up degrees of 'quantum dots' between the field/particle pairs of negative charges, to form a lasing medium, in the vertical mode. The latter acts like a diffraction gradient that is trapped between parallel crystal lattices. In other terms, an Even Middle Ground State (black donut) is a positive nucleophilic mass density with electrophilic substrates as its field/particle reactions (milk without & within). For example: 2 – *1 & 3*, concerning the slow electron insulator and a single-electron transistor (SET); 4 – *3 & 5*, in relation to the proton and a bipolar-joint transistor (BJT); 6 – *5 & 7*, a stable free radical with heterolytic electron reactants (odd pair); etc. I'm still thinking about 8 – *7 & 11*, because the 8th orbit is generally unstable and is associated with the high frequency gamma radiation of the 'ultraviolet catastrophe', beyond the fringe of existence, at the point of no return – after *crossing over* the Event Horizon, toward nonexistence. Importantly, the 8th orbit can easily pitch up or down, to a more complex or less complex atomic structure, depending upon environing conditions. Certainly, the 8th orbit is unstable and can never be completely filled. Finally, as infinity and singularity, which provides for the spin-2 standing waves of a potentially magnetostatic ground state, 10 – *11 & 9* is associated with 0 – *9 & 1*, so that *11 & 9* and *9 & 1* become the twin jets of Hawking radiation, for what Roger Penrose calls 'time asymmetric quantum gravity'. I think of *11 & 9* and *9 & 11* as, together, making up the diakinetic 'constant of kinetic velocity', which becomes the v.e.d of a heat signature within the true Doppler shift of supergravity, in deep space. So, the constant of kinetic velocity, as paraelectrical within a truly diamagnetic wave function convergence, is a special kind of fine structure constant (small red-to-green hourglass in No.7) called Planck time or Planck length, that involves the superconduction of c^2.

By way of summary, whether a mass density or an energy density, a given Middle Ground State (donut) is treated classically as *a polynomial development of algebraic numbers.* (The four seasonable qualities of algebra involve: subtraction for Phase I, multiplication for Phase II, addition for Phase III, and division for Phase IV.) Further, each of these integers, of classical Middle Ground States, whether a mass density or an energy density, has associated with it an Outer Field & Inner Particle that is treated *exponentially, in the manner of quantum operatives.* Thus the classical develops the polynomials of a horizontal cross channel, and the quantum works with the exponents of a vertical direct channel. Ergo! the question becomes whether or not SU(3) should be locked into the orthogonal plane of the Vertical Mosaic, as in Construct No.1, with the Horizontal Mosaic reduced to a threefold button hole, or should we go with Construct No.7 as the third system, because it is not only an associative production, but also includes both classical and quantum dimensions? If we restrict ourselves to the third-level integrals of the vertical Hyperplane, with SU(3) as a single symmetry classification, because it works well for the interactionism of particle accelerators, it could explode in our faces, by making SU(5) into a fission bomb! As Carl Gustav Jung intoned, "To think that energy is friendly, is naïve." Hence, if we go with Zeno of Elea, and exploit the soritetic syllogism of vertical triplets, as field around ground, and ground around particle, then 'rings within rings' extend infinitely from a macroscopic circumference, through a monolithic middle, down toward a microscopic center. Interestingly, any given 'ring', as in No.1, can, depending upon the triplet chosen, be a field, a ground, or a particle. Thus, shifting up or down in scale, exponentially, is covered by the Vertical Mosaic, but the *fourth dimension of polynomial experience* cannot be modeled by the idealism of the so-called three-dimensional plane, as the assumption of the 'aleph one'. In other words, if we try to consolidate the Paradigm shift & the Doppler shift, by reducing the latter to a mere button hole, then the metaphysical existentialism of empiricism takes over as structuralism, followed by the evolutionism of scientism as constructivism, and we are all in deep doo-doo. It's the contemptuousness of the static universe & the warmongering of cosmic censorship all over again. One cannot isolate the spiritual from the scientific.

To reprise, in contrast with the above, 4 & 6 + 5 is a *special case* where the paramagnetic weak force (4 & 6) is associated with the electromagnetic interaction of slow-breaking asymmetry, as the real Paradigm shift. That is to say, one does not fixate SU(5) (shown in No.12) as a nominal operation for a perfect state of existence, because 'aleph one' is ideally based upon + 5, which is a *transfinite real number* as the infrastructure of a *noncomputable ground state*, due to the law of excluded middles. (The White Donut as the Middle Ground State of the toroid of *special relativity*, is dunked in the coffee of its Outer Field & Inner Particle.) Hence, Theory itself, as pure Reason, is always shifting, and is unnamable, because it cannot be tied down to a particular Classification. (New donuts are being baked and old ones are being eaten away.) Classification has been traditionally interpreted in a hyper-theoretical, categorical manner, in that if the Hyperplane could really be fixed, it would be a single symmetry classification as the grand unified energy of the GUT. This would turn SU(5) into fissionable matter, like the single 'E' of the left side of Einstein's oft-quoted equation. Quite differently, I show + 5, in association with 4 & 6, as not allowing the perfect conservation of energy, and SU(5) as being of a totally indeterminate nature. Attempting to represent SU(5), as the scalar field of a quasiparticle, makes Construct No.12 into a very strange model indeed, because it is both infinitely small & infinitely large, as well as constantly finite in the middle. That is, No.12 can take on *any scale* and point in *any direction, at each and every null point*, whether an expansive intersection (x-shaped) or a reductive point, and thusly, one always maintains the unitarity of the universe. It is Just…that the Great Crystal of Light is at nobody's beck & call.

About 1967, the complete demonstrative set of QED was defined by Glashow, Salam and Weinberg, as the electroweak force, or, SU(2)-U(1). However, one might ask if this pattern follows the traditionally erroneous monism of the 'one', as in 4-5-6, or does it reflect 4 & 6 + 5, which has the asymmetrical, analytic chirality of a priori reason? Note that the 'one', as the electromagnetic interaction, seems to mimic the old hat, epistemological approach of the 'patio in the pool' (4-5-6), resembling the forging of Tolkien's One True Ring, in the fires of Moria. (Remember, My Sequence of Speciation has five basic messenger photons: 11 & 9, 9 & 0 and + 1.) Such a sententious statement marks the fallacious notion that the static universe provides for defining the exact energy rest frame of 'aleph-one', with SU(5) portrayed as the unfriendly fissionable Hyperplane of E_o, with the left side of Einstein's equation, as one term all alone, being much too inflationary. Further, there is nothing incorrect about the scientific observation, using Hubble's theory, that the light of objects receding from our point in space will be 'redshifted'. It's just that the erroneous conclusion, that the whole universe began in a hole somewhere close by, probably at our "6", is based upon Metaphysical Conceit.

If the reader finds these patterns difficult, just remember that *a posteriori reason* (11 & 9) is an implicit formation within & without the Explicit Function of *a priori logic* (10 -), &, *a posteriori logic* (4 & 6) is an implicit function within & without the Explicit Formation of *a priori reason* (+ 5). *A priori* simple pulls *a posteriori* along behind it, like the term implies, because reason & logic always remain associative. Hence, every wave train triplet must include both reasonable entities and logical events in a way that maintains unitarity, through what is called the gauge invariance of Constant Unity Factors. In other terms, nonlocal inductive reason (11 & 9) is without & within local deductive logic (10 -), &, nonlocal inductive logic (4 & 6) is without & within local deductive reason (+ 5). As a third example, one could also state that, a field & figure of reasonable interpretation (11 & 9) is associated with a ground of logical inference (10-), &, a field & figure of logical interpretation (4 & 6) is associated with a ground of reasonable inference (+ 5). What is important, as Einstein has stated, is to keep the two primary syllogistic patterns, for the first & second systems, independent, and to realize that 'what is a constituent doublet in one system is a single force in the other, and vice versa.' Plus: note that we are not following old figure-ground Gestalts, but the newer patterns that associate an Outer Field & Inner Particle with a Middle Ground State.

As per the erroneous triplet of No.4, a difficulty, bias or enigma occurs when the upper tautology (up/down) of *presuming* a perfectly associative analytic proposition (9-11 as a retrodictive one-to-one association) involves *assuming the direct definition of a theoretical law* (5). This represents the Metaphysical Conceit or Hubris of selective attention, which is telepathic and parapsychological, for the production of *paramnesia.* Discordantly, by sentimental conjunction, subjectivism produces realism, through the transcendent replacement of intellectual evasiveness. Freud referred to this aspect as the 'coalescence of the superego' (9-11-5, top of No.4). For Einstein such allegorical abstraction was 'affirmation'. *Separate sameness* seems to be explaining the lie that 'I have Reason' and that obviously 'my' predisposition is the right one…!? However, such an assertion could only be made by having a direct line to God; well beyond anybody's normal process of recognition. Discordantly, the synaesthetic 11 & 9 becomes the retrodictive déjà vu of 9-11 (Remember New York) as the alienation of naming before meaning, dissociated from any contextual clues. (God forbid that in a democracy that self-criticism be banished from society.) It is then that self-righteousness sets in as the obviation of *ethical equivalence*, through the elevated compensation of a Gestalt ultimatum, or, what is transcendent intellectualism. (Frankly, how much good has the snobbery of literary intellectualism done for the average person, and as Georg Cantor maintained, might we stumble when assuming that 4 & 6 is equivalent to + 5?) The special case looks to the opportunism of political inclusion, for the "right choices and right people". Then, the erroneous interpretation of explanation (9-11) leads deductively to the fallacious inference of a reasonable excuse for bad behavior (5-10). Like the 9-11-5 triumvirate, the traditional analytic proposition, of so-called enlightened reason, is really just the Three Stooges, or the Three Princes of Serendipity, or three men in a tub, or the three-corner hat, or three men on a bridge, etc. Me-myself-and-I becomes dumb-dumber-and-dumbest. And then, as might be expected, the unconscious presumption of the logical positivism, of having reason on one's own side, leads to the fatal mistake of accepting a contrived coincidence as being obviously right. We have to ask, does 'I' really know better? The fractious incompatibility of the Daemon, as the transcendent Assumption of Being, or Plato's Tauton, becomes the active aggressivity of the God of Wrath, whose predatory nature demands to be accommodated. (This is my 'proscription' as the Fourth Commandment, which concerns inordinate Metaphysical Conceit, just like the transfinite cardinal number of fundamental 'order', that is associated with the 'power set' of the 4th orbit.) Hence, as with forced extroversion, there is a tendency to act out an expected behaviorism as though it were preordained through telepathic parapsychology. Our mind plays tricks with our memory, when we project an obvious conclusion. 'This' is a question of heretical irrelevance, which shows a distinct lack of economy, by reflecting things such as neoliberalism and homosexuality, which require the constant revisionism of intellectual evasiveness. In other terms, the axiomatic self-righteousness of logical positivism gives the impression that, having the gold allows one to make the rules. 'I have my reasons.' A commonly used term is 'dickhead', which, of course, implies Freud's Phallic Stage, and can also cause difficulty for the ladies, if they have become 'White Witches'. This is the enigmatic pinnacle of the cone or triangle of stupidity, in the upper portion of No.4.

The 'subjective correlative' (9-11) of the behaviorism of acting out (5) unconsciously begs the 'objective correlative' (6-4) of introspectionism (10) as its subconscious, alter ego counterpart, which then produces a *schizothymic reaction* (a downer) that denotes the emotional degradation of prejudicial evidence. The telekinetically paranormal produces the anamnesia of selective retention. Discordantly, the street angel becomes the house devil, with the changeling returning to the underling, and, the middling vegging out, in between, through pococurantism. In other words, neoliberalism as political inclusion (up) reverts down to neoobjectivism as political exclusion (down), with affirmative action (between) setting the impersonal quotas of a fixed agenda, as though automatic progress has the right to grind people up into hamburger. The demagogue above & mystagogue below are centered in between by the idealogue, as 'doing something', like an assertive action that is justified upon ideological grounds. (Jung identified these inadvertent inversions as 'extroversion & introversion', which is just as uninformative as Karl Marx's dialectical materialism of upper & lower classes. However, Freud did identify the Latent Stage, progressively, as parasexual, rather than the unisexual center of ironic detachment.) A problem, prejudice or conundrum occurs when the lower tautology (down/up) of *presupposing* a perfectly dissociative synthetic proposition (6-4 as a retrograding one-to-one dissociation) involves the *supposition* of a directly derived general principle (10). Or, what is standing on principle, in a matter-of-fact manner, despite proof to the contrary – which is ignored. The evasive complicity of the analytic proposition spinflips down to the devious duplicity of the synthetic proposition. Then, pragmatically, the fascistic success of a predetermined practice (6) implicates a fundamental belief (4), which in turn induces prejudicial evidence through immutable naturalism, as if facts can actually speak for themselves (10). Thus, by sympathetic subjunction, predication produces suicidal altruism, through the idyllic displacement of a return-to-nature movement. That is, individualism 'complains' in order to give a personalized slant to a value judgement. Freud referred to this as the displacement of the id. It is a question of moral equivalence, such as the commoditization of values, bribery, pandering to baser needs, black humor, stubbornness, lateness and disinformation, etc. Therein, the pragmatic interpretation of complaining (6-4) leads deductively to the logical justification of self-indulgent apologizing (10), as basic to the permissiveness of the diva triformis (6-4-10). (Reminds me of the 1957 movie *The Three Faces of Eve.*) Then with accommodation above & indulgence below, appeasement reigns in between, which reflects the triplet neoliberalism, neoobjectivism and progressivism, or, opportunism, permissiveness and dictation. (Selective attention & selective retention combine to produce selective detachment: from the human community of well-meaning persons.) Subject to diatheism & object to dialetheism, the Styx of self-amputation & Lethe of self-oblivion do not flow together to produce self-redeeming actions such as *learning from experience.* The capriciousness of selective retention justifies the incompatibility of Lilith as the descendent concretism of Non-Being, or what is the Heteron of supposed natural perfection. Hence, the revolution of passive aggressivity undermines progressive modes through excessive attention to the parsimony details. This paranormal delusion is fundamentally conservative in nature and invokes the extremes of obsequious behavior, through the self-justification of Metaphysical Humility, or Bathos as the irreverent monster from the id.

Metathesis depends upon the pivotal interpolation of *reciprocity*, which allows the direct correlation of limited cooperation, but *does not permit* concomitance to pass through coherence, followed by congruence based upon commingling. There is organicism, but no concerted dialogue. That is, metathesis, like the chemistry of double decomposition, is an ideal center of interaction, with codependent subject/predicate & predicate/subject patterns circling about the unproductive verbosity of invariant transitions. The sorites syllogism becomes part & parcel of the Circles of Vengeance of the War of Sexes as a closed-loop system, or the hexagon of suspicion with the bipartisan paratactically cycling about the nonpartisan, and no possibility of a postpartisan resolution. Hence, metathesis is talk-the-talk without listening, and, no walk-the-walk.

As a third wheel, the abstract inclusion of *revisionism* (up, autocratic) & the parsimonious exclusion of *minutia* (down, meritocratic) combine inadvertently to produce the *gradualism* of special persons (theocracy) & special cases (technocracy), taken in isolation. That is, the fractious & capricious about the fastidious, could come to lead us by the nose, from precarious controversy to pernicious conflict. Unfortunately, the Metaphysical Certainty of such quodlibetical argumentation reduces the effectiveness of Associative Justice as a process, by subverting the discovery of evidentiary progressions that substantiate the legality of meaningful outcomes. In other terms, cinematic image above switches to kinetic animation below, from *aiding* inflation to *abetting* reduction, with the two seditiously *enabling* the perversion of the kinematic decision modes of Right Choice & Correct Action.

Tied to the limitations of a specific history & destiny, honor & duty merge as an unquestionable obligation, with the complicity of conjunction & duplicity of subjunction enforcing the conviction of injunction, followed by *inclusive & exclusive disjunction*. Or, fractious thoughts & capricious emotions are combined fastidiously to converge artificially upon the intractable entanglement of erroneous choices & actions. A vertical pair of tautologies, between enigma & conundrum, leads to the merger of two syndromes that are based upon collusion as the dilemma of contempt for others (either/or of inclusive disjunction) & conspiracy as the dilemma of the condemnation of others (neither/nor of exclusive disjunction). That is the ultimate gamester, as an Agent Provocateur, becomes caught up in the bipolar twin-paradox of intractable double standards that lead to Classical Alienation. (Inclusive disjunction does not realize the serialization of the rhetorical syllogism, &, exclusive disjunction does not recognize the sequence of the dialectical syllogism.) In other words, the maker of the cage becomes ensconced in minding his or her own miscreance. If 'all one needs is the will', then the apprehension of strong convictions leads to apprehensiveness, because of self-conviction. That is, trapped within the mirror of self-recursion, the two demiurgic alter egos of a doppelganger, through the resembling of an autocratic *demagogue* & the dissembling of a meritocratic *mystagogue*, remain disassociated. As a result, the artificer, as an *idealogue*, devises theocratic assemblage, which then leads to technocratic disassemblage. *In toto, with resemble & dissemble vertically, &, assemble & disassemble horizontally, the devil's window is closed to conscious reassemblage.* More wisely, the fifth element as a moving cause, based upon a constant vigilance against the enemy within, focuses upon the positive side of conscious recomposition. To paraphrase the French writer Jean-Paul Sartre, 'Things move along naturally toward the Verb.' Except that, the dualism of the 'one' usually leads to the misstatement of the third dimension, which locks 'us' into the cardinal sin of cruciform limit cycles, trapped on the wrong side of the window by a negative outlook. Discordantly then, metalepsis & prolepsis could & might turn away from conscious intermingling, toward the unconscionable interaction of the third person singular, if monistic individualism is translated through misrepresentation & misdirection, and thereby separated from the monotheistic self-sameness of the third person plural. The question that poses itself at this juncture is, if one comes to appreciate the *spiritual unicity* of such a Quest, what does that have to do with the *unitarity of science*, and, what is the role of *holistic philosophy* in relation to the other two?

Discordantly, misconstruing the spontaneity of the Divine Comedy could & might return upon itself as the dark humor of the Demonic Parody. By avoiding sarcasm, cynicism and farce, as laughing at, humor can play upon the brighter side of life, as laughing with, by walking the path of the golden mean, while entertaining the irenic repartee of mature satire. In contrast, the arrogance of unrealistic self-esteem tends to make mockery of others. Thus, the ironic detachment of the sardonic mocking of others is very different from the concerted dialogue of ironic interplay as friendly satire that seeks to share a more gentle approach. In contradistinction, the quixotic witticisms, of the hypersensitive love accidents of dramatic genius, through the eclectic dance of nonsensical counterpoint, merely produce *informality & dysfunction.* That is, dialect, shibboleth and neologism, like rumor, gossip and innuendo, do not encourage the diacritical vetting of meaningful progressions, or what is *synonymy.* The careful bringing together & separating out of likenesses & differences is central to all learning, by which one acquires a love of life, and of the living. Unfortunately, erroneous behavior gives love the appearance of resembling a car accident, when, through cross-purposes, at the wrong time (irrelevance) and in the wrong place (irreverence), one does the wrong thing (misrepresentation), in the wrong way (misdirection). In such a case, there might be, as Shakespeare remarked in *Hamlet*, "more honour in the breach than in the observance," which reflects Einstein's twin-paradox between unconscionable choices & actions, and those that are consciously recombinant. If we do not keep our wits about us, and thereby break faith with humane development, then the stand-alone absurdities of maniacal circumstance could & might take over.

In my theoretical search for Crossover Patterns, I built up the triplets that can be seen as an X-pattern within the Quarteron Pattern. Apparently, in terms of physics, the little squares of eight colors make up the 'strong color force' of the 'super-weak interaction' (Fritjof Capra). The odd & even pairings of quark triplets & gluon triplets become the third-level integrals of fundamental 'massless vector fermions & bosons', which, as SU(3), soon become part of bilateral neutral current processes, hidden within classically experienced, local matter ground states. It is also possible to appreciate that, instead of the axiological heterotic strings of SU(3) being limited to the center of the Quarteron Pattern, a pattern of five-ness seems to expand outward on an orthogonal Hyperplane, as the SU(5) of a quasicrystal. Thus, much to my surprise, I had hit upon the Crossover Patterns of what some theorists, such as Necia Apfel (*It's All Elementary*, 1985, p. 147), refer to as 'X-particles' – including both the orthogonal plane & the parametric string of SU(3), to make up SU(5). (Keep in mind that with Construct No.1, the fourth dimension is still missing.) The resurrected reformation of the X-pattern becomes a kind of fifth element as a scalar field, or the SU(5) of a grand unified energy, as show in Construct No.12. With four triplet colors for quarks & four for gluons, I have modeled a set of relationships similar to Necia Apfel's 24 X-particles. These particles could have only existed within Planck space-time, during the supposed inflationary period of the big bang, which eventually produced our neck of the woods. The real point to be made here concerns our incessant search for *implausible & impossible 'conversion factors'* as a way to control & deny the probabilities of the third alternative. Of course 'complexity theory' (M. Mitchell Waldrop, *Complexity*, 1992) is quick to recognize that real experience involves the accumulative addition of increasingly complex clusters, rather than the hypothetical solution of the three-body problem. This is why Darwin himself did not dwell upon the exact meaning of natural selection, but sought to work with selective evolution. In other terms, we must learn to work with *arbitrary precision*...and be patient. For all things will reveal themselves, in good time.

The caduceus, based upon the compatibility of Hermes Trismegistus & Hestia, must not attempt a coercive reassemblage of the Autonomous Complex, based upon the 'fearful symmetries' of a predetermined orthogonal button with a parametric hole as a cutoff point. The *rationalization* of 'knowing reason' is specious, and not reasonable, just as the *paralogism* of 'understanding logic' is spurious, and not logical. And yet traditionally, wisdom dominated by the reason of the analytic proposition, was isolated from recombinantly meaningful patterns of development. The recombinant approach is what Kant really wanted to advocate, but he was apparently unaware of the imbalance implicit within his reasoned notionality. If contrived, the combination of the *two systems* leads from a sense of conscious development to unconscionable disparities. Kant's categorical & hypothetical imperatives are properly rendered, and therefore compatible, but his positivism concerning the analytic proposition (No.4, 9-11-5), builds a house of cards which suborns of the synthetic proposition (No.4, down), and never allows anybody to go home. Thus, although Kant produced a remarkable thesis, for the peaceful, global development of supranational interdependence, his sense of substantial progress was reduced to 'synthetic equivalence' as a mere masculine sosie. Significantly, wisdom reflects the coextensive recombinance of reason & logic, not the speculative projection of the practical reason of strict application, in combination with the pragmatic logic of a limited methodology. Unfortunately, the same imbalance is generally felt to dwell in the irresolute patterns of Hegel's thesis, antithesis and synthesis, although he worked very hard to dispel such an unintended result.

Later, we will bring out the imbalance of Hegel's unnatural synthesis, as a third term that erroneously advocates the 'squared universe'. Remember the traditional confusion brought about by Newton's *spatium est absolutum*? The same 'hamartia' or tragic flaw, without a natural peripeteia, plagues both Kant's and Hegel's irresolute measures, and blocks the potential of anagnorisis. Even today, modern scientific philosophy has trouble realizing that the

First Principles of the Book of Nature, in Phase IV, require the other three Phases, to even intimate some kind of Certainty Principle. Big bang: my left foot!

As a small aside, True Trinitine Patterns are hard to manage. On April 4, 1999, in Canada, the democratic institution of the arctic Territory of Nunavut, with its capital in Iqualuit, was celebrated nationally as Happy Nunavut Day. I was particularly taken with the important role played by the elders, both men and women, among the native Inuit. Accordingly, focusing upon community development produced a remarkably generic action statement, based upon the TTP of caring, compassion and commitment. I couldn't have done better. Again, philosophy is the bridge, between the spirituality of the people and the science of social progress.

Frequently, the disproportionate treatment of analytic & synthetic propositions, in the vertical mode, prevents an adequate commingling of *analytic and synthetic infinities* in the horizontal mode. (Keep in mind the 'continuum problem' posed by the Theory of Transfinite Numbers.) Similarly, with physics there are generally problems with both the cross-reading (4 & 6) of the orthogonal juxtaposition of 'boundaries' & the cross-purposes (11 & 9) of the parametric linking of 'anomalies'. *Boundary difficulties* are created by the reciprocal interplay of vertical superstrings on minimal surfaces, between the interacting 'domain walls' of matter & antimatter variation. That is, both the positive emission resonances & the negative absorption resonances, of nonlocal quantum operatives, can & may interrupt the local variations of natural progressions. *Anomaly problems* are associated with asymptotic freedom within the heterotic strings of neutral current processes, which relate to 'quantum mechanical tunneling'. In contrast, *Recombinant troubles* deal with regulating the coextensive blending of empirically experienced complexity theory, by recombining the positive mathematics of real numbers with the negative mathematics of imaginary numbers. Psychologically, the conception of the fifth element & the perception of the tenth element make up the intractable intricacies of our psychological knot, which just might solve the ridiculous & sublime, as the ludicrous. That is, although we can generally experience the interlay of matter and antimatter variation, through the ground states of classically local waves, the *exact reciprocity* of field/particle patterns remains a quantum issue that is by and large, indeterminate. (Note that the field/particle interplay of Bell's inequality has proven to be intractable.) In other terms, + 5, as the tentative variation of the Identity of Matter Resonance, is generally evident (mode & median + mean or 4 & 6 + 5), but not specifically a computable 'position' for categorically verifying of the Test of Time. Likely then, the most important aspect of the vertical mode of Verification involves building-up credible *redundancies* that permit the assumption of being reasonably sure about the *resiliency and reliability* of something. Our awareness of the interaction of the autocratic & meritocratic, through the obviation & evidence of interpreting 'this' as the length of time, is usually accomplished by setting the 'constants' of artificial limit cycles, and never becomes an exact determination. (Georg Cantor showed that the fundamental magnitude implied by the orderly field positions of cardinal numbers [4], as a subset, can not be directly linked to the set of cardinal relational numbers [6], with the two as precedent to transfinite cardinal numbers that make up real numbers [+5].) Hence, a 'reasonable theory' is primarily a nominative pleonasm, like the circumstantial evidence of an anecdotal epithet, and therefore subject to *in situ* revision, depending upon the developing complexity of the classically local context. In terms of physics, the contragradient representation, or m* (4 & 6), is always masked by an indeterminate heat signature (+ 5).

In contrast, for 10 -, because of the contingent momentum of the Continuity of Antimatter Resonance, no cosmic censorship is allowed to turn the Trick of Space. That is, the enthalpic PRP of uniform inertia, as omniformity, is a non-computable Sequence that never allows experiment to provide an exactly predictable solution.

As the Distributive But/Not, the *falsification of the neither/nor* (exclusive disjunction) only allows limited recognition of the specific sequences. Hence, the Validation of Process permits one to be relatively sure about what will come next, providing that one avoids relying too heavily upon the veridicality of contingent evidence. We are always troubled with determining the natural facts of 'that', for a given 'distance of space'. Importantly, that doesn't make the irreverent subreption of the matter-of-fact approach, of standing on principle (6-4-10), into linear logical, as though an axiological inference makes it possible to absolutely prove something, through action at a distance. That buttonhole, of orthocentrism, is too restrictive to become a string.

To recoup, holistic philosophy, like mathematics, and other areas of human inquiry, must proceed through *ever-ascending sets of elaboration.* One begins with the one-ness of whole numbers and unitary measures, with the self-same monotheistic approach permeating the subsequent blending of the cardinal derivations of magnitudes, & the ordinal development of relationships (forms & functions). Thus, the self-sameness of *species* implies the supersymmetrical duality of the co-ordination of *genus*, as precedent to a triune pattern such as a third-level integral, when one considers the raising of powers & extracting of roots, pivoting about a hypothetical center. Then, from the rational *family* of three-ness, the quadrilateral fixation of a cardinal set, makes the four-ness of cardinal *order* seems a natural form of vertical serialization. Subsequently, the fivefold formalities of the planar transitions of quasiparticles become a theoretical moving cause that must naturally include the hexis of functional numbers, that are implicit without & within, as the reductive & expansive resonances of an antithetical nature. Importantly, with real flatness & imaginary curvature continuing duality, etc. that leaves us working with the tertiary recombinant space-time objects of the accumulative addictions of seven-ness, for the developmental sets of complex numbers. After seven-ness then, bringing in the indeterminate nature of eight-ness presents the problem of a harmonic spectrum, that must have both vertical (direct) & horizontal (cross) channels – which makes the Periodic Table of Elements partly indeterminate. Here, the flatness of 'four elements' must extend toward the full spectrum of 'four causes', after the five-ness of the 'moving cause' of real numbers blends with the six-ness of curvilinear imaginary numbers; through the associative development of compatibility; so that the seven-ness of complex numbers facilitates the eight-ness of legally viable harmonic progressions.

In the 1970s, physicists found that they could use the Crossover Patterns of the diacritical measures of 'isospin & hypercharge' (two-ness) to work out the vertical magnitudes of what was called the 'eightfold way'. The hexagonal patterns of Construct No.8 reflect the same type of octets, in which each family takes on a donut-like toroidal shape, based upon Outer Field, Middle Ground State and Inner Particle (three-ness). By convention, physicists find that subgroups of 8, 10 or 27 are effective for modeling particle identities within a given eightfold way, or family. My donut-like families work along the same line. Think of three buttons, for the 'three families of particles' (2 & 4 +3, 4 & 6 +5, 6 & 8 +7), on a string that makes up neutral current processes, formed by fundamental neutrinos combinations. As a Phase I relationship, Construct No.3 models three quartets for a total of 12 identities; four without, four within and four between. (Remember to add in, mentally, the four outer quadrants for the Outer Field, of the same resonant colors as the Inner Particle.) However, in No.3, black (likely a Z° particle) and white (a messenger photon) have not yet crossed over, through Event Inception, to become statistically viable, as the measurable *protomatter of leptons.* That leaves the 10 subgroups for the decuplet pattern that makes up the lepton family of *three generations*: 1) purple field (magnetic resonance), yellow ground (electron), purple particle (electron neutrino); 2) blue field (magnetic resonance), orange ground (muon), blue particle (muon neutrino); 3) green field (magnetic resonance), red ground (tauon), green particle (tauon neutrino). Finally, the black field (magnetic resonance), white ground (messenger photon) and black particle (?) have not yet crossed over, through Event Inception. All four field factors, along with the four particle factors in the center, make up the *nucleophilic substrate* of Magnetic Resonance, which supports the *electrophilic torus* of the lepton family. Accordingly, the center becomes a 'hole' which is made up of four neutrino particles that have fundamental mass when grouped together. Thus, for the three families of particles, Phase I is the lepton family of electronic nature (No.3), Phase II the hadron family of mesons and baryons (No.1), and Phase III the antilepton family – with positronic variables (No.5). And, neutral current processes are able to flow axiologically down the center of the three families of particles, with neutrinos centered in Phase I, 'pions' centered in Phase II, and electron antineutrinos centered in Phase III. Grouped tightly, as a sequence of quantum tunneling, these three centers are, respectively, 'holes' (of neutrinos), 'excitons' (of pions) and 'free electrons' (of antineutrinos), with the various kinds of neutrinos running down the center or all three families of particles, in support of the SU(3) of "braided" neutral current processes.

Horizontally, when considering the alternation of odd and even orbits, harmonic congruence produces the eight different 'symmetry families' shown in No.7. Vertically, each of the eight orbits is thought of as a *single symmetry classification*, which establishes the *inertial frame of reference* for that stage of development. Further, each symmetry family is considered an eightfold way from a vertical point of view, while all together the eight families together become the Eightfold Path, at a given scaling level, to make up the 'elements' within that particular horizontal range. As shown by the pattern of concentric rings in No.1, sets of three, as field-ground-particle, begin in the center, as subatomic, and move outward to the macroscopic, and, even to astronomical scales. Whether an Outer Field, an Inner Particle or a Middle Ground State, odd rings are dextrorotatory for the pattern orange-red-green-blue, &, even rings are levorotatory for the pattern yellow-white-black-purple (if viewed from the other side of the surface). Regardless then, of the viewpoint, contracting absorption patterns & expanding emission patterns are congruent with each other throughout the vertical demonstrative syllogisms of the direct, s-channels of superstrings, from smallest to largest, and vice versa. And, as Einstein maintained, this same compatibility occurs between the field-ground-particle patterns of all ten wave-train triplets (No.14), within the Eightfold Path of the horizontal dialectical syllogisms of the cross, t-channels of heterotic strings. Compatibility then, is also maintained in spite of the fact that synthetic chiralities are devolutionary and reductive, and, analytic chiralities are evolutionary and expansive. So whether moving eternally inward or outward (No.1), or, continually devolving or evolving (No.7), the universe remains relatively balanced, with special relativity & general relativity blending together. Thus a *series* is a vertical-style demonstrative syllogism, of two basic types that expand & contract in cooperation, exponentially, &, a *sequence* is made up of horizontal wave trains that grow and decay, in the bilateral manner of polynomial developments, while still working together associatively. So, the long and the short of it is that to really understand SU(3) is to realize that triplet patterns are an effective way of treating both the *reciprocal oppositions* of the Vertical Mosaic, as primarily quantum and nonlocal, &, the *associative appositions* of the Horizontal Mosaic, as primarily classical and local. It all fits together.

However, the real trick is to see how the finer scaling ranges act as a carrier medium for a given range of development. Thus, the full spectrum of classically local, electromagnetic waves has absorption & emission resonances that interrupt their flow, negatively & positively, on a quantum level, with the Outer Fields & Inner Particles made up of the *gamma wave spectrum*, for the emission & absorption of photons. So with 2 - 1 & 3, one has an even magnetic ground (wave), backed up or carried by the odd emission resonances of the field/particle radiation of photons. Hence, a magnetic black donut is dunked in photon milk, both on a higher scale as a field, & on a lower scale as a particle. Similarly, at a level higher than the electromagnetic spectrum, the hydrogen spectrum produces an infrastructure of harmonic elements, while it also has "fine" electrical emission resonances that are above & below even orbits (2 – 1 & 3, 4 – 3 & 5, 6 – 5 & 7, 8 – 7 & 11), and, "hyperfine" magnetic absorption resonances that are above & below odd orbits (0 & 2 + 1, 2 & 4 + 3, 4 & 6 + 5, 6 & 8 + 7). Thus, through the triplets of the SU(3) pattern, whether moving vertically or horizontally, when an even Middle Ground State becomes classically local, at a given level, it is always supervened & subvened by the quantum reciprocals of an odd Outer Field & Inner Particle, as a *nonlocal resonance.* That is, the odd exponential operatives of a quantum *emission resonance*, as the constituents of radiation normals, act like a higher-order interrupt for the locally classical toroid of an even Middle Ground State. Similarly, an odd Middle Ground State may have even constituents as a lower-order interrupt or *absorption resonance* of a quantum field/particle pattern. In other terms, a given donut, whether an 'Odd Wave' or an 'Even Wave', floats in its carrier medium of field/particle reciprocals, of opposite charge and nature, which are without & within it.

The whole process, of the natural system, begins to the left of No.7 with photons, keeping in mind that the odd orbits of positive matter dominate human awareness, as a kind of 'squared existence'. (The expression usually used is logical positivism, which in Christian terms is Adam's first bite of the apple, or 'my left foot'.) Naturally, the fundamental spectrum of the odd orbits of photons is associated with the even orbits of gravitons, so that one has, at this lowest or finest of ranges, both absorption & emission characteristics intertwined. (It is difficult to identify the characteristics of virtual phonons as different from those of gravitons, which resemble virtual phonons.) That is, both absorption & emission become important when dealing with higher-level spectra, because they influence how more complex elements interact, either positively or negatively. (In a way, the gamma wave spectrum is the ultimate carrier medium, having the finest "knitting needles".) On the positive side, one begins then with 'messenger photons' (0 & 2 + 1), which have not yet crossed over the Event Inception as the second orbit, and hence they remain relatively undetectable within plasmic emissions, although they produce cosmic rays that have measurable effects. (Plasma is a 'fourth phase of matter', while ideal gases are associated with Phase I, ideal solids with Phase II and ideal liquids with Phase III.) Next, it's on to 'virtual photons' (2 & 4 + 3), which tend to remain confined to or contained within higher-level processes, in the buildup of 'virtual particles' that support the development of other particles. Some examples of virtual particles are intermediate vector bosons, virtual phonons, neutrinos, mesons, pions, and quarks and gluons, etc. Here we are mostly within the range of Phase I relationships, for photon development. Importantly then, the next level, if No.7 is imagined as a complete gamma ray spectrum, is the 'real photon' (4 & 6 + 5) as beginning the *surface effect* of a narrow range of visible light that is associated with the five wavelengths of the 5th orbit. (Remember that as part of the Sequence of Speciation, there ought to be, in nonexistence, *at least five* of the most basic photons, as the uniform inertia of a penultimate diapason. The metaphor often used is *the greening of the gold*, which has a vainglorious flare [9/5] that links the preformationism of the ninth harmonic to the interactionism of the fifth harmonic, or the Acoustic to acoustics. However, I take umbrage with the *nine-to-five inference*, which implies a direct relationship between Oyama's 'preformationism and interactionism'.) Finally, one has the high-energy/high-frequency orbit of ultraviolet radiation (6 & 8 + 7), before the Event Horizon reaches the extremely high frequencies, of such things as x-rays and strong gamma radiation. In final analysis, kept in mind that the even orbits of the *gamma ray spectrum* are usually only detected indirectly, by how the implicit function affects other processes, especially through absorption resonances. Nevertheless, it is fundamental that any given natural system registers both the resonances of dark spectra and the resonances of light spectra, blended antithetically within the one self-same system of development.

A family is the third *taxonomical group*, after species and genus, and one might expect that particular *taxon* to be a precondition for the fourth taxon, of order. In relation to the Eightfold Path of Buddhist conception, we will be examining scientific *taxa* and comparing them with other orderly patterns, within a range eight harmonic progressions. (One must also add in the dyad of nonexistence, for a total of ten relationships.) For example, my rendering of the generality of scientific taxa is as follows: subspecies (10/0), species (1, white), genus (2, yellow), family (3, orange), order (4, red), class (5, green), subphylum (6, blue), phylum (7, purple), subkingdom (8, black), and kingdom (9/10). Other such *doctrinal ordinances* are: the mathematics of set theory, the system of transfinite numbers, Neils Bohr's seven allowed atomic orbits, and other more obvious harmonic patterns such as the diatonic music scale, etc. From an epistemological point of view, one must keep in mind that these propagation systems, that mirror the natural system, are not a dogmatic rendering, but an organizational device and memory aid.

At this juncture, I am not going to bring out the complete logic of my treatment of Einstein's ten field equations for complete phasal space, but an improved rendering – at least in my thoughts – of the Christian Ten Commandments, might be in order. To my way of thinking the Commandments cover the following range: inscription (10/0), prescription (1), ascription (2), conscription (3), proscription (4), subscription (5), description (6), rescription (7), postscription (8) and transcription (9/10). Certainly this progression takes a monotheistic approach, and importantly, it goes beyond the limitations of personal opinionation. Hence, I am very proud of this remarkable example of code breaking, although some people might find it very pedestrian.

As per No.7, for the Horizontal Mosaic I will be using a pathology similar to the Buddhist Eightfold Path: conch (1), umbrella (2), tent (3), knot (4), fish (5), flower (6), vase (7) and wheel (8). Interestingly, this spiritual progression seems to fit the same development as Niels Bohr's seven allowed orbits. Unfortunately, the rhetoric of the world's great charismatics usually goes fishing for the tokenism of the monistic one (9-11-5), in order to convince others to accommodate their own, special interests. To possess another's soul, between George Orwell's utopia & dystopia (No.4), is to attempt to sell him or her 'anything', as though the cornucopia of the *cockatrice* (4-5-6) could provide a free lunch for everyone, and lead directly to the panacea of the *chimera* (11-10-9). Hence, besides the metathesis of attempting to tie down the Paradigm shift (4 & 6 + 5), by defining Reason itself, there is the thorny issue of James Clerk Maxwell's (Scot. phys. 1831-1879) 'ultraviolet crisis' (8 - 7 & 11), which places the 9th orbit off limits. Logical positivism, as overly analytical, and therefore tending toward evolutionism, usually pushes determinism too far, by attempting to both *define* the monolithic Vertical Mosaic, &, *describe* the monopolistic Horizontal Mosaic. Fortunately, Bohr's seven allowed orbits seem to naturally cut themselves off, out on a limb, but not off the cliff. (We will eventually show that the mathematics of Bertrand Russell's three sevens is also naturally self-restrictive.) Hence, beyond the Event Horizon, with the 8th orbit as 'thou shalt not steal', one cannot cross over to the Great Seal of Logic itself, and therefore it is not possible to determine the exact experimental results of the true Doppler shift. For us, the Validation of Relation is a question of natural processes. Hence, modern science must not confuse the intimation of First Principles, within the plasmic emissions of Phase IV, as being able to encompass the Certainty Principle.

In the latter case, we have already examined the Phase IV Sequence of Speciation as being a kind of chimera, based upon the three fundamental outcomes of experiment. For nonexistence, the traditional Book of Nature, as Objectivity, antimatter, Mind, the dialectical syllogism, experiment, Logic, or, the Being of Sequence itself, has its equivalence in existence as the traditional Book of Scripture, as Subjectivity, matter, Body, the rhetorical syllogism, observation, Reason, or, the Becoming of Series itself. Naturally then, there ought to be, in that the metaphysics of Myth is central to the Means of Existence, some sort of temporal entity as equivalent to the spatial chimera. Blame it on the Greeks. As expected they had a myth concerning a ferret-like creature that could destroy plants and animals by a mere glance, or by simply breathing on them. (Again, the static universe of the cockatrice, as the traditional rhetorical syllogism, &, the cosmic censorship of the chimera, as the traditional dialectical syllogism.) Of course, there would have to be three-ness involved, like the statistical set of mode, mean and median, or the aesthetic transition of rat, mole and mouse, or my triplet of trivia, trice and trifle, or the politics of honor, duty and obligation, etc. Interestingly, a mole is similar to a ferret, and a trice is like 'splitting hairs in three', which also reflects SU(3). So if the Greeks came up with a special entity, called a *cockatrice*, one might not be surprised. As Construct No.4, we have already been dealing with this infernal creation, especially through the top/down pattern of partisan, nonpartisan, bipartisan, as the inverted heart shape. Interestingly, in modern society a postmodern trend has come about, in an attempt to reverse the nefarious influence of the *patristic apostasy* of this beastly creature, through what has become the popular sport of 'male bashing'. Nevertheless, as one might expect, reversing the biases & prejudices of something like Marx's dialectical materialism, is no simple question of eliminating masculine biases of the Apocalypse Now (red-white-green-black). Looking at Construct No.1, the upper apocalyptic hemisphere of the Quarteron pattern is my "good" example. (At least the field-ground-particle pattern avoids the stupidity of the 'wave/particle duality' – which most physicists still ascribe to.). As a sorites syllogism, the 'middle wave of the verb ground' always has a 'subject field' without it, & a 'predicate particle' within it. But, in keeping with the style of the sorites syllogism, the matrix of the triplet pattern can be shifted up in scale, or down in scale, without any theoretical limit. Here, the field-ground-figure pattern, or field-wave-particle triplet, is no longer a cockatrice...but we are not yet home free. That is because, most importantly, the final conclusion, in the very center, as the 'angel square', returns from the inside to the outside, by coming back as the 'squared universe' of a transcendental abstraction. (Why else would one conclude that the universe is constantly expanding? Science is also subject to the natural stupidity of partisan advocates, who are using the three little cups of the sorites syllogism, to play a shill-game with the rest of us.) It's as through the extreme ellipsis of the hole in the center forms an unholy alliance with the hyperbole of the button. Then, as a bipolar reaction formation, *repression leads to transference*, and vice versa: the brinkmanship of all bones (nothing) & skin (everything), but no flesh (anything). So who cares if men put butterflies on pins, & women collect stamps!? Well, the problem with the glorification of the cockatrice, as a single symmetry classification, is that, like Voltaire's best of all possible worlds, there is no fourth dimension *for learning from experience.* Men and women just get too personal and abuse each other, but there is no commitment to a long-term relationship. Like the cockatrice, it's all image & hot air whistling through the center, or a nasty look & flatulence. Fortunately, by not being too perfect, there is room for doing better.

As a child, I learned the universal meaning of 'I cut you choose; you cut I choose'. It works for grapefruit in the morning, as well as insider trading, boardroom politics and the tariffs and subsidies of the international market place. No Two Towers of double standards, as 'tails I win; heads you lose'.

Human personality conflicts come out in all walks of life, with spiritual liberation irrevocably tied to physical discoveries. For example, when Einstein came up with the 'homomorphic/isotropic' (10/9), as a Phase IV wave/particle pattern, he sent humanity down the wrong road. (The proper field-wave-particle pattern is 11-10-9 as isotopic-homomorphic-isotropic, or better yet, 10 – 11 & 9 as a more healthy dialectical syllogism. Interestingly, the latter matches Einstein's M_0c^2, but his E_0, to the left of his equation, is a *soritetic non sequitur*, because the reductive implicit function, of two cohomologous nonlocal quantum operatives, is missing. That is, there is a logical chimera for general relativity, but not a reasonable cockatrice for special relativity. And, because his equation is not completely balanced, 'us' remains trapped on one plane, in a superficial existence. It is only "natural" then, that humans would come *up* with a fission bomb, before learning to master 'cold fusion'.) This simple error is important, because it affects everybody's abilities to untie the psychological knot, by avoiding the twin-ultimatums, or Two Towers, of Gestalt brinkmanship, reflecting the repression of the static universe & transference of cosmic censorship. A wave/particle pattern just won't do the Trick, and leaves us, along with superman, trapped on a celluloid surface, getting 100% on the Test, but not able to act in a humane manner. Hence, we have a tendency to blow up the four elements, to an impossible dream, while reducing the four causes to a non-issue, in the center. The Thin Man is not a person of substance. (This is the 4-10 pattern of Hades, as my *decussate-decuplation.*) As per No.4, life becomes a fascist/communist conspiracy of superficial aesthetics (all image), with the 'god dot' of myopic individualism making everything a personal issue, through an accusative attitude that unjustly blows the whistle on others (arrogant flatulence), by constantly giving them the third degree. If the vertical cockatrice of subject-verb-predicate remains sententiously preclusive, the 'cumulative summation' of Temporal Infusion forecloses upon the progressive complexities of 'accumulative addition'. Structuring behavior is really part of an on-going process of development. Naturally then, despite strong-minded individuals, the psychogenic cannot reduce the 'four identities' to one plane of action, even if a dictator's pictures and statues are almost everywhere. The twin-paradox of the ultimatums of the control of the Test & denial of the Trick, make up the Gestalt brinkmanship of transference projected from preclusion & repression stemming from retroclusion: the squared universe. Such a reaction formation is the product of *superstition*, based upon the conceptual structuralism of empiricism & perceptual constructivism of scientism. In other words, the most difficult single moment in the life of any Human Being occurs within the Crux of Right Choice & Correct Action: resulting in the self-exorcism of personal revival – through the glass darkly. Importantly, without understanding such matters, 'higher education' is a great waste of time, and, *a real danger to Humanity!*

To get back to the source of quarks and gluon triplets, No.3 is the appropriate model of their 'confinement' within the protomatter of Phase I. That is, each of the three generations of the lepton family (electrons, muons and tauons) has its material cause (Aristotle) supported by the positive energy of a given quark species, which subtends the appropriate lepton generation. (I'm wondering if it isn't gluons that set up the neutrino-based hole in No.3? But, apparently, as the two basic 'flavors' generated by the strong color force, quarks & gluons change readily, from one into the other.) These dual-natured triplets of the fundamental SU(3) pattern resemble a *digital current* that radiates asymmetrically from within the strong color force, as basic to all other relationships, on a larger scale. The dyadic parity of that fundamental "diode" is based upon the Hypothesis of Homogeneity (10 - 11 & 9 and 0 - 9 & 1), as deuterotypical 'true photons' (10 and 0) and archetypal 'dilaton photons' (11 & 9 and 9 & 1). As previously stated, the messenger photon is associated with the 1st orbit of 0 & 2 + 1, which has not yet crossed over, from Phase IV, into the lepton family of Phase I. And, what I call a true photon likely relates to the gravitons of supergravity, which both Roger Penrose and Stephen Hawking seem to feel are at the center of the most fundamentally asymmetrical sets that one can imagine. That is, spontaneous symmetry breaking (10 and 0) seems to set up time-asymmetric quantum gravity (Penrose), and, 'there is no reversal of entropy within gravothermal collapse' (Hawking). Here, one has established the *direction of the distance of space itself*, for the Space Vector, as analogous to a diode that leads to the rectification of a 'direct current'. The prime question of sequential origination becomes how to relate the squared exponentials of the two *subspecies* of dilaton photons (11 & 9 and 9 & 1) to the *species* of messenger photons, in the 1st orbit of 0 & 2 + 1?

Resembling the chimeric pattern of true photon-dilaton photon-messenger photon, as deuterotype-archetype-genotype, the American biologist Seymour Benzer has his own fundamental sequence of recon-muton-cistron, which resembles my 10 – 11 & 9 (transformer), 0 – 9 & 1 (diode) and 0 & 2 + 1 (rectifier). Of course, these devicive triplets are just a way of dealing with fundamental causes, for the experimental outcomes of the Sequence of Speciation. Thus, my spiritual triplet of transcription-inscription-prescription also applies to the three fundamental relationships. In the mathematics of set theory, one has the most basic sequence of infinite set-null set-extension set. Biologically, 10 – 11 & 9 is the *cenospecies* of the allopatric 'gene pool' of accessible random traits, which I usually refer to as transcription (9/10), as an infinite set. That makes 0 – 9 & 1 into the expression of *subspecies* or what I term inscription (10/0), as the singularity of a null set. In a genetic sense, this most singular triplet – with zero as a null set – is a biological 'isolate' that has the greatest chance of producing the mutations of 'genetic drift', which agrees with Benzer's middle term as a muton. Nevertheless, both 10 – 11 & 9 and 0 – 9 & 1 exhibit, in their odd constituent resonances, an adaptive radiation that is called 'heterozygous dihybridization'. In simple terms, the even egg has odd parts, so that we get the combined sequence of cenospecies-subspecies-species. That is, the two deuterotypical triplets, 10 – 11 & 9 and 0 – 9 & 1, contain heterolytic pairs of odd archetypal constituents, which reflect the squared expansion of the sum of their allelic frequencies: Hardy-Weinberg law. (With so many other 'experts' having patterns similar to mine, I might not be crazy after all.) That is, despite that fact that, between 10 and 0, the factors of genetic mutation ought to be perfect hybrids, in a deuterotypical manner, archetypal patterns tend to favor the genetic drift of an odd *subspecies.* (This genetic tendency reflects the directionality, that

Penrose and Hawking maintain for physics, is not an *optical isomer* as a perfect mirror image.) These subspecies next support the third element of the Sequence of Speciation, as the triplet of the *species of genotype* (0 & 2 + 1). Hence, the source of the "arbitrary troubles" of Phase IV relationships occurs through the blending of the deuterotype and the archetype, as being in two places at once, within the measure-for-measure purview of dyadic parity, and yet still fundamentally asymmetrical for the production of the genotype. The pattern is deuterotype as cenospecies, archetype as subspecies, and genotype as species. Interestingly then, for humans there is a natural 'dimorphism', because of the need for sexual coupling between males & females, in order to reestablish the *diploid number* of a full set of 64 chromosomes. (Naturally, with the two systems, *haploid meiotic replication* is centered in Phase II, &, *diploid mitotic division* radiates from a Phase IV pattern. The first doubles down in the double up, &, the second doubles up in the double down. Once again, as in No.7, we have the Antithetical Vortices of the double light cone.) Consequently, some of the combined traits of parenting remain sexually specific, while still others can be transferred from mother to son or from father to daughter. However, although some traits are transmitted regularly through a relatively stable dominance, others are inherited recessively, and still others are acquired by random patterns due to haploid 'crossing over' (Phase II) or diploid 'criss-crossing' (Phase IV), from one parental group to another. Importantly, here, for the third system, if the supersymmetrical implications of the blending of haploid & diploid patterns are not deterministic, then that supports Darwin's attitude of not defining *natural selection*, and then more appropriately, paying attention to selective evolution.

In the year 2003, 50 years after James Watson and Francis Crick mapped out the fundamental polymerization of the double helix of DNA, Human Beings are celebrating the relative completion of the human genome project. That is, except for a few error gaps and about 1% of indeterminate characteristics, we have revealed the genetic code for nearly all, 25,000 to 30,000 human genes. Further, from the point of view of The Human Equation, as a natural system, one would expect mitosis radiating from Phase IV to mirror the Doppler shift, &, the meiosis centered in Phase II to reflect the Paradigm shift, or, what is the duplication of DNA & replication of RNA. Then, from the reduction division of Phase I, with crossing over, and the meiotic division of Phase II, with segregation, the recombination of energy and materials supports the polymerization of protein cells in the manner of the metabolic growth of Phase III. As usual, Construct No.7 gives us the General Guidelines for these helical Crossover Patterns.

I am certainly not the person to give a detailed account of the hereditary processes of human reproduction. However, the fact that the whole process is tied to the co-ordination of a heterosexual association is significant. In fact, the helical polymer of DNA is based upon the alternating, associative development of phosphates and sugars, about a central core of two nitrogenous compounds that have four basic nucleotides. We have already covered many similar sets of relationships in other areas of inquiry, and, it should be of no surprise that the biological theme follows the self-same process. Further, if one examines the radiation of mitosis, centered from within in the 'daughter cells' of Phase IV, the setting out of its four phasal relationships is self-evident. Phase IV itself mirrors the dyadic, duplicative sequencing of 'interphase' (no color, 9/10-10/0), which produces two relatively identical daughter nuclei. (Despite a natural tendency toward the mutations of genetic drift, a given species tends to remain remarkably stable, over many thousands of years.) Radiating from the duplication of interphase, mitosis progresses on to 'prophase' (white-yellow, 1-2), to 'metaphase' (orange-red, 3-4), to 'anaphase' (green-blue, 5-6), and finally to 'telophase' (purple-black, 7-8). Naturally then, mitosis stems from Phase IV relationships, wherein the duplication of DNA produces the root cause of the decalogical polymer. (Interestingly, about 1952, a British biologist and X-ray crystallographer, Rosalind Franklin produced an X-ray photo of wet DNA which not only made evident the spiral structure but also showed that each complete turn of the double helix had ten units of development!) However, because the unitarity of the universe must be maintained, if the reductive haploid pattern doubles down the chromosome count of the germ line, in Phase II, then it must be doubled up in Phase IV, by the diploid reunion of two haploid parental groups. The overall pattern is reminiscent of the four-dimensional double light cone, with the two kinds of variation interspersed associatively.

Normally, in relation to meiosis, centered in Phase II, one would expect the germ cells of each haploid gamete to have an equal number of the two parental types of genes, like the perfectly closed cycle implied by No.4. However, the crossing over of genes, between the separate parental groups, during the first stage of meiosis, in reduction division, is relatively common. And, at the same time environmental factors and other influences often introduce genetic aberrations that are unattended. Subsequently, the new germ line could contain many surprises, some of which are *not viable* when it comes to the later sexual reunion of male & female gametes. Further, with the rejoining of the two parental groups, to restore the full chromosome count, the ideal 'half transmission of acquired characteristics' usually undergoes further variational changes, from within the random *gene pool* of all possible traits. (Recent studies have indicated that the male y chromosome, because it doesn't double up, to determine sex, as with the female x chromosome, nevertheless has its every own built-in diploid, criss-cross pattern that "corrects" defects that occur accidentally.) Thus, although there are evident, in the offspring, natural inheritance patterns based upon the regular criss-crossing of the two parental groups, things like random mutation, environmental influences, and the unexpected interaction of dominant and recessive genes, tends to make the Sequencing of Speciation too troublesome to predict. Thus, hidden within the genetic code of the young of many species, there are often minor aberrations and deficiencies that go unnoticed, especially in early stages of growth. The full expression of inherited traits, as obvious behavioral characteristics, depends upon the organic relationships of many different genes, as well as the influences of environmental factors, and operant conditioning. Like a 'biological clock', over time, interacting genes are expressed as specific behavior patterns, usually at an appropriate stage of development. Naturally then, some young expire before birth, as well as immediately after birth, or, at a later stage of development, when the 'genetic clock' initiates a specific series of interactions. The point to be made here is that one cannot line up the dots, directly, from the preformation of inherited traits, to the full expression of the behavioral characteristics, for an adult body plan.

To get back to the Sequence of Speciation, the arbitrary encoding of the hidden variables of the Doppler shift, in Phase IV, makes up what is called *preformationism.* Traditional models have tended to reflect the dyadic character of the "split ends", by a simple transformation such as 9/10, as the 'end of the beginning', and 10/0, as the 'beginning of the end', or, infinity & singularity. For the set theory of mathematics, these are the infinite set as 'environment' and the null set as 'corpuscle'. And, that makes the two 10s into a 'homomorphism' that could be mapped back and forth, from one to the other, as ideal duplicates. (This hypothetical idealism is the source of the ultimate conundrum of spatial displacement, about whether or not 'Schrödinger's cat is dead or alive', as just ending the beginning or just beginning the end, or somewhere in between? Of course the logic of 'that event' is a spurious paralogism as an 'elliptical extremal' [Gauss].) Importantly, there is no 9th orbit for the ultimate Acoustic of First Principles, because the ninth harmonic cannot exist as a waveform that can be measured as a locally classical ground state, although, like a "special candle", the complementary acrostics of No.7 all reflect nine-ness. So, if the 10th orbit represents supergravity, what is the 9th dimension in relation to it? (Does it define antimatter relationships, or are antimatter sets better represented by the interplay of matter waves & antimatter waves?)

Similar to the traditional rendering of 9/10, Einstein referred to the 10th orbit as a homomorphism, and associated the 9th element with it as an 'isotropic corpuscle' or indeterminate particle. And yet his M_oc^2, as 10 – 11 & 9, shows 9 as being part of a heterolytic pair, as the fundamental recognition of a reciprocal permutation for 'isotopic field & isotropic particle'. Likely the traditional problem with figure/ground Gestalts force this erroneous recognition of the idiosyncratic cause of the untenable 'wave/particle duality'. What we are really talking about, all the way from Newton's mistake of ascribing absolute qualities to space, is Einstein's apparent inability of solve the riddle of the Validation of Process. (Later, working with Stayendra Bose, he came up with 'Bose-Einstein statistics'.) Nowadays, we know that most things come in threes, and so the Sequence of Speciation is bound to have three sets of triplets, to make up the Ninth Dream as a treasure that will never be found. Interestingly, Christian teachings recount these Phase IV sets of relationships as the parable of the wedding, where Christ was said to have changed water (immaculate evenness) into wine (sacred blood of conception), which surprisingly left the best wine for the last (reincarnation).

To continue in that vein, for physics the first part of Sequence reveals the Weyl tensor (11 & 9) and the next (9 & 1) the Ricci tensor. However, adding in the Reimann curvature tensor as infinity and the null set or zero set (10-0), all three 'tensorial vectors' may be tied together through the Riemann curvature tensor (Penrose, p. 271). All three tensors together are 10 – 11 & 9 and 0 – 9 & 1, and 0 & 2 + 1 is added on later, as a plasmic emission, to complete the Sequence of Speciation. Thus, although I have expressed nine-ness as the sequence of cenospecies, subspecies and species, the first triplet, governed by cenospecies (10), has been broken down biologically into 'echotype & echospecies' (11 & 9), like the isotopic field & isotropic particle mentioned above. In mathematics, the latter is referred to as a 'closed form integral', even though 10 - 11 & 9 and 0 – 9 & 1 make the Type II pattern into an Open System, split between the two Ends. Biologically, in total we now have echotype (11, as field), echospecies (9, as particle), subspecies (9 & 1, as field/particle), and species (+ 1, as a ground state). That is, like the Christian parable, the even cenospecies as "water" has been associated with the odd pair of echotype & echospecies as "old wine", while so far subspecies as "new wine" has not been divided up. Later, species naturally crosses over to existence, as the ever-single, first taxon. The important thing to keep in mind is whether or not *fundamental causality* is being effectively described, as a working model for the Validation of Process.

To make up an implicit *scalar point-function*, in the pattern 4 & 6, governing the weak force, the last number is descriptive of a *particle configuration*, which has been termed the Higgs boson (not yet validated). For one thing, it takes at least *six spatial dimensions* to describe a round shape, which, in this example, begins as a particulate center and extends outward to encompass the circumference of the galactic lens. That is, the inductive interpretation of the quantum field/particles nonlocalities of 4 & 6 would seem to make six-ness both impossibly small & impossibly large, or infinite in extent, as a principle of least action. (Like many physicists, I maintain that the apparently "instant" character of gravity is really due to a *subspace illusion*, created by the reductive effect of the carrier medium, of the 'fabric of the universe'.) Microscopically, such sphericity would make evident a nearly perfect periodic crystal, and in contrast, macroscopically, produce a gigantic black accretion disk with the supraperiodic traits of diamagnetic standing waves. Well then, in keeping with the idea that there is no effective limit to either largeness or smallness, Construct No.6 would naturally have to model an intermediate sphere of classical dimensions, made up of yes, 'intermediate vector bosons'. (In No.1, this is the middle, yellow-white-black-purple ring.) As represented in No.6, *gluon triplets* move inward toward a 'glueball' in the hypothetical center, like a gravitational well. However, at this point quarks have not yet been manifested because we are still dealing with the anomalous convergence of the condensation of *super-weak interactions* (orange-red-green-blue), as precedent to the strong color force of quantum chromodynamics or QCD. (Keep is mind two things: that the Higgs mechanism acts like a 'strange attractor' for microgravity, and, as Einstein maintained, gravity always remains attractive – even within a black hole. In the latter case, ironically, one might be dealing with 'massless vector bosons'.) However, as the third law of thermodynamics *does not allow absolutes*, approaching the temperature of absolute zero, at unimaginable pressures, a basic form of matter might suddenly spring forth to fill the void: because, *ex nihil, nihil es*, or out of nothing, nothing can come. Hence, in No.1, there is represented a rectangular center of adiabatic expansion that has an *antigravity affect*, because its odd traits naturally fold outward, to eventually make up quark triplets. (In deep space then, the enthalpic remnants of fundamental matter, as the PRP of omniformity, set up a paraelectrical worm hole of *quantum mechanical affects* that produce the fundamental heat signature of the v.e.d. without & the c.c. within. For this reason, mysteriously, blackbody radiation is not just limited to larger dimensions, but also emanates from what Einstein called inner illumination.) Here, we can envision how SU(3) allows quark triplets to radiate outward, associated with gluon triplets moving inward. Interestingly, in No.6, the toroid of the glueball seems to be made up of the messenger photon (0 & 2 + 1, white) and three heavier messenger particles: the Z_o (8, black), the W+ (7, purple) and the W- (2, yellow). (In No.3, look for the white messenger photon and black Z_o as having been emitted from No.6, but without either having crossed over to become part of the three generations of leptons.) My best guess is that the elusive graviton might be embedded within the very center of No.6, as an undetectable true photon, between infinity & singularity or 10 & 0. 'That is there', as the dyadic parity of the homomorphism of the spin-2 particle, which, in the past, has been referred to as 'aleph 2'. (Can ideally biomorphic binaries be without dimorphic similarities, with Schrödinger's cat both dead and alive, in two places at once, as within a perfectly round sphere, or is such a paralogism merely a figment of our imagination?) And, if we symbolize the glueball as the oblate condensate-prolate dilate (even water-odd wine) of spontaneous symmetry breaking, then fundamental *antiparticles*, in the center, appear to break left (blue-green) and right (orange-red). That is, from the rest mass of M_o, c^2 radiates as the superconducting properties of a paraelectrical worm hole that describe the constant of kinetic velocity. Accordingly, it doesn't take too much imagination to envision that the rightward chirality of positive matter, as a negative electron configuration (Note the balance of the 'positive-is-negative'.), would take up a clockwise dextrorotatory pattern, from Phase IV to Phase I, with natural emissions becoming embedded within the lepton family (No.3). And, antithetically, the analytic 'positive negation' of matter variation, to the right of Phase IV, would be accompanied by the synthetic 'negative summation' of antimatter variation, to the left of Phase IV, as a positron configuration in Phase III. (Note the balance of the 'negative-is-positive' when it comes to the opposing stream of particles.) Hence, the two commingling antiparticle streams, of rightward analytic infinities and leftward synthetic infinities, set up the associative emission-absorption patterns of No.7, based upon the compatible correspondence of matter & antimatter waves. In final analysis, as the Antithetical Vortices of the Transmodal Inference, not only is the rightward tendency analytically positive, while negative in nature, but the leftward tendency is synthetically negative, as positive in nature. Further, each and every wave train must have balanced triplets of either negative-Positive factors that are even-Odd, or Negative-positive factors that are Even-odd, in order to maintain the unitarity of the universe. This is called gauge invariance, which maintains the Constant Unity Factors of the full harmonic range of a *given level* of complete phasal space, and, there are many different levels of operation.

Importantly then, each of the eight quantum states shown in No.7, would be a blend of composite energy/mass densities, the character of which would depend upon the scaling level of the given polymer. That is, the light & dark spectrums, of positive negation and negative summation, blend together to produce the gray spectrum of associative production, as the kinematic double light cone. (We talk about the kinematic because we are dealing with the General Guidelines of angular momentum, and not the specific nature or scaling level of a given natural system.) In other terms, the positive grounds, with negative fields & figures, for *opaque matter*, and negative grounds, with positive fields & figures, for *transparent antimatter*, produce Einstein's blended compatibility, as the *translucent natural system.* (It's like running along a picket fence, with the pickets & spaces seemingly blending together.) In other terms, the formal temporal continuity of the light spectrum exhibits dark spectral lines as an implicit function, and the functional dark spectrum of spatial continuity has light spectral lines as an implicit formation.

Importantly, when we look at the wave characteristics of the Four Phases, all together co-ordination (recombinant), cooperation (quantum) and congruence (classical) establish a remarkably natural process, whether dealing with either religion or science. That is, the unitarity of science and unicity of spirituality are surprisingly similar. For example, Phases II & IV are antithetical when we compare their wave characteristics, while Phases I and III, as balanced symbionts, provide for buffer zones that compose the more gradual gradients of livable Side Effects. That is, Phase II is made up of *covariant wave fronts,* in contrast to Phase IV, made up of *contravariant standing waves.* And, more harmoniously, the *soliton travelling waves* of Phases I and III act as the two halves of the proverbial apple.

From a political point of view, how is it possible to tell whether or not 'one' is barking up the wrong tree? Here is the skinny on the Thin Man of politics. We have already touched upon how the dysfunctional heart of No.4 reflects the fatal triplet of the partisan (exploitation), the nonpartisan (coercion) and the bipartisan (manipulation). These are George Orwell's Ministry of Truth (enigma of truism), Ministry of Plenty (dilemma of gradualism) and Ministry of Love (conundrum of naturalism). Orwell was conscious of humanity's psychic rift, with his up/down-down/up pattern of *utopia & dystopia* having the potential to be resolved as a *cornucopia* of progressive measures (postpartisan) that go beyond his 'social democracy' (my pragmatic democracy). For Orwell, each person had the ability to *actively conjoin* his or her own controversial coplanar indecision & conflicting coterminal confusion, without resorting to the inhospitality of monolithic coincidence & violence of monopolistic convergence. That is, we don't give people 'freedom' like a Band-Aid solution, a name tag or a heart transplant, because self-liberation depends upon proactive involvement, through a resolute commitment to general democracy. In other terms, freedom must come from within the heart of each person, with the Maintenance of Innocence as basic to all emergent forms of democratic intercourse. The Autonomous Complex is the only way to go, with truly free persons working toward the general democracy of a postmodern New Wave, like the Third Testament of an ethological approach as the Heart of hearts.

If one takes the inverted heart of No.4, and overlays it with a quadrilateral pattern of four elements, frighteningly *Karl Marx's dialectical materialism* is made manifest. As per Construct No.1, transcendent realism is communism (red) paired with socialism (green). The implicit pattern is black-and-white, so that the Four Horsemen of the Apocalypse Now, as red-green-black-white, become inhospitable to human nature, by attempting the *complete assimilation* of the individual to the strict 'planification' of a fixed social order. This is Freud's Phallic Stage as the ancient City of Sodom, by which the patristic apostasy of a masculine hierarchy takes on an adductive role, by subjugating feminine modes. Logic becomes linear, as with economic imperialism, while Reason turns to the legalisms of defining human rights based upon the triplet of the irrelevant, irreverent and relativism. Believe it or not, in a "perfect society" there would be no room for the co-ordination of heterosexual behavior, which was what Orwell portrayed in the novel *1984*, because the unisexual legalisms of the dysfunctional nuclear family would stifle the Associative Justice of the democratic reforms of the Extended Family.

To further our argument against dialectical materialism, the lower hemisphere of No.1, as the antipodal alter ego of the upper hemisphere, based upon the colors of blue-orange-purple-yellow, is Armageddon as the City of Gomorrah, that mirrors the acculturation of strident individualism as an ideal melting pot. We all become the toy soldiers of moral rearmament, while real morality, for the humane treatment of others, is thrown out the window, into the dustbin of history. This is Freud's Anal Stage, with the two quadrants of the lower hemisphere, to match communism (red) and socialism (green) above, being pragmatic democracy (blue) and fascism (orange).

The long and the short of it is that Karl Marx's dialectical materialism; as the *four elements* of a closed society, based upon communism, socialism, pragmatic democracy and fascism; dictates that the combinatorial one-note person be a reflection of Orwell's Big Brother. And, the only innovation allowed must be channeled through a meat grinder of human egalitarianism, as the proverbial hole in the button. This is Orwell's 'memory hole', by which hypermnesia knows how to spell the words, but fails to see that Freud's Latent Stage, in the center, should have a parasexual potential for the meaningful co-ordination of democratic reforms. Reforms begin with the eudaemonic and extend to the eusocial. Thus, real reform is based upon the Heterosexual Stage of Ethos, in Phase III, which emphasizes the efficient cause of the phylogeny of the group (7th orbit, purple).

At this juncture I'm going to call Volume I finished. Both the complete set of fourteen Metalogical Constructs and the Glossary will be published with each volume.

We have cleaned out a lot of Augean stables, even though there is much more work to do – both from a scientific and a spiritual point of view. For example, we need to elaborate the seven stages of the Theory of Transfinite Numbers, which link Bertrand Russell's three sevens with the modern approach to complexity theory. Further, Volumes II and III will continue my emphasis on the ordinary language philosophy of taxonomical nomenclature, *as basic to all areas of human inquiry.* As well, we will continue to analyze some of the erroneous behaviorisms of Human Nature, which prevent us from developing a truly holistic philosophy that gives democratic freedoms their proper due. Without a comprehensive set of models for The Human Equation, we are more likely to continue to unconsciously advocate aberrant behavior, while terrorizing ourselves. And, because of *this* enemy within, our stay on *this* planet just might come to a sudden end.

As a token of my respect for the reader, here is the complete set of my numerological patterns, for the theory of everything. If the individual reading this work is capable of taking a truly comprehensive approach to learning, the methodology of this decalogical acrostic, although simplistic in nature, will always remain front and center.

Hopefully the reader will feel that Volume I is worth reading over again, many times. To really understand all of the natural progressions that I have presented herein is to be able to relate them to the following wave trains of associative development. This particular rendering is very effective for the physics of string theory.

0 & 2 + 1   2 & 4 + 3   4 & 6 + 5   6 & 8 + 7
0 – 9 & 1   10 – 11 & 9
2 – 1 & 3   4 – 3 & 5   6 – 5 & 7   8 – 7 & 11

For the *third system*, according to Construct No.14, the reader might like to identify the sets of numbers that occur *three times*; all of which follow the compatible absorption-emission pattern of particle-ground-field…and up to what orbit?

THE HUMAN EQUATION: SCIENCE AND SPIRITUALITY

VOLUME I

Glossary

Affective Domain: is considered the thesis of 'this', in relation to the antithesis of 'that' as the Effective Domain. Traditionally, one is looking at the Book of Scripture in existence, as observation, separate from the Book of Nature in nonexistence, as experiment. But, these two domains can not be properly treated as absolutes, in isolation. Materially, their diacritical, antithetical relationships, built up between Matter Resonance & Antimatter Resonance, are precedent to and supportive of all other recombinant patterns, through the Transmodal Inference. Nevertheless, the Subjectivity of the Affective Domain (4 & 6 + 5) tends to become bastardized as intellectual subjectivism (9-11-5), subtended by idyllic naturalism (6-4-10), with the Superego Self repressing the Sublime Self or Shadow Self. Thus, the Affective Domain, as *art for art's sake*, combines the unconscious intellectualism of an assimilating socialism with the subconscious emotionalism of an accultural individualism, to suborn progressive behavior through the disarming enabling of an idealistic aestheticism. Then, stemming from meaningless indifference, the inhospitality of ironic detachment often transfers from the repression of self, through idealistic passion, to the violence of activism. Discordantly then, the false authority of the Affective Domain, as the Test, tends to become a *misrepresentation* which demands the *misdirection* of the Effective Domain, by making First Principles into the Trick. The authoritative affectation of a theocratic approach begs the efficacy of technocratic release, or what is religiosity & violence.

Analogism: the Horizontal Mosaic as a paralogism that is isolated from the Vertical Mosaic, with logical positivism leading to evolutionism. Through the premature convergence of reductionism, a compensatory narrowing of perspective replaces ontological progressions within an axiological approach that implies direct channeling between the configurational spaces of separate states of existence. That is, the Effective Domain of the kinetic becomes isolated from the cinematic Affective Domain. Idealism implicates the possibility of a perfectly predictable, mechanical transformation from one state to another, without the need to undergo a process of natural development. The logical fallacy of the linear channeling, of action at a distance, implies that the synthetic proposition allows one to disprove the negative hypothesis, and present a perfect antithesis for establishing the detailed accuracy of evidence taken in isolation. Analogism makes evident the false belief syndrome, by inferring that a matter-of-fact approach produces immutable general principles that are a measure of the Certainty Principle. Naturalism provides prejudicial evidence.

Anaphasic Phobia: denial of the bilateral subsequent Side Effects of Phase III and the precedent Side Effects of Phase I, due to the ambivalent polemics of the Vertical Mosaic, based upon the antecedents of selective attention & consequents of selective retention. The paratactical polemics of vertical magnitudes are inadvertently substituted for the analogical progressions of natural polarities, with the *structuralism* of the conjunctive & subjunctive leading to the reductionism of an injunctive *constructivism.* Thus, through the reduction of Side Effects to narrow limit cycles, temporal frames of reference tend to magnify a **back-formation**, with abstract notions & concrete impulses imputed to be sufficient & necessary proof for the obviation & evidence of set legalisms. Then, as Armageddon, control & denial patterns produce empiricism followed by scientism. That is, *structuralism & constructivism* lead to an anaphasic contretemps of unrealistic expectations that retard the development of humanity. Hence, anaphasic phobia is based upon the bipolar twin-paradox of the two superstitious assertions of the Certainty Principle, that give the false impression that an exact science is not only obtainable but desirable.

Androgynous Reinversion: nonparasitic, symbiotic relationships of mutually beneficent inter-dependence, established through the associative production of congruent harmonics. That is, instead of asserting a bipartisan or nonpartisan solution to the partisan, a postpartisan approach is taken. In other words, rather than the disarming neutrality of an artificial, hermaphroditic union of unisexual indifference, cycling uniformly between the androgynous inversions of masculinism & feminism, the Dual Metaphor is rescued from the dualism of preclusive retrodiction (9-11-5) & retroclusive postdiction (6-4-10). Hence, by avoiding the reaction formation of coincidence & convergence, the heterosexual co-ordination of Androgynous Reinversion produces the natural progressions of meaningful measures that objectify experience in the fourth dimension of complete phasal space.

Anthropomorphic Projection: a surrealistic, mythological expression of desires, needs, wants and wishes, which dishonestly involves the speculative projections of both transference (from structuralism) & repression (from constructivism). Effectively, one builds up one's own prison as a virtual reality, based upon the fallacious arguments of specious reason & spurious logic, with the combination of the latter two merely getting more refined & more subtle, in the deceptive production of alternative lifestyles.

Antithetical Vortices: begin with two self-polarizing light waves and extend to all higher-level Crossover Patterns. Accordingly, *equivalent pairings* are not only evident supersymmetrically, but also establish the invariance of the internal consistency that holds within the field-ground-particle triplet of a given field equation, as well as between the naturally alternating states of associative development. In other words, Antithetical Vortices mean that the quantitative entities of essences & qualitative events of substances, are *always* objectively evident through compatible blending within *each and every space-time object*, as the elemental wave train triplets of the Recombinant Third System.

Anxiety Structures: legendary triumphalism lends itself to the self-righteous epistatization of a superego personality, through the intellectual proscription of universal sovereignty, based upon the affirmative axioms of masculine conceptualism. As Adam's first bite, the Pathos of the abstract intellectualism, of transcendent modes of reasoning, tend toward the nominalism of humanistic structuralism. Thus, through convincing rhetoric, the myth of a totemic, hierarchical synergism constantly refines the self-deception of the Vertical Mosaic, based upon the monolithic instantiation of Temporal Infusion. And, if we are constantly chasing, faster and faster, the Thin Man, one is always getting further and further away from a more viable approach to life.

Archetypal Patterns: based upon the uniform inertia of the lowest-energy state, for the perfectly random patterns of omniformity, as originating the natural emissions of the Sequence of allopatric preformation as the causal source of speciation. Thus, the First Principles of the Acoustic of the Ninth Dream, based upon Archetypal Patterns, trumpets the stentorian diapason of the unified field theory of the Holy Grail of physics. Nevertheless, there is no direct, vainglorious nine-to-five inference between the allopatric Acoustic and sympatric acoustics, by which to actually experience the so-called greening of the gold. That is, the Corpus Universalis does not dictate the exact appearance or body plan of intelligent creatures, nor what sort of lifestyle assures that simple survival has a value-added dimension.

Architectonic Design: represents the Event Horizon of natural extension, with the 8th orbit normally remaining incomplete, retrospective, dissociative and outlandish. For the human outcast as a retrovert, behavioral extremes reflect the apocryphal postscription of inopportune circumstances, with a tendency to resort to activism, violence and mechanistic solutions. Such utilitarianism often involves the theft of universal sovereignty, or another's territory, property, or intellectual authorship, and may even lead to the idealistic extinction of self & others as a "final solution". Architectonics reflect going beyond the point of no return, which might revert to the obsessive-compulsive self-indulgent and self-justifying attitudes of dogmatic Belief Structures, such as religious fundamentalism, idyllic romanticism, standing on principle or taking a matter-of-fact approach. The admonition of not stealing, in the 8th orbit, by going off the deep end, is a warning to avoid taking supraluminary dimensions for granted, through transference, because the resultant retroclusion of seeking to manifest the perfection of Nirvana might throw back to repressive measures such as legalism, personalism, empiricism and political brinkmanship. When encroaching upon the Sovereignty of God, using the tools of preformationism, the technocratic supposition of First

Principles does violence to human nature, by attempting to *monopolize* the unattainable Certainty Principle. Architectonic design ought naught *push its ideas too far*, because opening up that Pandora's box just might make Medea consume all human children.

Bifurcation Plane: a hypothetical 'aleph-null' for the field effect of existence as precedent to essence. Through the limited recursion of the reflection principle, an uncertainty relation builds up the parallelism of a natural chiasmus that often becomes a psychic, and possibly a social rift – if Big Brother has his way. Information theory, psychographic narrow-mindedness, bipartisan politics, the chemistry of double decomposition, sententious serialization, etc. all reflect the disarming 'population inversions' of actually seeking to place the Zen nail. Because of the implicit function of spatial discontinuity, the Bifurcation Plane represents the parametric reductionism of the before and after of temporal frames of reference, which seek to subsume the putative character of the periodic crystal as a fixed Certainty Principle. Such unprogressive Temporal Infusion tends to produce the instantiation of parallelism within the Vertical Mosaic, which, through the tragic flaw of the Divided Mind, is basic to Classical Alienation. An abstract ultimatum & a concrete ultimatum, together, alternating between the unconscious & the subconscious, merely set up the unprogressive patterns of Indecision-Confusion & Confusion-Indecision (5-10 & 10-5) as a psychotic break.

Belief Structures: represent the fundamentalism of pragmatic, linear modes of logical evaluation. Reflecting back anarchically through an architectonic overextension, such as millenarianism, the revolutionary Supposition of Innocence implies that one can concretize the perfection of Non-Being through the preciosity of objective values as a meritocratic gem of objectivism. The suspension of disbelief fixes prejudicial evidence, panders to the needs of others, excuses treating others in an undignified manner or seeks to delimit the destiny of the majority. The result is the idyllic instantiation of schizothymic introspectionism, which tends to undermine existent value systems, while producing the nihilistic tendencies of extreme altruism. Pragmatic success becomes its own measure, with the question begging its answer through the postdictive concretism of the synthetic proposition – by which the objective correlative fails the false belief test, and it appears possible to disprove the negative hypothesis in order to justify the anathematic thesis of logical positivism. Discordantly, the repression of guilt feelings, as action following upon emotion, in an obsessive-compulsive manner, tends to rebound as the rhetorics of philosophic extravagance. The collective subconsciousness of the purported solutions of Belief Structures is hyperbolically codependent with the collective unconsciousness of the affirmed answers of Anxiety Structures, with the two resulting in the ambivalent myth of an inviolable and untouchable political correctness. The latter slavishly follows the erroneous ABCs of honor, duty and obligation.

Crossover Patterns: produce recombinant correspondence between antithetical tendencies, but never allow the complete separation of temporal & spatial relationships, one from the other. Further, the Crossover Patterns of separate sameness & same separateness guarantee that the *stress of temporal characteristics* & the *strain of spatial traits* will never allow the *recombinant objectivity of torsion* to constitute the mutually inclusive or mutually exclusive as the psychotic break of politically correct legalisms. Hence, Subjectivity & Objectivity, in isolation, are untouchables, and only the heterosexual space-time objectivity of monotheistic humanity makes experience meaningful and measurable.

Certainty Principle: Traditionally, the ideal Being of First Principles mistakenly assumes that the Spatial Hypothesis of the Laws of Nature can & may blend perfectly with the Temporal Thesis of the Natural Language. (Not to be confused with the parasitic, metaphysical certainty of the Mimesis of an Iconographic Simulacrum, based upon the local reductionism of rationalism & paralogism.) The incorruptible Immaculate Conception of Mother Nature, which hides First Principles within the Great Seal of the Womb of Theotokos, seems to be crucial for The Human Equation, where the Objectivity of Being is traditionally isolated in the nonexistence of Spatiality, as the Book of Nature. Better yet, unknown Verification & unfathomable Validation make up the Haptic Extension of the Hands of God as the Forbidden Fruit of the authentic Certainty Principle as a unified field theory. That is, the Diacritical Consciousness of the Certainty Principle can & may only be appreciated by recombining temporal entities & spatial events, through the development of the recombinant space-time object. Rather than an exact science, based upon the isolation of the two systems, we continually build up more comprehensive relationships. Hence, self-evident, self-same relationships always display a measure of the Recombinant Third System, and are only known & understood by Human Beings through the consensual co-ordination of the Recombinant Third Person, as reflecting the heterosexual maturity of the four-dimensional double light cone.

The Death Wish: is based upon the coplanar & coterminal irony of the triplet of reductionism, which does not allow natural, coextensive development. As such, hyperbolic codependent relationships give the impression that all difficulties have obvious answers, all problems have transparent solutions and all troubles have clear results. Except that, because of the cognitive dissonance of evasiveness, deviousness and perversion, the first bite of structuralism leads to the second bite of constructivism. And then, bipolar irony will not allow the realization of the coextensive dialogical irony of the Living Metaphor. With the Death Wish, the ambiguous (unreasonable) & the arbitrary (unsound) advocate the ambivalent (incongruous), which leads to the absurd as the fourth nail in the coffin. As a more complicated pattern, that inscribes the bedeviled nature of a lost soul, the Four Pillars of Forgetfulness are: paramnesia, anamnesia, hypermnesia and kinetic amnesia. The *general amnesia* of the Death Wish encompasses all four of the aspects of the quadrupole knot of fatal unconsciousness.

Deviciveness: represents attempting to unduly prescribe the exact instrumental outcome of the natural contingencies of an objective experiment, in a perfectly predictable manner, as the Trick of technical or kinetic amnesia. The devicive pretense of factual objectivism returns to the meritocratic values of pragmatic methods, romanticism and the dogmatic naturalism of fixing general principles. Thus, following the expression of structuralism, with observation becoming obviation, the deviciveness of constructivism, with experiment becoming a simple mechanical extension, completes the other bite of the bipolar so-and-so. These double standards mark the Human Race for extinction. The divisive & devicive, together, are unconscionable.

The Double Blind: is based upon bad habits caused by looking without seeing & hearing without listening, with anamnesis & paramnesia vertically, and hypermnesia & kinetic amnesia horizontally, and, the four centered about the general amnesia of *uniform standards of conduct.* Discordantly then, the spiritualism of coincident structuralism & scientism of convergent constructivism produce the nefarious combination of temporal controversy & spatial violence. The Double Blind of such a twin-paradox is not conducive to establishing legitimately recombinant systems of development. Whereas, a truly supersymmetrical Universal Duality, beyond control & denial, engenders more viable relationships, through the co-ordination of General Guidelines that have built in checks & balances.

Double Dissolution: involves the Fusion of Antimatter Resonance within the extreme shearing gradients of the Doppler shift. Based upon the hypothetical possibility of a perfectly spherical event, that, somewhere between infinity & singularity, provides an apparently necessary but arbitrary judgement concerning the dyadic parity of spontaneous symmetry breaking. What one must keep in mind, is that Antimatter Resonance is only one of the Four Resonances which, all together, preserve the overall unitarity of the universe. And, that looking for the First Principles of objective 'experiment' does not coincide & converge to provide the Certainty Principle of Creation. In fact, expecting to know & understand the nature of creation is exactly what leads to the miscreance of the doppelganger. Hence, seeking out the Nirvana of a logical fallacy in the Nothingness of Being, simply makes people overly dissolute. In actuality, there is no perfect solution for the disproof for the synthetic proposition within the contravariant standing waves of nonexistence, as an ideal spin-2 particle for the Sequence of Speciation. Hence, duplication itself is beyond realization, as when our reach attempts to exceed our grasp, and then comes back to haunt us. Then, resembling the ghostly presence of the miscreant adaptationism of a doppelganger, a person becomes plagued by his or her inability to perform self-exorcism.

Double Reconstitution: involves the Fission of Matter Resonance, with the doubling up of covariant wave fronts, which, within an extreme formation, could produce a Hyperplane of sudden energy release. For a normal distribution, by recombining with Magnetic Resonance, Electronic Resonance and Antimatter Resonance, Matter Resonance passes through the Paradigm shift, like a free lunch, by overcoming the extreme affirmation of the Double Reconstitution of the analytic proposition, in order to espouse the emergence of slow-breaking asymmetry. Double Dissolution produces the ideal superstition of complete fusion & Double Reconstitution the formal superstition of perfect fission. However, we *cannot* have reason, give an exact explanation, live forever, be a special person, know gnosis, justify doing things on ideological grounds, impose personal standards, define an exact thesis, verify existence, prevent variation, etc.

The Dual Metaphor: reflects the co-ordination of the two antithetical systems interacting through the Transmodal Inference of Crossover Patterns, to reveal the Recombinant Third System as a natural progression.

The Superego Self: is the assertive alter ego of positivism, as an antipodal demiurge that represents paratactical optimism in relation to the pessimism and passivism of the Shadow Self or Sublime Self. The Superego Self is Freud's superego as the *homosexual replacement* of the Phallic Stage, in relation to the id as the *bisexual displacement* of the Anal Stage, with the two centered about Egocentrism as unisexually dissociative for his Latent Stage. (Freud's more viable ego love begins with a parasexual kernel.) The triplet pattern is Ego Self & Shadow Self, centered by Egocentrism, or *changeling* & underling about middling, or *behaviorism* & introspectionism about automatism, or *realism* & altruism about humanism, or *fractious* & capricious about precarious (entrap, confuse and entangle), or *foolish* & silly about whimsical, or *evasive* & devious about elusive, or *heretical atheism* & irreverent agnosticism about anathematic nominalism, etc. Some other dimensions of the imposition of the Ego Self reflect: the unconscious, Hubris, intellectualism, the transcendental, homicide, dismissiveness, unctuous piousness, being predatory, loving hate, etc.

Empathic Transference: depends upon Integrative Discipline providing anticipatory powers by which the 'one' becomes sensitized to the existence of the 'other', in a responsible manner that is not overly compromised by caring too much. Beginning with Integrative Discipline, by not trying too hard (disinterested), and incorporating Empathic Transference, by not caring too much (disengaged), one develops a feeling for General Guidelines (discernment). Thus the Double Blind of the Double Jeopardy passes through the Double Passover of the Double Indemnity, to become the Living Metaphor of the third person, in touch with her or his humanity, through truths that are co-ordained.

Enneagram: mirrors the vanity of an apolaustic wish to re-create the Jungian Ninth Dream, in an attempt to control the Continuity of the speciation of reincarnation, based upon seeking to interpret the Acoustic of the unrecognizable ninth harmonic. The enneagrammatical First Principles of consequentialism expect to probe the preformationism of the eschatological endgame, by seeking to find the Golden Fleece of Sequence as the Dance of Siva, Nirvana, the Gates of Heaven or the Holy Grail of physics, etc. The end result of such a vainglorious pursuit is the mechanism of kinetic amnesia as a monopolistic censorship that involves the technocratic abuse of Human Culture, while prostituting human nature to a fatalistic idealism.

Gestalt Brinkmanship: begins with autocratic answers & meritocratic solutions, and then results in twinned ultimatums, as the preclusion of theocratic misrepresentation (doubled by the projection of transference), & the retroclusion of technocratic misdirection (doubled by retrogressive repression). In simple terms, coplanar structuralism & coterminal constructivism become bipolar through general amnesia as a dissociative mode of conduct. Thus, telepathic parapsychology

& the telekinetically paranormal lock into the illusion of necromancy, which permits the dishonest pursuit of telepresent surveillance & teleportative interventionism. Using bipolar intractability, Gestalt brinkmanship not only hides the face of the fourfold psychological knot, but provides for the unbridled consumption of its kleptocratic apple core. That is, the autocratic & meritocratic show contempt for others, as the first bite, and are followed by the theocratic & technocratic, as the second bite of the condemnation of others, with the four becoming centered about a kleptocratic core. The latter occurs when an Agent Provocateur uses the Gestalt brinkmanship of the Demon Seed, somewhere between Eternity & Infinity, to control & deny others, by suborning their existence through an erroneous triplet (aiding, abetting and enabling) that renders absurd behavior.

The Haptic Extension: involves the interplay between local & global adaptations, to produce recombinant adaptations. For the individual entity, intangible haptic relationships touch upon a tactile link between proprioceptive sensations within, and then pass through kinesthetic extensions in between, to once again return within, based upon feedback from synaesthetic global intelligence without. Accordingly, the two systems of fundamental epistemological duality, as the local & global without & within each other, recombine associatively for the democratic ordinances of the third system. That is, the dynamic equilibrium of the teleological democracy of physics enhances natural adaptability through the asymmetrical equilibrium of phyletic recombinations, as the Autonomous Complex of the efficient cause. Thus, the theoretical & hypothetical aspects of natural selection, as Duplication-replication (10-11 & 9) & duplication-Replication (4 & 6-5), if not locked into a closed system of cladistic adaptationism, as neo-Darwinism (9-11-5 & 6-4-10), become experientially actualized through the accumulative addition of Darwin's descent with modification. Hence, the Haptic Extension of the Hands of God is not ours to control & deny…unless arrogance becomes diabolical.

Homologism: gives the false impression that the temporality of Quantitative Change, as the spiritual essence of Form for positive matter, can be treated as a *prima facie,* in isolation from all spatial characteristics. Thus, the Hyperplane of existence is imagined to be the isomorphism of an energy rest frame for the static universe. Hence, in isolation, the adaptationism of Homologism generates reductionism as the distorted perspective of evolutionism, which turns progressive measures into a form of violence. Instead of button & string, the pattern of button & hole becomes silver lining & silver bullet as a Hyphenated Person.

The Hyphenated Person: takes on the tokenistic existence of a psychopathological metalepsis in relation to the paranoid schizophrenia of a censorial prolepsis. This dualism distorts the prosyllogism of perilepsis, by turning away from a progressive ego love, toward a regressive agape. That is, the abstract enigma (9-11) & concrete conundrum (6-4), of obviation & evidence, combine to produce the paired dilemmas of the mutually inclusive 'one', of Indecision-Confusion (5-10), &, the mutually exclusive 'other', of Confusion-Indecision (10-5). Discordantly, the Hyphenated Person becomes a silver-tongued devil, with all the answers & solutions (metalepsis), leading to perfect results (prolepsis) without having to follow legally natural procedures. Discordantly, so-and-so develops a wicked limp, cycling viciously between the 'so' of monolithic metalepsis & the 'so' of monopolistic prolepsis, with the contrapuntal accidentals of a psychotic break blocking the realistic hopes of perilepsis.

The Life Cycle: a dynamic range of development based upon the Four Resonances, and experienced through the Four Phases of complete phasal space. The Life Cycle is fundamental to the natural system and produces an empirical set of ordinances that are evident from within the smallest imaginable system of propagation patterns, such as light waves themselves, all the way up to the largest imaginable system, the universe itself.

The Mind/Body Syndrome: Duality becomes reduced to a simple, closed-loop system within the dualism of Temporal Infusion, as a narrow range of limit cycles. The result is a paratactical chiasmus between mental & physical attributes, with the ridiculously intellectual & sublimely physical combining to produce whimsically intractable behavior. The mind/body syndrome represents a psychic rift caused by recursive reciprocals, with abstract entrapment & physical confusion as the closed limit cycles of metalepsis. Subsequent to preclusive metalepsis, the entanglement of retroclusive prolepsis inhibits the revelation of perilepsis – as mind and body working in harmony. As per Construct No.4, stupidity & ignorance are centered about the betrayal, of both self and others.

Missing Link & Necessary Link: The Missing Link is erroneously considered as sufficient to establish the exact Identity of Verification, & the Necessary Link is misinterpreted as able to actualize the precise necessity of Validation. Respectively, the tentativity of the Missing Link in existence, as asymmetrically indeterminate for the Paradigm shift, is a temporally continuous entity, and although non-computable as the Variation of Means, it is never really missing. And, the contingency of the Necessary Link in nonexistence, as asymmetrically indeterminate for the Doppler shift, is a spatially facilitated event, and as non-computable for the Continuity of Ends, it is never precisely necessary. Nevertheless, these two rather strange limitations to knowledge & understanding, are important. Otherwise *entity & event* would not allow 'us' to experience the *Objectivity of Living:* that 'we' sanctify the continual awakening of humanity.

The Nine-to-Five Inference: is a vainglorious channeling of axiomatic action at a distance, implying a direct deterministic link between the preformationism of Phase IV & the interactionism of Phase II. However, not only is each ground state non-computable, but various analytic transitions and synthetic transmutations, crossing over between separate ground states, are never an exact science. Therefore, one cannot infer directly from one ground state to another, let alone from the nonexistent Acoustic of Ninth Dream, to the existent acoustics of the fifth element. Attempting to do so, merely links the horizontal axis of spurious logic to the vertical plane of specious reason, which has a disarming effect for the progress of human nature. Hence, it is primarily a dishonest paralogism, to infer axiologically that a generic preformation, extending from the inscription of fundamental traits in Phase IV, might be able to predict the exact characteristics of a behavior field that will eventually come to exist in Phase II.

Omniformity: mirrors the opalescence of an infinity of possible values for the production of positive matter from within time-asymmetric quantum gravity, based upon the PRP of quantum chromodynamics, which reflect the inflationary characteristics of the v.e.d. as a lowest-energy state. The uniform inertia of omniformity is an implicit formation of enthalpic adiabatic expansion, as a fundamental kernel of matter that flows from within the Doppler shift of cold dark matter. This lowest energy state, as Planck time within nonexistence, is basic to the v.e.d., and, is not to be confused with the Planck space of a kernel of antimatter within existence, as the c.c. of the implicit function.

Phasal Delay: is based upon the accumulative addition of recombinant descent with modification, as a continuously dynamic process of development which reflects characteristics like: the teleological democracy of physics, the teleonomic survival of the fittest, the phyletic metamorphosis of organic life, the ethological phylogeny of the group, the development of in-depth learning and the natural evolution of the democratic state, etc. Today, the proactive politics of such relationships are said to depend up the expression of 'soft power'. Thus, with the Reconstruction of Phase III, symbiotic reagents emerge as the progressive Side Effect of a dynamic equilibrium, based upon natural processes that are persistent, resilient, reliable and viable. And, from the point of view of legality, the coordinated merging of compatible tendencies establishes the New Wave of the moral rule, as the Living Metaphor of a never-ending story.

Primary Experience: represents the neophytic development, through new knowledge & understanding, of fundamentally generic processes which introduce change into the human environment. Unfortunately, most people are not only unable to appreciate new research and development, but the educational system is not geared up to maintain more than a token, vicarious involvement in emergent processes. Thus Alvin Toffler's 'integration of the integrators' tends to place others into a virtual reality of secondary experiences that disenfranchise the individual.

Quantum Chromodynamics: stem from the contravariant gauge symmetries of the complementary antiparticle relationships of the Doppler shift centered within the external means of Antimatter Resonance. Time-asymmetric quantum gravity produces the quantum mechanical affects of the lowest-energy state as the adiabatic expansion of an implicit formation, basic to the subsequent development of more complex forms of positive protomatter. What quantum electrodynamics is to Matter Resonance, quantum chromodynamics is to Antimatter Resonance.

Quantum Electrodynamics: is the antithetical counterfoil of quantum chromodynamics, and is centered in the Means of Matter Resonance, where quantum mechanical effects are used to estimate electrodynamic interactions within the nuclear core, subject to the limitations of the uncertainty principle. One is mainly dealing with the covariant gauge wave fronts of the semiconducting properties of the slow-breaking asymmetry of the Paradigm shift, as an aspect of matter variation. The electro-weak theory relates to QED (4 & 6 + 5), but it is my concerted opinion that the term 'weak force' (4 & 6) is a misnomer, and, should read 'weak constituent'. The electrodynamic force (+ 5) of Matter Variation is the most representative aspect of QED.

Quantum Mechanical Effects: are an estimation of the wave mechanics of the position & momentum of the structures & interactions of fundamental particles, subject to the limitations of the uncertainty principle. One is mainly dealing with the imputable field effect of the 'aleph-null', through which inertial gravity & mass density vary in relation to the elementary nature of a given matter particle.

Retrojock: an individual, primarily masculine in outlook, who uses expressions like 'coming out, companion partnership, you're worth it, freedom', and, the triplet 'fairness, equality and tolerance', etc. in order to avoid commitment toward the natural maturity of a more humane approach. Retrojocks nearly always get their TTPs wrong and use quodlibetical debates, quarreling and the encouragement of conflict to disguise their real intentions, which never include the autonomous empowerment of others. Not including a feminine perspective, in full measure, and invoking the primacy of 'reason' are symptomatic of a retrojock.

Sensory Ratios: reflect the aesthetic exegesis of The Human Equation, by which it is possible to place the sensory response patterns of the five senses, and the imputable & reputable sixth sense, within the range of the complete phasal space of the Four Phases. Thus, the oral relates to Phase I; the visual, auditory (aural) and tactile/kinesthetic perceptions to Phase II; the olfactory to Phase III, and synaesthetic perception to the overall intelligence of Phase IV. The ironic interplay, from within to without, of the Haptic Extension of the sixth sense, between the Body & Mind, is internally a proprioceptive orientation, within the imputable tactile/kinesthetic sense, & is externally sensitive to global orientation without, as reputably synaesthetic intelligence. Thus, the Haptic Extension consciously recombines the universal & individual, global & local, mental & physical, etc. in a morally democratic manner, between the instinctual inner compass of personal motivation & the intuitive aspirations of globally intelligent response patterns.

The Shadow Self: is the nihilistic alter ego, Sublime Self as antipodal and paratactical in relation to the positivism of the Superego Self, or, the capricious deviousness of the id in relation to the fractious evasiveness of the superego. The Shadow Self as the underling of the lost soul, & the Superego Self as the changeling of the oversoul, are centered about Egocentrism as the disarming middling of token half measures.

The Shadow Self typifies self-indulgence, permissiveness, fascistic pragmatism, idyllic romanticism, immutable naturalism, pessimism, introspectionism, passivism, fundamentalism, feminism, hedonism, objectivism, prejudice, Bathos, parsimonious conservatism and self-justification, etc. One might say, 'Watch your six.'

The subliminal self: works as an implicit function of logical extension that supports the purposive *quiet revolution*, by enhancing the substantivity of change. In contrast, the Sublime Self relates to the prostitution of self to power and separation, while the subliminal self (never capitalized) supports restitution through acts of reconciliation, accountability and redressment, but never demands retribution. That is, progressively, the subliminal self inhabits the functional gaps (2 – 4 – 6 – 8) of the associative development of logical transitions, and by working with the positive identities of essential pickets (1 + 3 + 5 + 7), shares the fence of complex co-ordination, that is congruent with Associative Justice. Hence, with the use of the in situ, tacit evaluation of non-linear logic, cohesive measures pass through the glass darkly, in a dignified and appropriate manner, with the subliminal self balancing the 'third force' through the irenic methodology of 'soft power'.

Teleonomy: reflects the experiential exigencies of evolutionary patterns, without resorting to evolutionism and consequentialism – as though it were possible to know the exact consequences of one's actions. Teleonomy implies the tenuous recognition of purposive intent within the natural system, based upon the teleological democracy of physics, by which the persistence, resilience, reliability and viability of dynamic equilibria tend to favor the accumulative addition of in-depth learning. That is, the increasing complexity of changes based upon descent with modification tends to favor experiences which enhance the likelihood of survivability. In the long run, the naturally adaptive species are favored over entities influenced by the adaptationism of the artificial and the accidental, because, for the most part, short-term, uncoordinated gains have negative side effects and/or produce negative feedback patterns that prevent Local Adaptations & Global Adaptations from rendering the more viable progressions of the third system, through Recombinant Adaptations.

True Trinitine Patterns: are co-ordinated, correspondent triplet patterns which make up the monotheistic ordinances of empirical processes and developments, experienced through the natural system as a recombinant third alternative to the two fundamental systems. Accordingly, the Universal Triangle remains an indeterminate Autonomous Complex, wherein the 'third force' is not really a "force" as such. In other words, through the True Trinitine Patterns of The Human Equation, the process of discovery reveals the doctrinal ordinances of the irenic gender issue, with the complex compatibility of the two systems recombining to produce the Autonomous Complex of the Recombinant Third System. To argue viably, based upon TTPs such as energy, mass and momentum, or full, accurate and complete, or eminence, distinction and discernment, etc. shows that an individual has truly "come out" and is willing to avoid the brinkmanship of the politically correct, and of legalisms, when dealing with others. Accordingly, based upon Associative Justice, each natural stage of democratic development – in the manner of the gauge invariance of the wave train triplets of field equations – must maintain the dialogical checks & balances of legally viable processes.

The Two Determinisms: are based upon the egocentric defense mechanisms of Gestalt brinkmanship, which foster temporal disorder through the inadvertent cycling of figure/ground inversions. The deranged expressionism & reductionism of Temporal Infusion prevents access to in-depth learning, because of the reciprocal ratiocinations of the transference of preclusive selective attention & the repression of retroclusive selective retention, as the closed-loop cycles of psychopathological disorderliness. Discordantly then, the concept of the static universe & the percept of cosmic censorship are symptomatic of a general malaise, which produces ethnocentrism & individualism, rather than the coordinated correspondence of a more compatible approach to humane development. Breaking the incipient fatalism of figure/ground patterns, by rediscovering the nature of field-ground-figure triplet, prevents the twined ultimatums of brinkmanship from becoming the inhospitality & violence of inhumane conduct. In this manner, the fallacy that specious reason & spurious logic, as the Two Determinisms of exact Verification & precise Validation, could & might produce the legalisms of an exact science, is no longer considered to make up a viable third alternative.

Xenogeneic Contingencies: reflect the disruptive interplay of informal cinematics & dysfunctional kinetics, which tend not to promote general kinematic recombinance, through the natural progressions of the third system. Discordantly, such bipolar, directly coplanar & coterminal relationships tend to reduce the likelihood of human survivability, based upon the fatalistic MAD of a codependent, deranged dualism. Thus, the closed loop of temporal disorder combines a coplanar back-formation with coterminal reductionism, causing the psychotic breakdown of proper communication. Hence, in a spiritual sense, Xenogeneic Contingencies *are Sin*, because they break faith with the third system, by not making allowances for the co-ordination of naturally coextensive progressions. In other words, Styx & Lethe do not a river make. That is, through coincidence & convergence, they encroach upon The Human Equation, by turning it into a bipolar twin-paradox of division & discontinuity, divorced from the benefit of the measured response patterns of democratically evolving states. Unfortunately, in that misery loves company and superstition never comes home to roost, invoking agape only gives an impression of openness & generosity, while actually placing others under the duress of immoral liberties. Hence, Xenogeneic Contingencies; based upon aestheticism projecting consequentialism, through transference, and activism promoting deontology, through repression; produce the double standards of the twin-paradox of misrepresentation & misdirection. Discordantly then, with inhospitality exaggerating controversy and unnecessary conflict leading to cycles of violence, the self-preoccupied and self-serving become the well-intentioned gatekeepers of what adds up to inhumane conduct. In final analysis, then, with the cinematics of chromaticism not being conducive to Integrative Discipline, and the kinetics of modulationism not including Empathic Transference, the natural emergence of the kinematic process of discovery becomes denatured – thereby blocking the revelation of the all-important, progressive measures of General Guidelines. In more familiar terms, if an obvious agenda & a hidden agenda revolve around the politics of a fixed agenda, then one is only paying lip service to freedom.

Author index